Dismantling the League of Nations

Histories of Internationalism

Series Editors:
Jessica Reinisch, Professor of Modern History at Birkbeck, University of London, UK and David Brydan, Senior Lecturer of 20th Century History and International Relations at King's College London, UK.

Editorial Board:
Tomoko Akami, Australian National University, Australia
Martin Conway, University of Oxford, UK
Adom Getachew, University of Chicago, USA
Sandrine Kott, University of Geneva, Switzerland
Stephen Legg, University of Nottingham, UK
Su Lin Lewis, University of Bristol, UK
Erez Manela, Harvard University, USA
Samuel Moyn, Yale University, USA
Alanna O'Malley, Leiden University, The Netherlands
Kiran Patel, Ludwig Maximilian University Munich, Germany
Tehila Sasson, Emory University, USA
Frank Trentmann, Birkbeck University, USA
Heidi Tworek, University of British Columbia, Canada

This new book series features cutting-edge research on the history of international cooperation and internationalizing ambitions in the modern world. Providing an intellectual home for research into the many guises of internationalism, its titles draw on methods and insights from political, social, cultural, economic and intellectual history. It showcases a rapidly expanding scholarship which has begun to transform our understanding of internationalism.

Cutting across established academic fields such as European, World, International and Global History, the series will critically examine historical perceptions of geography, regions, centres, peripheries, borderlands and connections across space in the history of internationalism. It will include both monographs and edited volumes that shed new light on local and global contexts for international projects; the impact of class, race and gender on international aspirations; the roles played by a variety of international organisations and institutions; and the hopes, fears, tensions and conflicts underlying them.

The series is published in association with Birkbeck's Centre for the Study of Internationalism.

Published:

Organizing the 20th-Century World, ed. by Karen Gram-Skjoldager, Haakon Andreas Ikonomou, Torsten Kahlert

Placing Internationalism: International Conferences and the Making of the Modern World, ed. by Stephen Legg, Mike Heffernan, Jake Hodder, and Benjamin Thorpe

Inventing the Third World: In Search of Freedom for the Postwar Global South, ed. by Jeremy Adelman and Gyan Prakash

Internationalists in European History: Rethinking the Twentieth Century, ed. by Jessica Reinsich and David Brydan

International Cooperation in Cold War Europe, Daniel Stinsky

Socialist Internationalism and the Gritty Politics of the Particular, ed. by Kristin Roth-Ey

Relief and Rehabilitation for a Postwar World, ed. by Samantha K. Knapton and Katherine Rossy

Cosmopolitan Elites and the Making of Globality, Leonie Wolters

Forthcoming:

The Human Rights Breakthrough of the 1970s: The European Community and International Relations, ed. by Sara Lorenzini, Umberto Tulli, and Ilaria Zamburlini

Dismantling the League of Nations

The Quiet Death of an International Organization, 1945–8

Jane Mumby

BLOOMSBURY ACADEMIC
LONDON • NEW YORK • OXFORD • NEW DELHI • SYDNEY

BLOOMSBURY ACADEMIC
Bloomsbury Publishing Plc, 50 Bedford Square, London, WC1B 3DP, UK
Bloomsbury Publishing Inc, 1385 Broadway, New York, NY 10018, USA
Bloomsbury Publishing Ireland, 29 Earlsfort Terrace, Dublin 2, D02 AY28, Ireland

BLOOMSBURY, BLOOMSBURY ACADEMIC and the Diana logo are trademarks of
Bloomsbury Publishing Plc

First published in Great Britain 2024
This paperback edition published in 2025

Copyright © Jane Mumby, 2024

Jane Mumby has asserted her right under the Copyright, Designs and Patents Act,
1988, to be identified as Author of this work.

For legal purposes the Acknowledgements on pp. viii–ix constitute an extension
of this copyright page.

Series design: Tjaša Krivec.
Caricature by Derso and Kelen from a menu card for the journalists'
international association, 1936. Photo 12/Alamy Stock Photo.

All rights reserved. No part of this publication may be: i) reproduced or transmitted in any form, electronic or mechanical, including photocopying, recording or by means of any information storage or retrieval system without prior permission in writing from the publishers; or ii) used or reproduced in any way for the training, development or operation of artificial intelligence (AI) technologies, including generative AI technologies. The rights holders expressly reserve this publication from the text and data mining exception as per Article 4(3) of the Digital Single Market Directive (EU) 2019/790.

Bloomsbury Publishing Plc does not have any control over, or responsibility for, any third-party websites referred to or in this book. All internet addresses given in this book were correct at the time of going to press. The author and publisher regret any inconvenience caused if addresses have changed or sites have ceased to exist, but can accept no responsibility for any such changes.

A catalogue record for this book is available from the British Library.

A catalog record for this book is available from the Library of Congress.

ISBN: HB: 978-1-3503-7689-2
PB: 978-1-3503-7693-9
ePDF: 978-1-3503-7690-8
eBook: 978-1-3503-7692-2

Series: Histories of Internationalism

Typeset by Newgen KnowledgeWorks Pvt. Ltd., Chennai, India

For product safety related questions contact productsafety@bloomsbury.com.

To find out more about our authors and books visit www.bloomsbury.com
and sign up for our newsletters.

Contents

Acknowledgements	viii
Introduction	1
1 The beginning of the end, 1940–April 1946	23
2 Transfer troubles, April–July 1946	45
3 Geneva and New York, August–December 1946	75
4 (Un)Avoidable delays, January–July 1947	97
5 Many endings, August 1947 and beyond	133
Conclusions	163
Notes	179
Bibliography	235
Index	249

Acknowledgements

This book is the culmination of work started almost ten years ago, spanning master's study, doctoral research and beyond. As might be imagined, therefore, there are many individuals and institutions to whom I owe a debt of gratitude, and while I can't hope to adequately alleviate that debt in one acknowledgements section, I want to highlight just a small selection here.

I'd like to start by acknowledging the importance and value of Birkbeck College, especially its History, Classics, and Archaeology Department, in the development of my career thus far. The college's commitment to educating London's workers has deep roots – long may it continue – and without the support of both the college and the department, like many others, I could not have imagined the possibility of returning to academia. Along those lines I'd like to particularly pay tribute to the doctoral community of which I was a part at Birkbeck, which was a constant source of assistance, encouragement and laughter. This was especially true during the months and years in 2020–1 when Covid-19 forced us onto an array of different online collaboration tools, and their companionship was invaluable at what might otherwise have been a lonely time. Anna Cusack, Cora Salkovskis, Jack Watkins, Jennifer Putnam, Zehra Miah, Annalisa Martin and Nikki Clarke: that was your forty-five minutes, and thank you.

I also need to thank a number of people for their practical assistance over the past five years: Jacques Oberson, Lee Robertson and Nikolay Prensilevich at the UNOG Archives; Reynald Erard at the WHO Archives; and the staff at the UN Archives in New York all warrant a special mention. As do Karen Gram-Skjoldager, Daniel Laqua, Julia Laite and Joseph Viscomi, all of whom provided invaluable advice that helped shape this book. I'd particularly like to express my gratitude to the family of Connie Harris for their willingness to be interviewed by me on the basis of an unsolicited email to the Wilmslow Civic Trust, and to Stephen Barcroft, who not only shared many memories of his own doctoral research almost fifty years earlier but was also kind enough to show me around Dublin in the summer of 2019. I must also acknowledge the financial support provided by the Economic and Social Research Council for the doctoral research that underpins this work; the freedom to pursue this study on a full-time basis cannot be overvalued. I would also like to thank Maddie Holder and Meg Harris at Bloomsbury Academic for their help during the production of this book; they have been ideal guides to a world previously unknown to me and have been more than patient when my ignorance reared its head.

On a personal note, I'd like to thank my friends and family for their unending support, without which this book would undoubtedly not exist. When I decided on a career change some years ago, I received nothing but smiles and offers of help – something I will never be able to thank them for sufficiently. Finally, but by no means least, I need to find an appropriate way to thank Jessica Reinisch for almost a decade of encouragement and reassurance. I never imagined, when I returned to academic study as a 'fun evening hobby', that it would turn into a new career, and I know that would not have been possible without her guidance and commitment; I have been lucky indeed to have such a mentor in my life.

Introduction

On the second day of the League of Nations' last Assembly – its twenty-first – Robert Cecil, long-time devotee of the organization and one of the few attendees present at both that final session and its first, stridently proclaimed the League's death like the passing of a monarch: 'The League is dead. Long live the United Nations!'[1] The organization's membership gathered in April 1946 to solemnize the end of an endeavour they had already forsworn. The League of Nations experiment had drawn to a close by the will of its creators, and those same governments turned their attention to their next attempt at global cooperation: the United Nations (UN).

For the first time in almost six-and-a-half years, the Assembly Hall at the Palais des Nations in Geneva, a space designed for over 1,500 people, was once again being used as its designers had intended. Over 170 member delegates, alongside representatives from new and existing international organizations, the media and other observers, were supported by 397 Secretariat staff, many of whom had been recruited especially for the occasion. The Ariana Estate in which the Palais was housed had, in essence, been in hibernation for much of the intervening years while the Second World War occupied the hearts and minds of almost everyone in Europe, but the hallways of the League of Nations were busy once more.[2] Representatives from the League's remaining members had gathered in one place to officially euthanize this remnant of an interwar world that no longer existed. Although it was a gathering with practical ends in mind focused on the League's liquidation, much of the Assembly was dominated by reflections on the organization's history and its place, or lack thereof, in the post-war world. It was not an ordinary Assembly; it was a funeral and, as tradition dictated, it was considered inappropriate to speak ill of the dead.

A younger and better-looking model had replaced the League, and the twenty-first Assembly granted those governments that were still members of the organization the opportunity to reflect, pontificate and, as appropriate for a funeral, give eulogies for the dead. Cecil's speech, noted at the start of this chapter, was one of the first given as part of the General Discussion of the Report on the League of Nations during the war and, like those given by the twenty speakers that followed him, was characterized by rose-tinted contemplation of the League as a great experiment, consideration of the reasons for the organization's supposed failures and gratitude to those within its Secretariat that had ensured its survival during the Second World War. Despite the shared recognition among those in attendance that government failures and an unwillingness to commit to action had led to the League's irrelevancy and ultimate replacement, there was also an unwillingness to recognize that they, official delegates, were representatives of those same governments that had decided to leave the League behind and create something new – it was a convenient fiction for a funeral at which, on 18 April, after committee meetings and plenary sessions, the gathered dignitaries agreed to close the League effective from the next day.[3]

Yet there's the rub, because this was not the League's funeral, if only because the League of Nations was not dead. Cecil's defiant exclamation, a neat sound bite, is often mistakenly used as a sign of the organization's end, but the twenty-first Assembly only represented the death of members' active involvement in the League. The organization was, although not anywhere near the same scale as the UN, an intergovernmental institution composed of different elements – it was a workplace, a means of securing world peace, a focus point for socio-economic cooperation – and these facets did not cease to exist simultaneously. The final Assembly was a public funeral for delegates and governments, but to the people working inside the League, as part of its Secretariat, April 1946 merely marked the beginning of the end.

It was almost eighteen months before member governments received the expected final report on the liquidation process, the last Secretariat officials did not officially leave the Palais until October 1947 and League business was still conducted into the spring of 1948. These two years remain, for the most part, unexplored – what happened between the twenty-first Assembly and the final fragments of liquidation activity? Who was left to dismantle the League and why did it take two years? This book is about the last days, months and years of the League of Nations after its official death in 1946 and demonstrates that, contrary to opinion both at the time and in later literature, closing the League, an experimental organization with a wide remit and a broad membership, was neither straightforward nor painless.[4]

While many international organizations have come and gone over the past century, the League of Nations, with its global focus, broad remit centred on both security and socio-economic concerns and numerous membership – albeit one dominated by white, Western countries and not on the same scale as its successor, the UN – is one of only a handful of major international organizations to have faced a large-scale dissolution.[5] It is therefore an invaluable case study from which we can further infer how these organizations close, and the kind of challenges that might be expected should other international bodies follow suit in the future.

The League's position as one of the only large-scale intergovernmental organizations (IGOs) to close also provides the opportunity to explore whether the end of an institution like this indicated a repudiation of the form of internationalism that underpinned it. The League of Nations is often presented as both the manifestation and downfall of early-twentieth-century liberal internationalism, but the death of the League did not necessarily equate to the death of internationalism. The commitment of the organization's remaining members, and the members of the new UN, to the continuation of international cooperation in technical areas, as well as to a carefully managed liquidation process, demonstrated that nation states were not entirely ready to dismiss the League's brand of internationalism in 1946. Indeed, a by-product of examining the end of the League of Nations is an increased appreciation for the continuities between that organization and its successor, the UN, and, more specifically, how those continuities came about on a practical level. Do IGOs simply cease to be when they die or do they merge into what followed? To what extent should successor organizations be considered new? The relationship between the League and the UN, two international organizations that existed side by side for over eighteen months, provides an insight into the practical experience of institutional succession.

This is an exploration of what is involved in liquidating an IGO in practice. With no previous experience or precedent to draw from, the League of Nations was once again a guinea pig for large-scale international cooperation, although on this occasion, instead of having the opportunity to build something new and positive, the League of Nations was forced to pick itself apart. As the organization's last secretary general, Seán Lester, and its Secretariat discovered, dismantling the League with no best practice to observe offered both the freedom to approach it in the manner they chose and also the risks that came with that freedom.

Context

The League of Nations, officially formed in 1919, was both a step change from and a continuation of the Great Power States System that dominated European diplomatic relations in the nineteenth century. As a permanent organization, with an official headquarters and full-time Secretariat, it represented a significant departure from the intermittent conference structure that preceded it. Yet it was never envisaged as a supranational organization – national sovereignty was entrenched in its structure – and its reliance on arbitration and great power decision-making meant it was more evolution than revolution. The institution's central purpose, as outlined in its Covenant, was 'to promote international co-operation and to achieve international peace and security', and its structure and processes were designed to specifically address circumstances akin to those that led to the events of 1914. As a result, the League of Nations was formed with a heavy emphasis on open treaty diplomacy, disarmament and protection for minority groups following the creation of new states in Central and Eastern Europe.[6]

The 1920s, initially dominated by a post-war optimism, were relatively positive for the League despite the disappointment surrounding the US Government decision not to join its ranks. The League Secretariat, developed under secretary general Eric Drummond, expanded rapidly to meet new demands, and membership of the organization rose across the decade.[7] However, the global economic downturn that began in 1929 brought unwelcome financial consequences for governments around the world, and an increase in nationalist policies proved counter to the League's push for mediated international cooperation. Rising territorial aggression in Europe, Asia and Africa from both members of the League and non-members alike put the organization's membership under pressure to take action. Nevertheless, faced with these uncertain times, the dominant members of the organization – Britain and France – decided that the most prudent course of action was to avoid confrontation as much as possible, concerned it might lead to further armed conflict.[8] This reluctance to act in defence of its own membership gave rise to a subsequent and increasing lack of faith in the organization's security machinery, and, believing the League was no longer fit for purpose, states including Venezuela, Chile, Spain and Peru withdrew as members in 1938–9. Fewer members meant fewer contributions, and the organization's budget felt the ramifications. In 1932, the Secretariat budget was its highest with 19.2m

Swiss francs, but by 1940 it had fallen to 10.8m Swiss francs and would later dwindle to only 3.1m Swiss francs in 1945.[9]

The 1930s were a difficult time for the League's efforts to contain international aggression, but as the decade progressed it became clear the organization excelled at a different aspect of international cooperation. By the early part of that decade the Secretariat's work coordinating international health, economics, dangerous drug control, intellectual cooperation and modern slavery, among others, had overtaken that of its security apparatus. As these endeavours were considered less 'political' than the security elements of the organization, non-members became actively involved in the technical committees, including the United States, and this was reflected in the increasing number of officials employed to oversee these areas. Figures show that Secretariat staff employed in technical services almost trebled between 1923 and 1932, and former official Egon Ranshofen-Wertheimer estimated that the cost of the technical services rose from approximately 25–30 per cent of the Secretariat budget in 1921 to over 50 per cent by the 1930s onwards.[10] By May 1939, following earlier endeavours to bolster the League's socio-economic elements, Joseph Avenol – Drummond's successor as secretary general – had become increasingly focused on insulating the technical side of the organization from its faltering political work. He and the League's Council invited Stanley Bruce – former Australian Prime Minister and then High Commissioner in London – to form and lead a committee tasked with no specific directive beyond the production of recommendations as to how the League of Nations might reorganize itself to survive the current crisis in Europe. Non-members were invited to express their opinion on the subject, and the US Government inferred it might be willing to increase its levels of collaboration should the Committee produce viable recommendations.[11] The Bruce Committee, as it became known, published its report – centred on the creation of a Central Committee for Economic and Social Questions – on 22 August 1939, unfortunately too late for its suggestions to be put into practice.[12]

When Europe fell into all-out war just ten days later, it could easily have been followed by a quick death for the League of Nations. However, the organization was prepared, to an extent, for problems that might arise as a result of a European conflict. Back on 30 September 1938, the nineteenth Assembly agreed to delegate decision-making powers to the secretary general and the Supervisory Commission; any exceptional measures or decisions made would have the weight of the membership behind them, even if government delegates were unable to meet in person.[13] Nevertheless, it was the League's success in, and the demonstrative enthusiasm for, continued multilateral cooperation in 'non-political' arenas that proved the beacon of hope for the organization's survival. The hope that, one day, governments might once again collaborate on health, education and economics did not save the League of Nations from its inevitable end, but it did keep it on life support for a little while longer.

Memory and scholarship

The League of Nations has long been the subject of academic scrutiny, both during its existence and in the years following its demise, but the organization has seen a particular increase in interest from scholarly circles over the past twenty years. This book is inspired, in part, by this renaissance, not only in terms of its acknowledgement of the League as a valuable case study of IGO and internationalism in action but also in the continued disinterest that surrounds its disintegration following the Second World War.

The decision to distance the UN from the League of Nations, and the dismissal of the latter's legacy in order to prop up the former, has had lasting repercussions for the way in which writers have examined the organization in the decades since it closed. Most of the earliest writings on the League were couched in terms of either only success or failure, without nuance or consideration of alternative perspectives. Individuals previously involved with the organization, either as prominent supporters or as Secretariat officials, dominated those early writers both explaining and defending the League. Ranshofen-Wertheimer, who worked in several departments between 1933 and 1940, wrote *The International Secretariat* in 1945 which, although not the first text written by a member of staff, is still the most in-depth analysis of the League Secretariat and its inner workings.[14] The Carnegie Endowment for International Peace's (CEIP) Division of International Law funded Wertheimer's work as part of a project dedicated to capturing the experience of international civil servants – like those who had been part of the League of Nations Secretariat – and recording it in such a way that it might be useful to the new IGOs formed in the wake of the Second World War. The CEIP project provided a gateway for other former Secretariat officials to represent the League's legacy, including Bertil Renborg, formerly of the Drug Control Service, and Martin Hill of the Economic and Financial Organisation (EFO), both of whom compiled studies of their respective sections under the Carnegie banner, as did Manley O. Hudson (Permanent Court of International Justice) and Pablo de Azcárate (Minorities Section).[15] Another individual and writer connected with the League – for a time at least – was Raymond Fosdick, a devotee of Woodrow Wilson and later director of the Rockefeller Foundation, who held the role of undersecretary general for several months in 1919 before the US Government decided against membership of the new institution. Fosdick did not have a lengthy relationship with the League, but his fondness for the organization and its commitment to multilateralism was reflected in his writings throughout the 1960s and 1970s.[16]

A former senior League official also wrote the most comprehensive history of the organization. Frank Walters, part of the Secretariat for over twenty years before his departure in 1940, published *A History of the League of Nations* in 1952, and at over 800 pages it exhaustively covered the institution's history. Walters's connection with the League ran deep, and he was granted exclusive early access to the organization's Archives in 1946 while liquidation work was still underway.[17] Like his former colleagues, he demonstrated a reluctance to overly criticize the League's Secretariat, but his thoroughness and commitment to chronicling the organization was, and is, unmatched. At a time when advocating for the League was considered unfashionable, Walters highlighted previously unknown areas of effort, especially the socio-economic work of the Secretariat, which was lost in the wider public disparagement of the organization.[18]

These early assessments of the League of Nations, and the attempts to build a positive legacy for the organization, were not, however, sufficient to counter the predominant aura of failure, bolstered as it was by the organization's inability to prevent the Second World War. Whether apportioning blame to either the League's machinery or its membership, this undeniable fact ensured the negative perspective dominated much of the discourse for the rest of the twentieth century. Eric Hobsbawm called it 'an almost total failure' in *The Age of Extremes*, Mark Mazower suggested the League experience was a 'failure' and, in his well-regarded story of the UN's creation, Stephen Schlesinger referred to the League variously as a 'fiasco' and 'failed'.[19] Thinking and writing about the League of Nations only in terms of success or failure meant this perspective permeated not only through academic literature but also into contemporary public consciousness and politics. In 2005, Alexandru Grigorescu, in his work comparing the Iraq debates in the UN Security Council in 2003 to Nazi appeasement in the late 1930s, noted that US President George W. Bush used this analogy and the 'failures of the League of Nations' over forty times in the period leading up to the occupation of Iraq.[20] Grigorescu concluded that the analogy was not particularly relevant to the situation in 2003, but not because he believed the League's story had been unfairly maligned or simplified. Instead, demonstrating how the failure narrative had permeated academic circles beyond the discipline of history, he suggested the situations should not be compared because the UN was not as 'useless' as its predecessor.[21]

Scholars of international relations, for the most part and like many historians before them, have been similarly unconcerned with the League's place in the evolution of international organization. The academic field expanded rapidly in the wake of the Second World War, and this was accompanied by the popularity of the realist school, which stressed the inherently selfish nature of the state and thus the inevitable conflicts between them. It was the dominant movement of the post-war academy, and the events of the 1930s through to the 1950s supposedly justified the argument that the League of Nations was an ill-conceived attempt to manifest a utopian world order. One of these academics was E. H. Carr, a British scholar and journalist, who remains one of the most quoted realist international relations theorists, despite his waning interest in the field from the mid-1940s onwards. *The Twenty Years' Crisis* was initially published in 1939, the contents of which saw Carr launch a fiery criticism of the 'abstract theory' that dominated the structures of the League of Nations and the unrealistic belief that states could be compelled to act for the wider greater good via the power of reason.[22] As the realist school of thought gained influence and exposure, the academy came to think of international organizations as wasteful fantasies, and as there was little point in studying institutions with no value, the League became an increasingly discarded topic in the field in the latter half of the twentieth century.[23]

Over the past twenty years, however, the League of Nations has seen increased attention from those eager to revisit the organization, moving away from topics of disarmament or security and instead focusing on its lesser-known and ostensibly non-political work facilitating international cooperation in socio-economic fields.[24] The work of individuals such as Patricia Clavin and Susan Pedersen inspired, and continues to inspire, a rekindled interest in the League of Nations, its unusual position as a dead IGO and its impact on the shape of contemporary multilateral cooperation. However, several of these newer accounts have used the merits of the organization's functions and activities to counteract the prevailing fifty-year narrative of failure and, as a consequence, have compounded the view that the League can only be thought about in terms of success or failure. Iris Borowy, for example, noted that she would like the League of Nations Health Organization to receive more praise than it previously had, and that its continued legacy via the World Health Organization is testament to its success.[25] The choice to focus on the lesser-recognized achievements of the League's Secretariat in an effort to rescue the reputation of the institution continues to result in a scholarship still frequently focused on its relative merits, and while the eagerness to scrutinize lesser-known elements of its history helps to expand our knowledge of the League, research focused on the organization should not be confined to assessing its supposed worthiness.

A further common simplification of the League's story – one directly addressed in this book – surrounds the means and timeline by which the organization closed. The traditional fixation on security and balance of military power in the League's story means much of the earliest literature claimed the organization was defunct by the start of the Second World War.[26] As many of the new studies of the past twenty years have demonstrated, the League's security apparatus was only one element of the organization, and the continuation of the technical functions and activities, which overtook the former in terms of Secretariat time and resources during the 1930s, was largely responsible for its survival throughout the conflict. However, those more contemporary scholars who argue for the continued relevance of the League during the Second World War frequently fall into a different trap by reiterating the narrative put forth by the organization's leaders at the time: that the twenty-first Assembly in April 1946 marked the end of the institution. Leading figures in the movement to reassess the League of Nations in the recent past – such as Susan Pedersen, Patricia Clavin and Mark Mazower – have all made reference to the organization's final Assembly as the natural point at which to conclude the League of Nations' story.[27]

Much of the blame for this oversight can be laid at the feet of those overseeing the League's liquidation. The twenty-first Assembly was presented to the world as the organization's funeral, and the decision-making body responsible for supervising the closure process – the Board of Liquidation – was understandably invested in presenting the liquidation in as positive a light as possible when it issued its Final Report to Members in 1947. However, by accepting the version of events put forth at the time – either completely overlooking League activity after the twenty-first Assembly or relegating the period to a few sentences – scholars have unintentionally made the organization's closure look straightforward, uninteresting and unimportant. Furthermore, it has simplified the complexity inherent in the transfer of assets, activities and people from one organization to another. Restoring these events to our consciousness contradicts this assumption and demonstrates how the League's own leadership underestimated the challenges of a process that had never been attempted before. The way in which existing literature has presented the League's closure suggests a neatness to proceedings that was missing from reality, and subsequently misses how frustrating the experience often was for those working in the Secretariat from 1946 to 1948. The orderliness projected by the League's leadership at the time, and in historiography since, hides the truth that both the UN and the League were entwined for much of 1946, occupying a grey area during which one organization was not quite closed and the other was not fully in place.

For the time being, only a handful of writers have addressed the dismantling of the League of Nations after its final Assembly in April 1946. Notable examples include Douglas Gageby's biography of Seán Lester, Victor-Yves Ghebali's review of the League and the International Labour Organization (ILO) during the Second World War, Torsten Kahlert's brief look at the transfer of estates and assets, the unpublished doctoral thesis of Emma Edwards and Carolyn Biltoft's work on asset transfer; however, none of these explored the closure of the organization in its totality. Gageby referred to the closure process as 'a slow, onerous, slogging and pettifogging business' as part of his larger study focused on the last secretary general, while Kahlert's review of asset transfer, by virtue of its brevity, did not interrogate the process in-depth.[28] Meanwhile, completed in 2013, Edwards's *The Wartime Experience of the League of Nations, 1940–1947* went some way to rectify the scholarly oversight of the organization's wartime experience and closure but, in covering an eight-year period, did not feature the events following April 1946 in any detail.[29] More recently, Carolyn Biltoft touched on the end of the League in *A Violent Peace* and examined aspects of the dissolution in greater depth in 'Decoding the Balance Sheet', in which she scrutinized the relationship between the Board of Liquidation's decision to transfer gifts gratis to the UN and that decision-making body's efforts to construct and preserve the League's legacy.[30]

The closest the League of Nations' liquidation has come to an in-depth review, however, was courtesy of Victor-Yves Ghebali's *Organisation Internationale et Guerre Mondiale: Le Cas de la Société des Nations et de l'Organisation Internationale du Travail Pendant la Second Guerre Mondiale*, edited and published in 2013 by his colleague Richard Kolb following the author's death in 2009. Based on Ghebali's 1975 thesis, the work methodically reviewed each transferred function or service in turn, but his analysis came unquestionably from a UN perspective – supported by his primary use of UN Archives source material in this regard – and his focus was on transfer to the new organization, which was only part of the League's work after its last Assembly. Despite this, Ghebali stands out as one of the only scholars to acknowledge the significant efforts involved in bringing about the transfer between the League and the UN, and this review of the organization's wider dissolution builds on those foundations.[31]

The end of IGOs has been conspicuous by its absence from the academic fields of international organizations and international relations, although there have been more recent moves to address not only this oversight but also the misconception that institutions like the League of Nations are overwhelmingly resilient and almost exclusively survive any threats to their existence.[32] The extent to which the wider field has validated this approach in the past is perhaps best evidenced in Susan Strange's contribution to Bob Reinalda and Bertjan Verbeek's edited volume *Autonomous Policy Making by International Organizations*, titled 'Why Do International Organisations Never Die?' The basis of Strange and others' argument centred on the idea that international organizations evolve rather than end, and that it is typically employees of these institutions who bring about this change in order to protect their positions. Reinalda further suggested this is borne out either by officials changing the organization's remit or by the same officials making themselves indispensable to the international community they serve, either consciously or unconsciously.[33]

The League of Nations does not fit into this narrative and therefore reinforces the argument that the dissolution of international organizations needs to be studied with greater rigour. This is a position backed up by the recent work of scholars such as Mette Eilstrup-Sangiovanni, Hylke Dijkstra and Maria J. Debre, all of whom have shown that, in opposition to the prevailing opinion, these institutions can, and have, come to an end. Eilstrup-Sangiovanni's findings suggested that international organizations can close via a number of different means and identified some of the more common characteristics of these ill-fated bodies in an attempt to understand why some institutions are able to survive when others do not, also known as their 'stickiness'. Data has suggested that the larger the international organization in terms of funding and membership, and the wider its remit, the more likely it is to survive, and in this respect the League of Nations has been recognized as an anomaly. Dijkstra and Debre have addressed the reasons behind the League's lack of stickiness, and Eilstrup-Sangiovanni categorized the end of the organization as a prime illustration of what she called 'institutional succession' – whereby one international organization is replaced by another – but there remains restricted understanding of how both this and dissolution work in practice.[34]

The study of international organizations has also evolved in other ways over the past ten years, as writers have moved away from institutional histories in the more traditional sense to also focus on less tangible, if no less important, elements of international governance. Ilaria Scaglia has emphasized the centrality of emotion in internationalism and how emotions can drive decision-making in IGOs. The League, as Scaglia explained, was founded as a manifestation of post-war hope, its survival dependent on the faith of its membership and the wider public, but it was ultimately undone by the slow erosion of that trust and the sense of disappointment, and even betrayal, that replaced it.[35] Attention has also turned to a key pillar of organizations like the League: the international secretariat or civil service. The work of Karen Gram-Skjoldager and Haakon Ikonomou in particular has highlighted the value in studying secretariats as institutions, their practices and characteristics, and as the home of a new kind of international profession.[36] Before Assemblies, Councils and Committees, the League of Nations began with its Secretariat – arguably the first large-scale and permanent international civil service – and it was the element that remained once everything else had fallen away. The individuals within it were ultimately responsible for the tasks that made up the dissolution process, and the Secretariat itself was the last structural element of the organization to be dismantled. Bob Reinalda has suggested that, despite the belief that international secretariats were dull bureaucratic institutions, they also held the potential to be actors in their own right, and in few other circumstances was this as much in evidence as it was at the end of the League of Nations. Acting, for the most part, without direct oversight or guidance, especially in the organization's final months, the changing role and influence of the League's Secretariat are key elements in understanding the shape of liquidation.[37]

The increased focus on international secretariats has understandably coincided with an interest in the international civil servant. Ranshofen-Wertheimer's *The International Secretariat* was concerned with the logistics and procedures of that body, but it also examined biographical features of Secretariat officials in order to better understand what kind of individual became an international official. These included age, nationality distribution and gender, but the lack of data available during the volume's compilation meant Wertheimer was unable to produce as full and as rigorous an account as he would have liked.[38] Almost seventy years after Wertheimer first attempted his analysis, Klaas Dykmann embarked on a similar study, publishing 'How International Was the League of Nations Secretariat' in 2014 and, as the title suggests, Dykmann focused almost exclusively on the topic of nationality.[39] More recently, Torsten Kahlert published his prosopographical study of the Secretariat during the League's lifetime – looking at nationality, gender and career trajectories – while Myriam Piguet has looked at the organization's female officials and demonstrated how a roughly equal gender distribution did not necessarily mean equal opportunities.[40] Other studies, meanwhile, have used Secretariat officials, in part at least, as a means of illuminating commonality with the past. Clavin took this approach several times, highlighting key Secretariat figures such as Rachel Crowdy and Ludwik Rajachman, as well as Alexander Loveday and Ragnar Nurkse, while Borowy's review of the League Health Organisation used the experience of two of the remaining Secretariat officials in the department during the Second World War – Raymond Gautier and Yves Biraud – to illuminate those years.[41]

Our lack of understanding of the League of Nation's closure is therefore doubtless influenced, and mirrored, by our ignorance of its last secretary general, Seán Lester. The former League High Commissioner to Danzig has not been entirely forgotten by history, having been featured by both Raymond Fosdick and Arthur Rovine in their respective reviews of the League and UN secretaries general, but both of these accounts are over fifty years old and were dominated by the turbulent events surrounding his succession to the role in 1940.[42] Irish writers have tried to draw attention to Lester's eclectic professional history and his role in international governance in the twentieth century – including Gerard Keown and Stephen Barcroft – but his final months as secretary general remained elusive even to those with personal knowledge of him. The major published work of note to focus exclusively on Lester was not written by an academic but by journalist Douglas Gageby in 1999. A former editor of the *Evening Press* and the *Irish Times*, Gageby was also Lester's son-in-law, and thus had privileged access to Lester's diary and personal papers before they were later entrusted to the UN Office at Geneva and University College Dublin.[43] Stephen Barcroft was similarly granted early access to the former secretary general's papers; however, he was crucially able to supplement the diaries with interviews of several of Lester's Secretariat colleagues, including Martin Hill and Valentin Stencek, the latter of whom was another critical figure in the League's liquidation. Both Gageby and Barcroft's accounts provide much-needed background to Lester's life; however, neither were able to probe, in any depth, into his experiences of the League's closure, limited as they were by the dwindling number of personal papers available for 1946 onwards.

For too long the choice to scrutinize the League in terms of either success or failure dominated much of our collective memory around the organization – George W. Bush's comments in 2003 standing as a case in point – but this is not the only generalization from which the organization has suffered, and many of the most sweeping statements come from writers for whom the League is tangential to their particular focus of study.[44] Both historians and scholars from other fields present the organization as a stepping stone in the wider, and supposedly more interesting, history of other institutions, or in the field of international politics.

This is especially true of those interested in both international organizations in general, as well as the UN, accounts of which often tend to dismiss the League as either irrelevant or as a fleeting preface to be discussed before moving on to more attention-grabbing subjects.[45]

One of the key findings of an examination of the League of Nations' final months and years is the extent of the links between the organization and the UN, and the interweaving of the former's liquidation with the latter's creation. Clearly the UN is a much larger, more complex and now longer-lasting organization than the League was – at the end of 2020 the UN Secretariat was made up of over 36,000 officials; at its peak in 1931, the League had 707.[46] However, sources reveal that very few of the League's remaining assets in 1946, physical and otherwise, were fully liquidated; the vast majority became part, in one way or another, of the UN and its agencies. The links between the two are not necessarily dismissed by writers – the work by Macfadyen, Davies, Carr and Burley on the legacy of Eric Drummond is a more recent example – but many of those who do recognize the continuation between the organizations, such as Reinalda or Hinsley, have seemed reluctant to interrogate the connections in any depth or rigour.[47] Another example is Evan Luard's *The United Nations: How It Works*, in which Luard acknowledged that the UN learnt lessons from the League and implemented them accordingly, but did not expand on these any further.[48] A review of the League's liquidation does not yield results for those interested in the history of that organization alone. The extent to which the League and the UN were entwined, especially during 1946, challenges many of the existing origin stories of the latter institution as well as the persistent idea that international organizations exist in delineated silos, entirely separate from one another. It also shows the willingness of the post-war institutions, away from the public eye, to take advantage of the resources the League of Nations had to offer, from physical assets to Secretariat officials' experience.[49]

The League of Nations has inspired an array of scholarship in the seventy-five years since its death – including reviews of specific Secretariat functions, a revival of interest in internationalism and studies centred on the international civil servant – and while these have demonstrated the many different entry points into studying the League, they are all small parts of a much larger whole.[50] The closure process has been missing from the League's story for too long; understanding this period in the organization's narrative not only challenges many of the mistaken assumptions about the institution's life but also encourages us to think differently about its legacy.

Approach and structure

In order to establish what happened to the League of Nations after its funeral, why it took twice as long as planned and what it is really like to liquidate an IGO, this book focuses on the two-year period, from the final Assembly in April 1946 to the culmination of its business in 1948, in significantly greater detail than it has up until now. The results shed new light on a range of subjects, including the extent to which the League and the UN lived and worked side by side during this time, and the impact of not only the latter on the former's closure but also how the end of the League was an important factor in the UN Secretariat's formation. This is alongside discoveries about the complexities of the League's liquidation, the importance of precedent in the administration of international organizations and how individual actors could both make, and break, the closure process.

A central element of this examination, as might be expected, scrutinizes the practical aspects of the League's closure. This includes a review of the decision-making structures in place – specifically the Board of Liquidation created by the twenty-first Assembly – and the organization's ultimately unwise choice to implement only a light framework for dissolution, essentially based on the same design as that used during the Second World War. Understanding the motivations behind some of the League leadership's more puzzling, and often counterintuitive, choices not only explains why closure unfolded as it did but also demonstrates how decision-makers can be swayed by pridefulness and unwitting ignorance. Also important was the role played by outside parties in the process and how the rush to build a new UN Secretariat in 1946 had an unexpected impact on the League's ability to be proactive and methodical about its closure. The latter organization's efforts to liquidate were hampered from the start by external timetables, a lack of strategic direction and, perhaps most importantly, the challenge of an unknowable task. No one had ever closed an organization like the League of Nations before, and the shortage of practical advice or precedent proved a difficult task to overcome, even for a Secretariat as experienced as the League's.

Dissecting the practical framework put in place to close the League of Nations is obviously a vital part of understanding how and why its liquidation unfolded in the manner it did, but it is not the only means of shedding light on the process. Just as it is important to view the dissolution of the League from above, so too is it imperative to take the perspective from below. This book centres the individuals working in and around the League of Nations' Secretariat, regardless of their position in the organizational hierarchy, to demonstrate how the liquidation impacted, and was viewed by, them. Their experience and comprehension of the dissolution process was often significantly more extensive than that of the organization's decision-makers, especially the Board of Liquidation set up to oversee proceedings. Although the latter group met over forty times between April 1946 and July 1947, these meetings were often conducted on consecutive days in small sessions and included a six-month hiatus in the latter half of 1946. While the proceedings of these meetings give us rare insight into how and why certain decisions were made, they do not provide the full story of what liquidation was like for those responsible for making it happen. The official picture of the League's liquidation, painted in the organization's formal publications, represented a fraction of the real story that can only be revealed by looking at the perspective of those 'living' liquidation on a daily basis.

It is perhaps easy to portray the League of Nations as a faceless institution or as a collection of clinical scaffolding designed to enable international collaboration. However, like any other organization, that same scaffolding was built and maintained by a collection of individuals working quietly behind the scenes. In the League's case this task fell to its Secretariat, of which a much-reduced element stayed with the institution during the Second World War and in the lead-up to the final Assembly – many others having left in the late 1930s and 1940 – but as the organization's end drew closer, a significant proportion left to join the UN or similar international bodies. Leaving the organization before it was fully closed was understandable: some were disaffected knowing their work to keep the League of Nations alive was in vain, many were frustrated with the uncertainty surrounding their roles and others had no choice when their contracts were terminated. Yet despite the obstacles, a core group of dedicated officials stayed in Geneva, working alongside their replacements from the UN, through 1947. A closer examination of the mindset of these employees, and their participation in a one-of-a-kind change, brings new insight into the ways of working at international organizations. The ingrained working practices at the League of Nations – the commitment to procedure and propriety, the positioning of public relations at the forefront of decision-making – did not evaporate because the organization was in liquidation and instead had a significant impact on the progression, or lack thereof, of the closure process. The experiences of these individuals, their daily hopes and frustrations, and their relationships with one another provide a vital insight into the social history of the League, away from the high-level world of committees, reports and meetings.

The person in the Secretariat we know the most about, and one of the most prominent figures in this book, is Seán Lester. Secretary general for seven years – albeit with a significantly smaller budget and set of responsibilities than his predecessors – he, like the final years of the League, is often relegated to a passing mention at the end of a concluding chapter, even in more recent works. More than a mere caretaker, he was responsible for the liquidation of an IGO and thus occupies a unique position in our understanding of these institutions.[51] Why did Lester make particular choices, and how did his colleagues, both internal and external to the organization, view these decisions? The League of Nations was unlike any other IGO that came before it, and with no precedent to draw upon or guide him through liquidation, Lester's work and decisions are vitally important in understanding why the closure unfolded as it did. The culture of an organization is heavily influenced by its leadership, and the case of the League of Nations was no different.[52]

Yet leadership does not need to be solely embodied by the person in charge, or by one person alone. There was a small collection of individuals whose commitment to the League was often more pronounced than those senior to them and who were left behind when the organization's leaders believed closure work was complete in 1947. Take, for example, Valentin Stencek, director of Internal Administration – and effectively Lester's second-in-command – who bore increasing levels of responsibility while Lester was away from Geneva during 1946 and was the last official to leave the Secretariat in 1947.[53] He effectively managed the day-to-day running of the Secretariat for months during 1946–7, performed a key role in the organization's liquidation and consequently plays an important part in this book's exploration of that time. The same was true of Percy Watterson, a long-serving accountant with the League Treasury who worked for the organization in his spare evenings and weekends following his official departure in October 1946 and acted as the League's trustee and liquidating agent into 1948.

The 'trivialities' of the Secretariat's life help us to look beyond the institutional aspects of liquidation not only to understand how that process manifests in day-to-day reality but also to illuminate what it means to be an international civil servant of a dead IGO.[54] These figures were not passive bystanders; they were far from nonchalant about the chaotic, uncertain and often unappreciated circumstances in which they found themselves.

The prospect of future employment with the UN or its agencies was uncertain – many of the opportunities in the new secretariats were filled by the time the liquidation was complete – and with minimal prestige in working for an organization publicly declared dead and globally decried as a failure, it might seem difficult to understand why anyone continued working for the League after 1946. The loyalty demonstrated by these officials was due to a combination of factors, but most specifically a dedication to the concept of international civil service as well as a sense of allegiance to colleagues with whom they had endured years of isolation and later repudiation in Geneva. These officials' concerns, their commitment to an institution cast aside by the international community and their relationships with one another – both supportive and fractious – demonstrate how international organizations, away from the talk of bank accounts and buildings, work on an everyday basis and are the foundation on which this book is built.

The book is presented across five main chapters in a predominantly chronological order. The first of these provides an overview of both the League of Nations' experience during the Second World War and the initially surreptitious, then overt, plans to create a new intergovernmental body. The former is key to understanding how certain elements of the League survived the global war it was created to prevent, and why other areas seemingly blinked out of existence. The development of the UN in 1945 meanwhile explains the depth of that organization's later influence on the League's liquidation, especially during 1946, and how that influence also infringed on the morale and mindset of the older organization's officials. The first chapter concludes with the League's twenty-first Assembly in April 1946, the organization's funeral and the point at which it is most commonly believed to have ended, but which, in reality, represented only the start of the League's final phase: liquidation.

The second chapter looks at the months following the organization's final Assembly – and public death – in April 1946, through to the transfer of the League's Genevan estates to the UN at the end of July. This period lasted little more than three months, but was also one of the busiest, dominated as it was by the handover of fixed assets and ill-prepared attempts at technical function transfer to the UN, as well as the exodus of the majority of League Secretariat officials. The chapter examines these three elements of transfer in detail and uses the dismantling of the EFO's office at Princeton University as an example of transfer in microcosm. Finally, the chapter introduces the Board of Liquidation, which was established in April 1946 as the oversight body responsible for dissolution and whose presence, and absence, played a vital part in the progression of the League's closure.

The third chapter moves on to cover the official handover in August 1946 of the League headquarters to the UN, and the remaining months of that year. The arena of international cooperation and governance shifted its attention to the UN and New York in the latter half of 1946, leading to a relatively 'quiet' time for the League of Nations' Secretariat. However, 'quiet' should not be interpreted as meaningless, as the lure of the UN General Assembly and the development of that organization's Secretariat gifted League officials the literal and figurative space to both contemplate, and evade, the enormity of the task ahead of them. The chapter exposes the structural inadequacies of the framework established to dismantle the League of Nations and how the relative success of transfer to the UN effectively put the brakes on the momentum needed to drive the rest of the liquidation process.

The fourth chapter scrutinizes the remaining actions of Seán Lester and his colleagues, up to the dissolution of the Board of Liquidation at its last – and forty-second – meeting at the end of July 1947. Originally intending to dissolve the last remaining elements of the League of Nations by the end of 1946, and then March 1947, the reasons for delay can frequently be found rooted in the pridefulness of the organization's leaders. For good and for ill, many of the decisions taken in the first half of 1947 were motivated by very human and subjective reasoning, including attempts to forge a positive legacy for the League in the long term and long-running negotiations with the ILO in relation to staff pensions.

If the League of Nation's twenty-first Assembly signified the start of the organization's closure, the fifth and final chapter of this book attempts to establish when that closure process was complete. Looking at the drawn-out events following the Board's dissolution in July 1947, it posits a number of different points at which the League of Nations 'died', including the issuance of the Board of Liquidation's Final Report at the end of August 1947, the closure of the Secretariat in October and the last official communication sent to members in January 1948. The final chapter also looks beyond the tangible elements of what remained of the League to consider its institutional memory – especially the knowledge and experience of its rearguard of Secretariat officials – and how some elements of the great experiment have endured.

The well-preserved Archives of the League of Nations at the United Nations Office in Geneva (UNOG) are the primary source of information about the detailed elements of the organization's closure, including Board of Liquidation reports, internal Secretariat correspondence and other official documentation. However, wary of investigating events exclusively from the League's perspective, this book also makes use of an expanded range of sources beyond the bounds of what is held at the Palais des Nations. Sections of the extensive UN Archives in New York and the UNOG Archives in Geneva provide a useful counterpoint view of the transfer and liquidation process, as well as offering an external standpoint on the League's actions and its decision-makers during this period; the correspondence of Adriaan Pelt and Włodzimierz Moderow is of particular interest, due to their close proximity to events in Geneva.[55] Material gathered by the British Government at the time, and now held at the UK National Archives, further illuminates our knowledge of the events, as well as the British Library's collection of both British and international news media – particularly *Tribune de Genève* – to explore the League's closure from the viewpoint of those beyond the immediate inner circle of international governance.

A central tenet of this examination of the League's dissolution is the actor-focused perspective it applies to these events, and consequently it employs a number of personal papers from both those working within the Secretariat and those looking at proceedings from the outside. These include: Seán Lester (secretary general of the League's Secretariat), Włodzimierz Moderow (director of the UN in Geneva) and Trygve Lie (secretary general of the UN Secretariat). Although no personal papers exist for Connie Harris (interim head of personnel from late 1946 onwards), I have conducted an interview, and liaised, with her family in order to gain their personal perspective on her experience of living and working in Geneva. Finally, this work makes use of existing oral history gathered by Stephen Barcroft in the early 1970s for his unpublished thesis. Although records of these interviews are no longer available, I have held my own interview with Barcroft, and this book makes use of his recollections.

Closing

While the past twenty years have produced a wealth of new and valuable studies of the League, it remains an understudied and misunderstood entity. There is so much more to the organization than a set of successes and failures to be weighed against one another. This binary approach belies the League's importance in the history of international relations in the twentieth century: it was the first international institution of its kind, the only sizeable example to undergo a complete and thorough liquidation process, and remains relevant as a result of its relationship with the IGO that followed. The League of Nations' small stature in its final years did not mean it was without impact on the people working there or on the wider developments in international politics, and analysing its closure allows scholars – for the first time – not only to understand the organization's complete story but also to grasp the full life cycle of intergovernmental institutions from birth to death. Closing an international organization like the League was not as simple as turning off the lights; it was a complex process that threw up heretofore-unknown problems, complicated by distinctly human issues, all taking place in a unique set of circumstances.

Many of the commonly accepted assumptions about the League of Nations – the efficacy of its bureaucracy, its delineation from the UN and even the date of its closure – are contradicted by closer scrutiny of its demise. Looking closely at these months and years reveals much that has been forgotten about the League, its liquidation and, consequently, its legacy: the perils of setting precedent, the commitment of officials in the face of personal and professional sacrifice, and the long-lasting impression the organization made on the international institutions that followed. This was a liquidation process unlike any other attempted before, characterized by quiet determination, frustrated attempts to exert control and a desire to see the League remembered as something other than a global pariah.

For too long the final months and years of the League of Nations have been either dismissed or forgotten, and the unfortunate consequence has been the belief that these events have no historical merit and are unworthy of academic scrutiny. The League's death may have taken place quietly and behind closed doors, but it was also drawn out, frequently aimless and at odds with the neat conclusion the organization itself liked to project. The League was one of the first great trials of international administration and it is time to get to grips with the end of the experiment.

1

The beginning of the end, 1940–April 1946

When the League of Nations started to dismantle itself in April 1946, it had already spent the past six-and-a-half years in a wilderness of sorts. In 1939, the organization was undoubtedly under threat and had already taken steps to ensure its continuity if, and when, broader conflict spread across Europe. When those worst fears came true, the League did not crumble but instead endured – much diminished – in the heart of Europe while the Second World War devastated the rest of the continent. The organization's unlikely survival, and its relative readiness for the post-war order, not only ensured a full and equitable liquidation could take place but also shaped the formation and rapid start of the UN.

This chapter provides much needed context for the League of Nations' closure after 1946. The Second World War obviously had a great impact on the organization's ability to perform even the most basic of functions and influenced which elements remained for liquidation, but the isolation and frustrations bred during those years help explain the mood, morale and camaraderie that would define the dissolution. The conflict also created an alliance that became the foundation of a new IGO, whose establishment quietly condemned the League of Nations to death. As the League Secretariat's officials got to grips with their impending demise, they found themselves helping their lauded successors build the organization that would replace them. This chapter explains how a seemingly forgotten and derided international organization was able to survive a global war, help a new institution establish itself and attempt to put its own affairs in order before its membership pulled the plug on its existence.

The League during the Second World War

Little immediately changed for the League of Nations after the invasion of Poland, but in December 1939 an Assembly was convened to address a plea for assistance from Finland following the Soviet invasion of its territory. In spite of its previous inaction in both Manchuria and Ethiopia, the twentieth Assembly expelled the USSR from the ranks of the League membership – a decision that would have later ramifications for the organization's fate.[1] Perhaps the Assembly delegates in Geneva that December considered the expulsion a matter of principle in line with the organization's Covenant, but to many, both at the time and more recently, it looked like racist hypocrisy – having refused to act for its non-European members – and the Soviet Government's ignominy at its expulsion did not diminish with time. This lingering resentment would later seal the League's fate as a doomed institution and increased the pressure from the UN leadership in 1945–6 to dissolve the League as quickly as possible.

The expansion of the Second World War into Western Europe would later provoke massive change in the League Secretariat but, during the so-called 'Phoney War', Geneva was left in limbo. Aware of the political firestorm brewing in the rest of Europe, but attempting to work as normally as possible, the mood in the Secretariat was increasingly uneasy. Egon Ranshofen-Wertheimer, an official who would go on to write one of the most extensive reviews of the League of Nations Secretariat, described the 'gloom' among officials as they continued to fulfil their duties in the usual manner, awaiting their fate with 'a policy of wait and see'.[2] The League's technical committees continued to meet,[3] and some Sections even began to consider war-related issues. This included Alexander Loveday and the Economic and Financial Organisation (EFO) who, as outlined in greater detail in Patricia Clavin's *Securing the World Economy*, were busy working on gathering economic intelligence and analysing potential post-war problems.[4] At the same time the Social Questions Section prepared for its upcoming Advisory Committee meeting by preparing briefing papers on the social problems that might arise as a result of conflict-related population movements.[5] However, the calm before the storm could not last forever.

The extension of war into north-western Europe in May 1940 brought an end to any complacency still lingering among the League's leadership as Axis or Axis-friendly forces surrounded Geneva on three sides within weeks.[6] Committee meetings were postponed indefinitely, and the conflict's expansion accelerated a reduction in the Secretariat's size that had started in 1938 when the newly empowered League of Nations Supervisory Commission agreed to reduce overall budgets.[7] On 15 May 1940, an internal circular was distributed among the Secretariat, sorting all officials into one of several categories. Those on List A were considered indispensable to the new 'efficient organising centre of the Secretariat', while List B officials were given paid leave for six weeks and instructed to remain on standby should the secretary general require them.[8] Many of those placed on List B left and never returned to Geneva, although some on the list remained with the Secretariat until the end of the war, such as Léon Steinig of the Permanent Central Opium Board (PCOB) and Constance (Connie) Harris of Department I.[9] Those in List C, on which there were 203 names, were given two options: opt for either an indefinite suspension of contract or resign, and their decision needed to be made within forty-eight hours.[10] By the end of 1940, Secretariat numbers had reduced to 108 from a high point of 707 in October 1931, with many leaving by choice to reunite with their families abroad or for places of safety away from continental Europe, while others who wished to stay were forced to leave as a result of Avenol's cuts.[11]

Joseph Avenol took over the role of secretary general in 1933 and the majority of his tenure – as described in the work of James Barros among others – while not met with the same enthusiasm from some Secretariat officials as that of Eric Drummond, was by no means disastrous.[12] By 1940, however, under pressure from the new Vichy regime as well as League members, Avenol was increasingly agitated and unnerved by events in Europe.[13] In the first six months of 1940, he threatened senior staff with dismissal, suggested closer liaison with Nazi Germany and covertly despatched Secretariat files to France for 'safekeeping'. In his final months as secretary general, Avenol wrote to the League of Nations' Council President, Adolfo Costa du Rels of Bolivia, suggesting the Secretariat had to be dissolved, if informally, as a budget for 1941 could not be agreed. The letter was later declared void by both men but the episode was evidence of Avenol's loss of faith in the League and his increasingly tenuous relationship with the rest of the Secretariat.[14] Contemporaries of Avenol, including Ranshofen-Wertheimer, were not afraid to later place blame at the secretary general's feet: 'it appeared as though he were bent upon the destruction of the machinery which had been entrusted to his care'.[15] This was echoed by Jaromír Kopecky, the Czech delegate to the twenty-first Assembly in 1946 and later Board of Liquidation member, who declared: 'I cannot refrain from mentioning the fact that, had a change not occurred in 1940 as regards the person at the head of the Secretariat, this nefarious tendency and state of paralysis would have continued.'[16]

Other senior figures in the Secretariat, including deputy secretary general Seán Lester, EFO director Alexander Loveday, and undersecretary general Thanassis Aghnides, worked together as best they could to prevent Avenol's repeated attempts to, as they saw it, sabotage the League, and instead encouraged the erratic secretary general's resignation.[17] In a personal diary entry dated 17 July 1940, Lester expressed his frustration:

Will the bumptious bubble be burst (his morale is not really good), or (more likely) will he try – even from spite – to put his plan into force before he goes. Am assuming he will have to go despite all his high-fallutin' and legal arguments of four days ago! According to that theory of his, if he goes no one will have the authority to give him his pension money!!![18]

When Avenol was eventually convinced to fully resign in August 1940, he was succeeded by Lester, despite the latter's initial reluctance.[19] In another private journal entry written before he took up the post, he recalled a discussion with Costa du Rels about the possibility: 'I explained my personal views, pointing out that the job was not an enviable one ... I said I would think it over and I had never yet refused moral responsibilities.'[20] Previously a journalist, Irish Free State politician and delegate to the Assembly before becoming League High Commissioner to Danzig in 1934,[21] he became utterly devoted to the League of Nations, recognizing that leadership was needed to lead the Secretariat if work were to continue, and not even crippling loneliness – he was a devoted family man and missed them deeply during the war – would deter him from his obligation. In a lecture given in April 1997, Lester's son-in-law, Douglas Gageby, referenced a letter the secretary general wrote to Seymour Jacklin in the midst of his isolation:

> I do not believe we are merely pumping a doomed ship. (If we are, I'd still go on pumping till we get an order to abandon it.) All the glory and great activity may be going elsewhere – which of us expects thanks in the end? But as far as I can see, the value of this little side show in the war cannot yet be determined. Decisions may be taken in the future that will give our work an air of past futility but that is not yet and in certain political circumstances the damaged ship may come in damned useful ... Whatever the end may be, I, for one shall not regret the personal effort and sacrifice in the years which have seemed stolen out of my life.[22]

One of the acting secretary general's first acts – he kept that title until he was officially declared secretary general by the Assembly in 1946 – was to ensure the Supervisory Commission met in Lisbon in 1940, agreeing the budget for 1941 that Avenol had declared impossible. The delegation of the Assembly's powers to the Commission in 1938 kept the League and the Secretariat in operation throughout the war, as the group attempted to maintain a quorum in either Britain or America. Navigating the unusual routes enforced by conflict, including trips via Newfoundland, Bermuda and Senegal, the Commission members showed a level of fortitude equal to that of the

Secretariat itself, never refusing to make a journey, approving budgets and saving the League from death by defaulted management.[23] Another early act on Lester's part was to grant approval for elements of the League Secretariat to leave Geneva and pursue their work overseas.[24] A 'mission' of experts from Department II, led by Alexander Loveday, moved to Princeton University's Institute for Advanced Study in 1940, while the ILO – staffed by its own Secretariat but closely associated with the League – moved to Montreal. The Treasury, managed by Seymour Jacklin, relocated to London, and a branch office was established in Washington, DC for several officials working in drug control. The moves were justified as a way to ensure ongoing key activity, and the improved communications outside continental Europe, plus the significantly reduced risk of invasion would, and did, improve capacity.[25]

Once the immediate threat to the League of Nations' survival was dispensed with via Avenol's resignation, the Secretariat's attention turned to maintaining the organization's services and activities as best it could. The EFO officials based at Princeton were, relatively speaking, able to thrive away from the restrictions of wartime Europe. As detailed by Clavin, the Statistical Yearbook was published as normal, as was the Monthly Bulletin of Statistics,[26] and the staff at Princeton were able to focus on post-war issues, including reconstruction, trade, economic security and demography.[27]

It was not as straightforward, however, for other parts of the Secretariat. In January 1943 the number of officials at Geneva dropped to its lowest point thus far – eighty-one staff members – and postal communications beyond Switzerland were erratic, with one League official reporting an interruption in contact between Washington, DC and Geneva of almost fifteen months.[28] For individuals who had worked together so closely for the past two decades, this isolation was difficult. The international civil service experiment they were part of provided them with an experience unlike any other, and wartime separation and isolation threatened their shared determination. Work dominated correspondence, but there was also a sense of camaraderie and even friendship between officials. The group supported one another, keeping each other going when it would have been more than reasonable to give up and go home. In a statement at the twenty-first Assembly in April 1946, Lester paid glowing tribute to his colleagues: 'It is due to them that I have been able to carry out the duties entrusted to me throughout the war and that the international work entrusted to the League never broke down during those dark years.' Unable to name all those who assisted him, he singled out figures such as Seymour Jacklin, Alexander Loveday, Valentin Stencek (director of Internal Administration) and Henri

Vigier (head of Department I), the latter two of whom remained with Lester in Geneva throughout the war.[29]

Despite the restrictions in staff numbers, communications and physical isolation, the technical Sections of the League of Nations published over 130 reports and documents between 1 January 1940 and 31 October 1945, yet this number alone gives a distorted view of productivity levels and the fortunes of different Secretariat services. Of those reports, 118 related to the work of only four areas: Economics, Finance and Transit; Health; Social Questions; and Traffic in Opium and other Dangerous Drugs.[30] For every Section producing a relatively high volume of publishable work, there were other areas that suffered, including Legal Questions, Intellectual Co-operation, Mandates and Slavery. Even the number of publications was not a clear indication of productivity, as was the case with the Social Questions Section.

The Section had always been small in comparison to others in the Secretariat, but by the end of 1940 only one member of staff remained when Egon Ranshofen-Wertheimer was stranded in London after a trip there in early May, and another two officials left during Joseph Avenol's staff cuts.[31] When Andrée Colin, the last woman standing, passed away suddenly in August 1941 the Secretariat's senior leaders kept the Section's activities alive as much as possible – with much assistance from Connie Harris of Department I – but with no full-time resources available to manage the work, even producing the annual reports on trafficking and pornography was an achievement.[32]

One recurrent theme in the thinking of Lester and others during the war was the perceived importance of keeping the League of Nations alive for the post-war world, whatever that might look like. Any opportunity to become involved in reconstruction and war-related issues justified the organization's continued existence, and thus the League leadership jumped on a potential opportunity in 1941 to become involved in a US-led study on the immediate welfare problems caused by war. Suggested by Social Questions Advisory Committee member Katharine Lenroot, chief of the Children's Bureau at the US Department of Labor, Lester and Arthur Sweetser – an American Information Section official until 1942 – were eager at the prospect of not only facilitating a useful discussion on the effects of conflict, but also increasing the role of the United States in international work.[33] However, their enthusiasm was thwarted again when Lenroot chose to take the study elsewhere, leaving the League of Nations out of proceedings. Lester found himself in command of an organization that was becoming increasingly acceptable to ignore, and his anger was palpable in his choice of sign-off in a letter to Sweetser – a close friend – on the subject, curtly stating, 'That is all.'[34]

The Drug Control Service, split between Washington, DC and Geneva, had a similar experience. Bertil Renborg, head of the Service, produced numerous memoranda on the subject of reconstruction and what needed to be done before the war was over, in spite of the increasing involvement of the United States and Harry Anslinger at the Bureau of Narcotics.[35] In a letter to Seymour Jacklin, dated 10 February 1943, Renborg wrote:

> Alexander [Loveday] suggested to me the other day that the Bureau of Narcotics (Mr. Anslinger) might be approached with the suggestion of lending somebody for this purpose [post-war planning]. This does not appeal to me because I feel that we ought to be completely free in our work. I am sure that you appreciate this … I think it is important that the Secretariat should steer a middle course and be perfectly impartial.[36]

Renborg, like Lester, was fighting a losing battle for relevance in a changing world. The League was becoming increasingly immaterial as new international organizations were being established, and fewer and fewer people wanted a post-war world tainted by the failures of the League of Nations. The early part of the Second World War, dominated by budget cuts, the loss of staff and a leadership crisis, was a fight for survival for the League and its Secretariat. By 1942 and 1943, the fight became one of staying relevant, and ultimately a battle to remain useful to those leading the world into the UN. Some found it easier than others to relinquish that power, but the decision was beyond the control of the Secretariat, including Seán Lester.

Plans for a new organization

Rumours began to swirl as early as 1942 that Allied leaders were planning some kind of international organization for the post-war world, and both the US and British governments were secretly working to design the shape and guidelines of a new IGO. A pilot or test case for this post-war intergovernmental cooperation was soon underway in the form of the United Nations Relief and Rehabilitation Administration (UNRRA), which was established formally in November 1943 with forty-four member states. UNRRA was founded before the United Nations Organization, but its success in planning and organizing relief in post-war Europe lent credence to the idea that multilateral collaboration, including both the United States and the Soviet Union, could still flourish in the future.[37]

While Seán Lester and his colleagues were aware early on that discussions on the subject were taking place, it wasn't until early 1944, when planning became more official and open, that it became apparent that a resurrected or evolved League of Nations was not an option, despite planners actively using the organization as a template.[38] Clark Eichelberger, executive director of the US-based Committee to Study the Organization of Peace, recalled a planning meeting in 1942 during which those in attendance used the League's machinery as a basis from which to make their recommendations, identifying synonyms so as to avoid too many direct comparisons. For example, the League Assembly became the General Assembly, and the Council became the Security Council.[39] What was clear was that the League would be replaced by something new, although it was not yet obvious what that was, what it would be responsible for and what its creation would mean for the Secretariat officials still working in Geneva and beyond.[40]

Lester and Alexander Loveday, director of Department I, watched the Dumbarton Oaks and Bretton Woods Conferences closely as it became clear the decisions made by the attendees could have an effect on what remained of the League.[41] Would they agree to include socio-economic international cooperation in their new organization? Would this mean a direct transfer of League resources? Lester even allowed himself a moment of cautious optimism at the prospect of the UN planners using the League of Nations as the basis from which to formulate their vision for the future.[42] As it was, the discussions at Dumbarton Oaks, between representatives of the United States, the United Kingdom, the Soviet Union and later China, were ultimately focused more on the security and political aspects of the future organization than any non-political or technical functions. Consequently, there was little in the way of concrete outcomes the League's leadership could use for their own planning, although the announcement of a conference for all UN states at least identified the next step in proceedings.

The subsequent United Nations Conference on International Organization, held at San Francisco between April and June 1945, was designed to be a historic affair, with delegations from every proposed member state, as well as interested lobby groups and the world's press. As only five of the League's remaining thirty-five member states were not part of the UN – Finland, Ireland, Portugal, Sweden and Switzerland – the proceedings would give an indication of the attitudes of the League's own members. The foundation of a new organization would mean at least some elements of the League of Nations would have to be liquidated – what these areas would be was a key question from the League leadership's perspective – and Lester was both optimistic and realistic about the extent of the answers from the Conference.⁴³ The secretary general expressed a strong disinclination to personally attend the conference, but he also understood how important his presence might be in providing advice on the management of an IGO, as well as being present at the forefront of the discussions and their prospective impact on the League.⁴⁴ The decision was nevertheless taken out of Lester's hands when an unofficial invite for three representatives arrived just thirteen days before the Conference opened, and the League's leadership agreed the secretary general should attend alongside Loveday and Seymour Jacklin, League treasurer.⁴⁵ The backhanded nature of the invitation – they were not permitted to form an official delegation; the representatives were there purely to make themselves available for any informal consultations required – was a warning sign of what would be a wasted few weeks for Lester, Loveday and Jacklin.⁴⁶ Upon their arrival in San Francisco, the League trio found themselves without accreditation for the conference, later receiving just one ticket for the opening session which, when Loveday decided to attend, was found to be so high up in the theatre that he left after just thirty minutes complaining of dizziness.⁴⁷ At a later point Jacklin was invited to a committee meeting to give testimony, only to be left outside in a foyer for two hours in the middle of the night, before being told to return in the morning.⁴⁸

The US government did not hide its desire to keep the League of Nations, or anyone related to it, away from plans for its new organization. The war was not yet over when the San Francisco Conference began, and the UN was deliberately framed as a fresh start; they did not want to taint the events or the new institution with the League's supposed failure.⁴⁹ The same was true, to an extent, with the Soviet leadership. Still reeling from the government's expulsion from the organization in December 1939, the Soviet representatives made it clear they considered the League a failed experiment and raised objections to Lester's presence at the conference as the citizen of a neutral, non-member state, that is, Ireland.⁵⁰ The issue was eventually settled after nearly three weeks, but it was a strong indication of the power dynamic that would dictate both the plans for and the progress of the League's closure: the UN was now making the decisions and working to its own timetable, while the League's leadership had no choice but to sit at the bottom of the pecking order and wait.⁵¹

The eventual outcomes of the San Francisco Conference were not particularly useful for planning the dissolution process from the Secretariat's viewpoint. The possibility of transferring the functions, assets and staff of the League to the new organization was not discussed – the emphasis was on the new rather than the old – and instead the focal points of proceedings were the signing of the new Charter and the interim arrangements established to set up the Security Council, Trusteeship Council, and Economic and Social Council (ECOSOC) as well as planning for the first General Assembly. The body created to manage this process, the UN Preparatory Commission, had a large number of responsibilities beyond these primary tasks, only one of which was a pledge to consider a transfer of the League's non-political functions, activities and assets.[52] Closing the League of Nations before the UN was fully established was not an option – the shared membership of the two organizations wanted to see some degree of transfer between the two – so Lester and his colleagues were forced to remain in limbo while the new United Nations Organization solidified its own strategy.

The UN Preparatory Commission was made up of representatives from every member of the UN, and discussions began only days after the Charter was signed at San Francisco.[53] The interim arrangements agreed at the Conference recognized, however, that it would be nigh impossible to keep a group so large sitting for months at a time, as well as being an unwieldy size for constructive discussions, and as such a smaller Executive Committee was created to manage and plan on behalf of the Preparatory Commission in between meetings.[54] In session from 16 August until 24 November 1945,[55] and made up of delegates from Australia, Brazil, Canada, Chile, China, Czechoslovakia, France, Iran, Mexico, the Netherlands, the Soviet Union, the UK, the United States and Yugoslavia – the same countries comprising the Executive Committee at San Francisco – the work of the Committee was managed on a day-to-day basis by a small Secretariat recruited, and led, by Gladwyn Jebb.[56] Jebb and David Owen, his deputy, were both British civil servants, and the former was well-acquainted with early proposals for the UN, having being involved in post-war planning for some years before assuming his new post.[57]

Lester correctly assumed any initial liaison between the League and the UN planners would be informal and mostly carried out on the former's behalf by himself and Seymour Jacklin. Both were resident in London at the time and with the League's administrative body, the Supervisory Commission, not in session, they were best placed to negotiate terms.[58] While some of this took place in the shape of informal meetings between Jebb, Owen and Lester, the vast majority of the Executive Committee's relationship with the League was carried out via letter and the passing of documentation. A request for details on the League's powers and duties relating to international conventions, its assets and liabilities situation, and the organization's current technical activities was just the first of many to come over the later months of 1945.[59] The Secretariat in Geneva spent significant portions of time preparing reports on a range of subjects, but it was an inefficient process and increasingly wearisome for Lester. He was convinced, perhaps rightly, that posting written documentation was not the most effective means of communicating the knowledge and experience within the League's Secretariat, and despite making this point to Jebb on several occasions, he made little progress in changing the format of their interactions.[60]

The flow of information between the League and the Executive Committee was also decidedly one-way; the Executive Committee requested material and the Secretariat provided it. As time passed throughout the autumn of 1945, Lester and his colleagues were still none-the-wiser regarding the UN plans and thus no further with their own efforts to plan for dissolution. The Executive Committee refused to let Lester see League-related minutes or documentation from their meetings on confidentiality grounds, although it was difficult to enforce complete secrecy when several of the Executive Committee delegates were also still involved with the League.[61] Jonkheer Beelaerts van Blokland, a Dutch delegate to the Executive Committee as well as a member of the League's Drug Supervisory Body (DSB), offered to send Lester details from his committee meetings when he discovered the secretary general was still in the dark as regards plans.[62]

The first concrete outcome from Preparatory Commission planning, relevant to the League, was the UN decision to consider transfer of the League's assets separately from that of its activities, services and functions. To this end, the UN planners created another body, the United Nations Committee on League of Nations Assets, to engage and negotiate with the League's leadership to agree an approach for asset transfer.[63] Established on 18 December 1945, this new committee was chaired by Włodzimierz Moderow, the Polish delegate to the Preparatory Commission – and later the director of the UN Office in Geneva – and comprised representatives from Chile, China, France, Poland, South Africa, the USSR, the United States and the UK.[64]

The skewed power dynamics between the UN representatives and those of the League were, however, on display before the discussions even began. The meeting date of 8 January 1946 was set only days in advance, and the Preparatory Commission's report, which detailed its recommendations on asset transfer, had not been seen by anyone at the League, let alone published to a wider audience. While Gladwyn Jebb reassured Lester that the document would be available to Supervisory Commission members at the meeting, this approach hardly allowed for advanced preparation on their part.[65] To make matters even more difficult for the Supervisory Commission, Moderow, chairman of the UN Committee, passed along a message with a mere three days' notice, asking the League representatives to take the initiative in making the proposals.[66] There was no doubt as to who was in charge of the negotiations, and the League of Nations was not in a position to object. Lester expressed his concerns to Jacklin just a few days later, fearing the League was 'being rushed' into agreement with the UN Committee, but realized there was little to be done and instead could only hope for the best.[67]

Fewer than three weeks and four joint meetings later, Moderow reported back to the UN General Assembly's League of Nations Committee on the *Common Plan for the Transfer of League of Nations Assets Established by the United Nations Committee and the Supervisory Commission of the League of Nations*. An eight-point plan, albeit fewer than two pages in length, it was a document of compromise. The Supervisory Commission described it as providing the 'broad outlines' of a means to facilitate transfer,[68] although the original draft of the report downgraded any original enthusiasm the group had: the Supervisory Commission went from 'convinced' of its 'fair and reasonable' nature, to only 'considering' it as such.[69] The UN Committee likewise reported 'difficulties and divergences of opinion' during proceedings, not referring to a particular discussion by name, but the wording suggested the ILO may have proved a stubborn negotiating partner.[70]

The Common Plan agreed a transfer of all fixed assets from the League to the UN 'on or about' 1 August 1946; the degree of elasticity for this date included to avoid any embarrassment should it need to change.[71] Agreeing values for the assets was a more tricky prospect due to the unknown future use of the buildings and land, so the original cost price was taken as the basis on which the agreement was settled. A share of the transfer proceeds would be granted to each League member, and the size of this portion would depend on a distribution scheme to be established by the League of Nations – this was later agreed by the final Assembly as a percentage of each member's contributions to the organization across its lifetime. Those states that were also members of the UN would have their share credited to them in their UN accounts. The latter organization committed itself to determining how and when these 'credits' could be used by a date no later than 31 December 1948. Finland, Ireland, Portugal, Sweden and Switzerland, the members of the League not yet part of the UN, would receive their share of the proceeds as a direct transfer from the League itself. This was one of several responsibilities attributed to the League alone – a list which also included transferring the archives and any gifts free of charge; settling the accounts of those members in arrears; separating the interests of the ILO from the rest of the League before transfer; and dissolving as quickly as possible. Finally, the UN and League would also work together to make arrangements, as needed, with the Swiss authorities on issues relating to the transfer of assets on Swiss soil.[72] There were no definite plans as to how this transfer would take place or who was responsible for managing it at either organization, but it was some much-needed progress. Most importantly, the agreement laid out the high-level principles months before any transfer was meant to take place, ensuring any further refinement and detail could be settled in plenty of time.

UN planners were, however, less forthcoming about the future of the League's non-political functions and activities. The former were areas of work delegated to the League of Nations by international agreement, such as the provision of secretariats for the PCOB and the DSB or acting as a custodian for original signed documents and international treaties, commonly referred to as the Treaty Series. As these functions were administered by the League, but not directed by it, they were often supported by many governments outside its membership – the United States, in particular, was a strong advocate of drug control work.[73] The Preparatory Commission's recommendation, which was approved by the General Assembly two months later, was to transfer these functions – the PCOB, the DSB and the Treaty Series – to the UN, albeit with the right to review this decision at a later date should it choose, and without a schedule or scheme as to how the handover would be managed.[74]

The potential transfer of activities, however, was a more contentious subject. Sometimes described as technical activity, the League's work in this arena typically took the form of facilitating international collaboration in socio-economic fields such as public health, social welfare and intellectual cooperation. The areas of focus were decided upon by the League's many technical committees – made up of delegates from countries both part of, and outside, the organization – and carried out by officials of the Secretariat. The recommendations of the Bruce Report, published in August 1939 and commissioned by former Secretary General Joseph Avenol, strongly suggested there was backing for this kind of activity beyond the League's membership, but support for a direct transfer to the UN was not universal. Both the Soviet Union and the United States were hesitant to link the new organization with the supposed failure of its predecessor. It took considerable cajoling at Dumbarton Oaks to convince the Soviet representative Gromyko to agree to the formation of an ECOSOC – heavily modelled on the League-commissioned Bruce Committee Report – and an unnamed source in the US delegation to the Preparatory Commission told Seán Lester that there was a strong disinclination to take on much of the technical work to avoid the idea that the UN was merely a remodelled League.[75]

And they were not alone in their concerns about linking the new with the old, despite many government representatives expressing positivity towards some of the League's technical work. Delegates to Committee 7 of the Preparatory Commission found it difficult to reach agreement on terminology, let alone approach, in their review of the Executive Committee's work and formulation of further recommendations for the possible transfer of functions. The group met seven times across three weeks, for a total time of over thirteen hours, and spent at least a portion of that time assessing the use of the word 'transfer', ultimately replacing it with 'assumption of' for fear of linking the new UN with the League.[76]

As to how any activities might be transferred, the UN was forced to take a compromise approach. While the majority of the new organization's members favoured a mass transfer – as did the League – the Soviet government was wary of inadvertently agreeing to internationalist encroachment within its borders, preferring to review each function or activity on a case-by-case basis. At a discussion in late November 1945, the USSR representative Boris Shtein argued convincingly that 'no distinction could be drawn between political and non-political functions'.[77] Like its predecessor, the UN was not a monolith; ideological cracks were already beginning to form among the wartime Allies, and both the Preparatory Commission and the first officials of the UN Secretariat had to tread lightly if their new experiment was to avoid falling at the first hurdle. With that in mind, the Preparatory Commission agreed that the new ECOSOC would provisionally assume several activities, pending a later review during which the UN could choose to discontinue the former League work if so desired.[78] Nevertheless, like the agreement to transfer some of the League's functions and much to the frustration of Seán Lester, the process of how and when this would happen was yet to be determined. In a letter sent to Carl Hambro in February 1946, the League's secretary general relayed the details of a recent conversation with the UN Executive Committee's David Owen:

> In our conversation however, pointing out the difficulties created by the absence of decisions by the United Nations I asked if he could yet indicate any date on which the assumption of League activities could take place ... For the present he said both organizations had to face all the troubles of this indefiniteness.[79]

The number of staff working for the League increased steadily through the final months of the war. From a low point of only 81 officials in January 1943, the Secretariat contained 124 members of staff by the summer of 1945.[80] The easing of communication and travel restrictions across Western Europe allowed the

League of Nations to begin actively recruiting both new and former officials, as it became clear the numbers needed to liquidate the organization would be greater than those currently on hand.[81] Valentin Stencek, director of Internal Administration and Lester's right-hand man in Geneva, instructed Janet Smith, an official working at the League Treasury in London, to enquire as to the availability of former staff to work as stenographers, translators, copyists and more.[82] By January 1946, 132 officials were employed by the Secretariat, but Lester was concerned this increase would not last long.[83] His fears centred on the possibility that officials would leave the League before liquidation was complete, either for the UN or for different opportunities, leaving them with the individuals the new organization did not want and the League in a 'chaotic situation'.[84] Despite a valiant effort to keep the Secretariat alive during the war, Lester was now uneasy about his ability to see the organization continue long enough to both deliver a successful handover to the UN and wind up appropriately.[85]

The Executive Committee of the UN Preparatory Commissions made it clear in its recommendations that League Secretariat officials would not be directly transferred to UN management.[86] There was a possibility that people might be approached directly – the UN was well aware of the experience and knowledge held by League staff – but there were no guarantees. Individuals not approached in this manner were welcomed to apply directly to the UN, but Preparatory Commission delegates made it clear that recruitment to the Secretariat was the purview of the UN secretary general. Any such recruitment would also be made on the basis of new UN contracts, meaning previous League contracts must be terminated first.[87] To make this 'cherry-picking' of League staff even more challenging for Lester, the Supervisory Commission agreed in the Common Plan that the League would not stand in the way of any official joining the UN and would release personnel from contracts if requested.[88]

Lester's concerns about the capability and capacity of the Secretariat to effectively deliver a transfer to a still-in-development successor, while also dismantling an IGO, were exacerbated by the League's own personnel circumstances. While the secretary general knew notice of termination of employment would have to be issued to League staff at some point during 1946, much remained unknown in regard to UN decision-making, and he was wary of losing officials before the real work of liquidation could begin. However, his apprehensions were not shared by all his colleagues, and on this particular issue he found himself in opposition to Carl Hambro, president of the Supervisory Commission, who was concerned with the outward appearance of the League's progress with dissolution. He made enquiries with Lester in mid-January 1946 about issuing notice to all staff in 'the immediate future' and was talked down at the time by the acting secretary general, but he brought up the issue again in a Supervisory Commission meeting just over a month later.[89] In Lester's notes on the meeting, he recorded that Hambro suggested notice should be given as soon as possible to stop the 'ill-founded and unpleasant gossip' among government officials that the remaining League officials were trying to prolong their jobs. Hambro's position was that the League must at least be seen to be dismantling, regardless of the UN delays, arguing that key officials could be re-engaged on short-term contracts once their permanent status had ended.[90]

Lester was vehemently opposed to what he believed was a premature action. He reiterated his concerns to Hambro on several occasions, explaining that it was unnecessarily risky to terminate contracts when the UN had not made it clear when activity transfer might take place, and emphasizing the practical difficulties in issuing a mass notice to staff on different contracts with different terms. Lester was further vexed when Seymour Jacklin, League treasurer, indirectly suggested the acting secretary general was engaging in 'petty tyranny' by attempting to hold onto members of staff by making them wait for an indemnity payment.[91] Lester was infuriated by his colleagues' seeming lack of common sense, especially as he tried hard to implement a measure of order and structure to what was otherwise a chaotic set of circumstances. He longed for a dignified and 'orderly disbandment' which balanced both the needs of the service as well as the interests of his colleagues.[92]

In due course, however, Hambro and the Supervisory Commission enforced their position and ordered Lester to give notice to all staff. The secretary general did not contest the instruction nor refuse to carry it out, although he composed a letter to the president on 26 February 1946, explaining that he would of course attempt to avert any negative consequences arising from the decision, but prepare for their occurrence regardless, reminding Hambro that they were all 'acting in the dark'. It was an uncharacteristically formal piece of correspondence and strongly suggests a desire on Lester's part to 'cover his back' if the endeavour went poorly.[93]

And thus, the purgatory period that began one year earlier dragged on into the spring of 1946. Almost a year after the San Francisco Conference opened, the League of Nations and its officials had little sense of what the coming months would hold. They had expected, or hoped, to better understand the aims of the transfer process, as well as how and when it would take place. As one UN General Assembly delegate noted in a report to his colleagues in January 1946, there was 'an intimate connection' between the transfer to the UN of certain assets and functions, and the League's dissolution: the latter could not take place until the UN effected the former.[94] Instead the League had only a vague commitment to purchase its estates, a collection of loose promises to take on some of its work and absolutely no idea how any of this would be managed. Staff did not know if they had jobs in the long term, the organization could not undertake any liquidation activity and senior UN figures could provide little reassurance. All of this left the League and its Secretariat in an ambiguous position with the organization's first Assembly in over six years rapidly approaching. This gathering was supposed to be the institution's funeral, but the League's administration could neither close the organization nor carry on as before. The end of the League was supposedly nigh, but in reality the upcoming twenty-first Assembly would merely mark the start of another chapter in the organization's history.

The twenty-first Assembly

The League leadership, including Seán Lester and the Supervisory Commission, initially thought – in line with organizational precedent – that two Assemblies were required to close the League of Nations. The first would take place in 1945 to agree the budget for 1946, approve potential transfer to the UN, review the Secretariat's wartime work and authorize discussions with UN planners.[95] The subsequent and final Assembly would be held after the first UN General Assembly, likely in the spring of 1946, to ceremonially dissolve the organization as per the earlier discussions with the UN planners.[96] However, the cautious pace at which UN planning was unfolding meant it was increasingly unrealistic to hold an Assembly before the end of 1945, and the limited understanding of liquidation processes for an organization of its size and complexity meant the League leadership still believed the dissolution could be managed with relative ease and minimal oversight. Instead, Lester and Hambro suggested to member states that the Supervisory Commission should be empowered to begin negotiations without the Assembly's explicit approval, and by October 1945 this approach was formally adopted.[97]

Thus, it came to be that, despite the lack of progress in discussions with the UN, the convocation for the League's twenty-first, and final, Assembly was despatched to members in late January 1946.[98] This would be the organization's last hurrah, and those both in and outside the Secretariat wanted to go out with their heads held high. Arthur Sweetser, a former Secretariat official and vocal advocate for the organization in his native United States, wrote to Carl Hambro, the president of the Supervisory Commission, suggesting they host an elaborate event to fly in the faces of those who sought to 'scapegoat' the League for their own shortcomings.[99] Lester was all in favour of the proposal; he wanted the League to close with dignity and with pride in what it had achieved, even if the rest of the world had moved on.

The pivotal Assembly agenda item centred on the closure of the organization, and this measure was the only instance in which the agreement to dismantle the League of Nations was formalized. The decision to create a new global organization obviously made the League redundant, but at no point prior to the final Assembly was the organization's demise ratified by either the UN or the League's leadership. So why was the League able to solemnize its closure, when other institutions might have quietly fizzled away? The answer lay in the organization's valuable assets, worth millions of dollars, and over thirty governments all hoping for a share. An Assembly resolution, approved by all members, would therefore be needed to legally close the organization and agree an equitable process for liquidation of said assets. Members were not expected to oppose dissolving the League, but it was deemed appropriate – and in line with the League's championing of due process – to create a resolution that would capture any outstanding issues while also bringing the organization to a close. There was, however, no legal precedent from which to draw. While this allowed for a degree of freedom in its design, it also meant starting from scratch. Consequently, despite significant assistance from the British Government, there was a large amount of work to complete within a short space of time, and it was a rush to finalize the text; as late as 6 April, only two days before proceedings began, Seán Lester and Seymour Jacklin were still reviewing the latest draft.[100] The fixed deadline meant those working on the resolution were obliged to view its contents through a short-term lens, that is, focusing only on what was needed to ensure its passage through the Assembly, leaving little space or time to also consider what the text might helpfully reflect, such as the objectives of the dissolution process or the practical means by which it should take place. The tight timeline in place for both the Assembly and the months that followed was a blow to long-term planning for liquidation and wrought much frustration on the heads of those labouring to make it a reality.

The last-minute rush to draw up the resolution was not the only work carried out by the Secretariat in preparation for the grand affair. The formulation of a report reviewing the work carried out by officials during the Second World War took substantial resources, as did the agreement of the agenda and preparing Hambro's speech for the opening session, alongside other menial but protracted tasks such as arranging hotel accommodations and upgrading the interpreter earphone system.[101] In contrast to what might be expected, closing the organization increased the workload rather than diminishing it. The result was a scramble to re-engage former officials, new staff and even UN Secretariat members to meet the need.[102] By 1 April 1946, one week before the Assembly began, 232 new staff had been brought on board, bringing the total number of League employees to 397, the majority of whom worked in support roles such as clerks, ushers, cleaners and shorthand-typists.[103]

The twenty-first Assembly did not fail to attract attendees. A total of thirty-five member states were in attendance, plus one observer state, and representatives from the UN, the ILO and the International Institute for Intellectual Co-operation – among others – with 173 delegates in total.[104] While the numbers were smaller than previous Assemblies, it was notable that every member had at least one delegate present; even the organization's first Assembly, held in 1920, failed to attract full attendance in that regard.[105] Delegates, members of the press and the bolstered Secretariat saw the great halls of the Palais des Nations busy again after years of quiet seclusion. The home of the League was built to impress, and the sense of grandeur it was designed to instil – as a representation of international cooperation – was at its most radiant when the Assembly was in session. April 1946 was no different, even if the main Assembly Hall was a little emptier than it had been in the past.[106]

Proceedings began on 8 April 1946 and lasted for twelve days, made up of committee meetings considering specific issues, as well as a number of plenary sessions of the Assembly as a whole.[107] These latter sessions were not designed as forums for productive debate – there were too many delegates to foster decision-making – and instead took the form of lengthy speeches given by representatives. This being the final Assembly, these speeches were mostly dedicated to the end of the organization, its history and the hopes for its legacy in the future. The outpouring of lament for this fallen endeavour was a comfort to those still working for the League Secretariat, but the credibility of the eulogizers was also undercut by their abandonment of that same organization for the newer, shinier model that was the UN. Much like a romantic relationship the League was founded on hope and depended on trust for its survival. The organization's members did not necessarily bear the League ill-will but that trust was gone, something Sweetser recognized in a speech just days before the Assembly when he said 'I feel a bit like a man on his second honeymoon who is asked to speak about his first wife.'[108]

The eventual outcomes of the Assembly were mostly as expected. The Permanent Court of International Justice was officially closed which, in all respects other than the formal resolution of the Assembly, had already taken place.[109] Seán Lester was retroactively promoted to full secretary general of the organization, a position in which he had been 'acting' since the resignation of Joseph Avenol in the summer of 1940.[110] Accounts were approved up to the end of 1945, decisions taken by the Supervisory Commission during the war were validated and tribute was paid to the US institutions responsible for housing League missions during the war, as well as to the Soviet Union for its role in 'the overthrow of the Fascist enemies of civilisation'.[111] Delegates also rubber-stamped the UN decisions agreed at its General Assembly two months earlier, essentially allowing the new organization to adopt whichever functions and activities it wished – explicitly naming only the Treaty Series – but providing no specific means of oversight for these transfers. Instead the Assembly instructed Lester to 'afford every facility' to the UN in any transfer work. This specific instruction, interpreted to mean Lester should take special pains to assist the UN, would quickly cause problems as it clashed with his responsibility to the League and its closure.[112]

The resolution to dissolve the organization was approved unanimously on 18 April 1946 at the close of proceedings. Framed by the argument that the Charter of the UN had created a new international organization serving the same purpose as the League, and as most League members had already joined, the League of Nations would cease to exist – barring liquidation activities – from the day following the Assembly's end. It was a ten-point statement, thin on detail, covering the ratification of the Common Plan – a moot point considering the UN General Assembly had already started to act on the agreement – as well as transferring several specific funds to the ILO, outlining the responsibilities of the secretary general, confirming the distribution of assets to members and the formation of a Board of Liquidation to oversee what remained.[113]

The resolution did little more than provide some high-level principles for what would follow. There was no timetable for fixed assets set beyond the suggested date of transfer, no guidance on which areas took precedence over others and no discussion of how any of the liquidation or transfer would manifest on a practical, day-to-day basis. If anything, the resolution was contradictory in parts, leaving it difficult to conclude what a successful liquidation looked like. The importance of continuity in activities was stressed both within the resolution itself, as well as in committee meetings.[114] Any interruption to services was cautioned against in the strongest terms, and the resolution empowered the secretary general to ensure this work continued 'to whatever extent is necessary' to guarantee a smooth transition to the UN, including the extension of staff contracts and prolongation of negotiations. Yet the same resolution also called for liquidation to be enacted quickly, as well as allowing the UN to employ any current League officials as, and when, it wanted. So, what could Seán Lester and his colleagues take from this? The resolution conveyed a mixed message: dissolve the organization as quickly as possible, give the UN whatever it needed, but also ensure the League's legacy by managing a smooth handover, with minimal interruption, at all costs.[115]

Conclusions

The twenty-first Assembly was outwardly a success, and some vindication for those in and outside the League's Administration in regard to the organization's legacy. The proceedings were lauded in the UK press, described as 'a dignified end for a great international institution' by the *Belfast Telegraph*, while both the *Manchester Guardian* and *The Times of London* issued daily reports on events.[116] The organization's virtues were extolled, praise was lauded upon its lofty ambitions, but it was foolish to pretend this was the definitive end of the organization. It was an exercise in box-ticking, and perhaps a well-deserved morale boost for those who had spent years in isolation working for a maligned institution, but there was much more to be done, and no concrete plans for how it would be managed.

Decision-makers at both the League and the UN were reluctant to admit the truth to their members: the creation and liquidation of IGOs was complicated, especially when there were numerous interested parties with divergent agendas to contend with, and where precedent was non-existent. These tasks could not be effected quickly, especially when the liquidation of one body was dependent on the fully realized creation of the other. Consequently, despite the two-year gap between the initial indications the League would be replaced in 1944 and the final Assembly in April 1946, the League of Nations, through no real fault of its own, went into its official closure period quite unprepared for what lay ahead. A scheme for asset transfer and distribution had been agreed, but the logistics of administering these schemes, as well as the handover to the new ECOSOC of technical functions and activities, were an unknown. Add to this the concerns about staffing levels, the liquidation of the Nansen Office, the high levels of member contributions in arrears and the administration of League loans – the organization's final months looked like they would be anything other than quiet. Instead, the League's officials found themselves entering into one of the busiest and more chaotic periods they had experienced in years.

2

Transfer troubles, April–July 1946

According to delegates at the organization's twenty-first Assembly, the League of Nations was dead. The eulogies were delivered, respects had been paid and the 173 attendees went their separate ways. Left behind at the Palais des Nations, Seán Lester, the League's last secretary general, and what remained of the organization's Secretariat now faced an unprecedented challenge: the dismantling of a wide-remit, large-scale IGO. A tentative agreement had been reached with the UN in relation to the transfer of fixed assets and some vague assurances had been made regarding the assumption of League functions, but there was little in the way of concrete plans or specifics to guide them on their journey. This chapter outlines the work and challenges faced by the League of Nations in the period that began with the organization's official closure at its final Assembly in April 1946 and ended with the transfer of its Geneva properties at the end of July 1946. The events of this short fifteen-week period quash the narrative that the League of Nations experienced a peaceful closure in the calm of Geneva, free of stress or worry. In its place, the second quarter of 1946 comprised not only some of the most active months the organization had experienced in a long time but was also frequently governed by events beyond its control.

The months between April and July 1946 were the busiest of the League's closure, dominated by activity centred on transfer to the UN. While more recent scholarship on the League and, more widely, the evolution of international organizations has recognized the links between it and the UN in terms of structure, functions and even personnel, the practicalities of these links remain unknown. The League of Nations and the UN existed in parallel with one another during the former's liquidation, and the months between April and July 1946 were witness to the majority of transfer activity between the two organizations. Eilstrup-Sangiovanni posited the concept of institutional succession in 'Death of International Organizations', but how does this happen in practice? This chapter shows that the assumption of League activity was much more of a direct transfer than has previously been suggested, and that the two organizations were interwoven until the League's eventual end, especially during 1946.[1]

This chapter focuses on the three main elements of the transfer from the League to the UN: assets, activities and people. Before doing so however, an introduction is required for one of the twenty-first Assembly's most important directives in relation to the closure of the organization: the creation of a Board of Liquidation. This was the only official structure established to oversee the closure, and its focus on purely strategic issues and inability to react quickly to problems severely limited its effectiveness. By way of illustration, the chapter examines how the three different features of transfer were experienced by the small group of officials still working in Princeton, United States, following their decampment there during the Second World War. This served as a microcosm of the changes taking place on a wider scale in Geneva.

Both the UN and the League of Nations were complex, bureaucratic institutions in the 1940s, yet neither organization's leadership were able to appreciate the level of planning and precision needed to effect a smooth transition between them. Liquidating an organization on this scale had never taken place before, and this chapter demonstrates what happened when the League attempted to do so without any experience to draw from. It also explores the negative effect that presentism, and the lack of time for long-term thinking that often accompanies it, had on the League's ability to deliver liquidation in an orderly and efficient manner.

The events of these three-and-a-half months after the twenty-first Assembly cannot solely be explained by the structures and institutions put in place to manage liquidation. The chapter also focuses on the role of people in the process; the decisions made, the relationships cultivated and impact of change were all felt, or manifested, by individuals in the League and beyond. A significant conclusion of this chapter concentrates on the importance of personal rapport between colleagues and the negative impact a poor relationship can have on a much wider scale when it exists between senior figures, limiting what can be achieved during a turbulent time. The flawed personal connection in this instance was that between Seán Lester – last secretary general of the League – and Włodzimierz Moderow – senior UN representative in Geneva from May 1946. The nature of their relationship, and the effect it had on them and the transfer process, can be gleaned not only from the explicit dislike expressed in personal papers but also from their formal day-to-day correspondence, the reliance on written communication instead of meeting in person – despite working in close physical proximity – and their use of intermediaries to conduct discussions.

This chapter therefore challenges several commonly held assumptions about the League and its closure that have persisted for over seventy-five years. The twenty-first Assembly was not the end for the organization: it was merely the end of involvement for its members. The period following the public funeral was not quiet or without incident: it was haphazard and only scratched the surface of actual liquidation. The UN was not a completely new organization but instead had significant ties to its predecessor, receiving assets, activities, people and experience worth millions of dollars. The League was more than just a framework for intergovernmental cooperation; it was made up of, and managed by, individuals who faced both personal and professional uncertainty. The last chapter of the League of Nations did not end in April 1946; instead, that is where it began.

The Board of Liquidation

A central tenet to understanding how the League liquidated lies in the structure established to manage the process. The idea of a Board of Liquidation was first proposed in the draft dissolution resolution prepared by the British Government, which argued that a board or committee would be best placed to oversee wind-up activities and control the actual end date of the League in lieu of the Supervisory Commission. Providing oversight and decision-making machinery for the Secretariat in the Assembly's absence, its suggested responsibilities included the dispersal of staff, liquidating affairs as quickly as possible and issuing progress reports to members.[2] The Board of Liquidation sat separately from the League's Secretariat and was infrequently present in Geneva, but its decisions and priorities are critical in grasping why the dissolution progressed as it did.

The Assembly's First Committee quickly agreed to the British proposal and decided on the Board's membership using four criteria: continuity in the management of the League from the Supervisory Commission, personal qualifications and experience, the financial relationship between the candidate's home state and the League, and a geographical representation of membership. As might, therefore, be expected, there was significant continuity between the memberships of the Board of Liquidation and the Supervisory Commission, with Cecil Kisch (UK), Carl Hambro (Norway), Émile Charvériat (France) and Adolfo Costa du Rels (Bolivia) all elected to the new body. Also nominated to the Board were Atul Chatterjee – chairman of the PCOB and delegate from

India – F. T. Cheng (China), Jaromír Kopecky (Czechoslovakia), Daniel Secrétan (Switzerland) and Seymour Jacklin (South Africa).[3]

The Board was officially created by the Assembly's dissolution resolution, which also set out some protocols by which it should be managed. Terms were agreed regarding its full power in decision-making, setting a quorum of five members, granting Board members the international status of League officials and, notably, instituting a generous remuneration package. The group's chair was entitled to a monthly subsistence allowance of 3,000 Swiss francs per month, and 2,000 Swiss francs for other members, as well as recompense for travel and accommodation. Stephen Barcroft, during interviews with former Secretariat officials in the early 1970s, found that not everyone was happy about these arrangements, especially as officials were, until the summer of 1946, still expected to pay a subset of their own salaries towards the League budget as voluntary contributions.[4] In addition to these agreed protocols, the Board would later set its own terms of reference covering the preparation of agendas, the regular location of meetings and, in the first meeting of the Board on 23 April, nominating Hambro to the role of chair, with Kisch as his deputy.[5]

In practice, the Board's effectiveness in dealing with problems as they arose was severely compromised by the irregularity of its meetings. The group was not a sitting Board – they met when the members' schedules allowed it – and this meant its guidance was often unavailable when it was most needed. There were three meetings at the end of April following the Assembly, and then no more until mid-/late July, when seven meetings were held over a number of days – although four additional secret meetings were also held across the April and July sessions, usually to discuss a matter which the members did not want appearing in regular meeting minutes.[6] Chester Purves, a respected former Secretariat official with the Personnel Office, forced to leave like many others in May 1940, was re-engaged to lead a small Secretariat supporting the Board. Together this group was responsible for preparing agendas, ensuring Board members were paid, writing minutes and preparing fortnightly progress reports. These latter reports were not initially part of the Board's terms of reference, but as the group met so sporadically, it was suggested a report – issued via postal services – covering recent developments and updates on closure would be of use to members.[7] They were not, however, very useful for the Secretariat on a day-to-day basis, resulting in an increased workload to issue them every two weeks, and there was no mechanism by which Board members could take action on the reports beyond writing to Lester or Purves. The Board's inability to function when it was not in session was a fundamental problem, and it was one that would especially rear its head in the later months of 1946.

In lieu of the Assembly, Lester reported directly to the Board, and issues for discussion were tabled as official Board of Liquidation Documents. There were eventually 147 in total, usually prepared by a relevant member of the Secretariat in the secretary general's name. The first B.L. document for example – using the League's own referencing acronym – was a letter from the Italian Government asking to be included in the distribution of proceeds from asset liquidation, not scheduled to take place until 1947.[8] Secretariat officials were frequently reminded that the Board of Liquidation was only interested in high-level issues pertaining to closure – no supposedly routine issues were to be included in the fortnightly reports. It was a strategic body rather than a working group; it was less concerned with practical matters and more with issues of policy and approach. Any problems or issues falling outside this high-level remit – including liaison with the UN – were considered the secretary general's responsibility, leaving Lester with no recourse to, or back-up from, a higher authority when needed.[9]

Yet despite its removal from routine issues, the Board of Liquidation – made up of individuals long associated with the League of Nations – also had a quasi-emotional connection with the organization. Like other organizational bodies, it is easy to think of the Board as an impersonal institution, but like all these other groups, it was made up of people with their own motivations and attachments. For example, ensuring the ongoing use of the Palais des Nations, specifically built for the organization in the 1930s, was a priority for the group – they were concerned the UN would vandalize the building – as were certain issues they believed they had a 'moral duty' to oversee, such as aiding League-associated bodies, even when they had no official mandate to do so.[10]

Nonetheless, with hindsight, it is difficult to rectify these personal motivations and the group's focus on strategic matters with the organization's day-to-day decision-making needs. While the Board was undeniably made up of experienced individuals, who shared a great familiarity with the high-level management of the League, it was also disconnected from the practical work of its officials. There were some established working relationships between the Board and certain members of the Secretariat – particularly Seán Lester – that were undoubtedly useful and supportive, but there was little in the way of contact with those not in the highest echelons of the organization.[11] There were some in the Secretariat who believed the group was overpaid, exacerbated by the infrequency with which it met, and the seeming lack of concern about their absence from Geneva did not improve that perception. In their final meeting during this period, on

24 July 1946, the Board noted that a meeting in September was unlikely due to their expected presence at the second half of the UN's first General Assembly. While it was suggested they might meet in New York for a session should they be able to gather a quorum, there was a distinct lack of anxiety about being unable to provide oversight to the League for several months.[12] The members did not appreciate it at the time, but they should have been worried: the Board would not meet again until 1947.

Fixed assets

The League of Nations fulfilled many roles in international cooperation in the interwar period – as a forum for debating territorial disputes, acting as the guardian of treaties and providing secretarial support for committees – but the organization was also the owner of significant and valuable possessions that needed to be disposed of. The League's fixed assets were defined as those held by the organization that could not be quickly turned into cash, including fixtures, fittings and buildings, and agreement of the Common Plan confirmed that these assets would be transferred to the UN. To give a small insight into what this meant, the League had eight different estates in Geneva, totalling an area of over 200,000 m^2. The Ariana Park estate, within which stood the Palais des Nations, had buildings with a cubic content of approximately 440,000 m^3, containing nearly 600 offices, an assembly room with space for over 1,500 people, two bars and a cinema. Filling these rooms were all the organization's furniture and fittings, with more than 4,000 chairs, 113 sofas, 103 ladders and 23 vacuum cleaners.[13] All of these were accounted for in the Common Plan, approved by both the UN General Assembly in February 1946 and the League's Assembly two months later. It was high level and lacking in explicit detail, but it contained three crucial elements that helped the transfer of assets to the UN proceed much more smoothly than other areas of work.

Firstly, it provided a deadline to work towards. The Common Plan committed both organizations to a transfer date of 'on or about' 1 August 1946, and something as simple as setting a deadline gave an impetus to the work that was needed to put this Plan into effect. Having both Assemblies agree to this date meant both organizations' Secretariats were accountable for making it happen – it provided a critical level of momentum that would prove lacking in other parts of transfer.[14] Secondly it provided a basis from which work could start. Unlike the transfer of functions or the liquidation of other elements of the League, the

Common Plan's existence meant that the two Secretariats did not start with a blank sheet of paper. There was little in the way of practicalities in the agreement, and neither side thought it perfect, but it was the result of appropriately senior individuals from both parties ironing out the high-level decisions between them during the face-to-face negotiations in January. This meant there was agreement on the strategic direction of the transfer, something the Secretariats would not necessarily have had the authority to settle on their own.

Finally, it established a working relationship between the relevant elements of the UN and the League. The UN Committee on League of Nations Assets disbanded following the agreement of the Common Plan, but in its place the General Assembly created another group, the UN Negotiating Committee, to liaise with both the Swiss Government and the League as agreed in the Plan.[15] In doing so, the lines of communication between the organizations were clear; League officials knew who was responsible for what, and who they needed to liaise with on a daily basis.[16] Importantly, both this Committee and its predecessor were led by Włodzimierz Moderow, the Polish delegate to the UN Preparatory Commission, which provided valuable continuity not just between the two UN Committees but also between the UN and the League.

Moderow was a lawyer and former member of the General Prosecutor's Office in Poland before working for the Polish Government in Exile in London during the Second World War. He had also acted as a member of the League's Communications and Transit Committee in the past, so he was not a stranger to the organization. The working relationship between Lester and Moderow was the practical expression of the theoretical liaison between the two Secretariats, and official documentation suggests a formal but cordial affinity between the two men.[17] However, when Moderow was appointed by Trygve Lie, the new UN secretary general, as his representative in Geneva from mid-May, while his professional relationship with Lester continued in much the same vein as before, privately it became more strained. A last-minute request from the UN Negotiating Committee for a tour of La Pelouse, the secretary general's official residence, earned a passive-aggressive written rebuke from Lester, who responded that he would be happy for the Committee to visit the grounds, but in regard to the house he said, 'I was sure they would not wish to walk in on such short notice' and politely asked for more notice in future.[18] The secretary general also later expressed his frustration with Moderow's perceived lack of respect for the League of Nations during the handover events in early August – referring to him as 'a bloody fool' in his diaries – which was in great contrast with Lie, whom Lester thought well of.[19] The secretary general's private feelings did not spill over into the public sphere – and there is no indication in Moderow's papers that Lester's vexations were reciprocated – but the limits they placed on the relationship were significant. The League's Archives show that the pair rarely met in person to discuss issues during these months, choosing instead to conduct their business through memos or letters, or via a third party, usually director of Internal Administration Valentin Stencek.[20] While this was more than acceptable when either man was away from Geneva, for the two months in this period when both were working in the same building, it was a hindrance on productivity, especially in regard to the more controversial elements of transfer.

With so many of the strategic principles agreed in advance, discussions on asset transfer were fortunately not curtailed by Lester and Moderow's differences. The momentum generated by the agreement of the Common Plan meant work could begin on the finer details of asset transfer quickly. The UN Negotiating Committee remained in Geneva until 2 May 1946 – reviewing the inventories in the Common Plan and, for the most part, negotiating terms with the authorities in both Bern and Geneva. The League's chief legal adviser, Émile Giraud, was also working on the subject before the Assembly ended its ruminations in mid-April. He advised his colleagues that three essential things were needed to realize the transfer envisaged in the Common Plan. Firstly, the UN General Assembly and the League Assembly would need to pass resolutions agreeing to the transfer, both of which had already been done by 18 April. Secondly, a change would need to be made with the Swiss Land Registry – management of which was already underway in the joint negotiations with the Swiss. Finally, they needed a documented agreement between the UN and the League that would formally hand over possession of the assets and lay out the terms under which this transfer would take place.[21]

This closely defined process ran relatively smoothly as a consequence. There was no controversy around the transfer of these fixed assets; the UN was happy to take on the palatial facilities and were particularly complimentary of the state of the buildings, noting that they were 'in perfect condition'.[22] The energy driving this work meant a draft agreement was already in place by 1 May 1946, and while it went through a number of iterations as it was passed between representatives of the two organizations, the main substance of the document did not alter.[23] The only changes of note were the addition of a point agreeing to Lester's continued use of La Pelouse, and the actual nature of the document itself, as Moderow suggested and Giraud agreed, that it might be considered an executive agreement rather than a stand-alone legal contract. The lawful basis of the transfer was therefore bound in the combination of this document and the approval of both Assemblies.[24]

By the end of May the UN concluded its negotiations with the Swiss and an agreement was approved. Contract details relating to Palais des Nations utilities were passed to UN representatives in June, covering insurance, heating, water and more, and by the end of that month the final Agreement between the two organizations was settled.[25] The document contained ten articles over just six pages and covered the transfer of the land, buildings, fixtures and fittings, as well as the free-of-charge transfer of gifts bequeathed to the League, the latter of which has been explored in greater detail by Carolyn Biltoft.[26] The agreement also set terms by which the ILO would be able to use the Palais Assembly Room, as well as granting ILO staff access to the Library. It committed the UN to adhere to certain obligations on the land – specifically no additional building beyond agreed terms with the local government – granted the League continued use of the Palais while the organization closed down and agreed to a process by which any further issues would be managed. Finally, the agreement was noted as taking effect from the day of signature: 1 August 1946, the original date identified by the Common Plan six months earlier.[27]

On 1 August, as planned, Moderow, Lester and J. Lachavanne – representing the Geneva Canton – signed the Agreement Concerning the Execution of the Transfer to the UN of Certain Assets of the League of Nations.[28] The relative ease of these proceedings was a tribute to the value of methodical planning: setting out the actions to be taken, agreeing who was responsible for what and allocating sufficient time and resources to see it through. However, the transfer of these assets was not an exercise that could be conducted in isolation; only moving the League's estates to the UN meant the Palais would be owned by one organization but administered by another. Of course this was highly impractical: asset transfer would have to be accompanied by a similar transfer of Palais services, and this meant people and activities.

Activities, functions and services

As successful as the League's technical activities were, even with those countries not members of the organization, the continuation of this work in the UN was significantly more contentious and chaotic for two reasons. The first was the opposition of the USSR to the direct transfer of all supposedly non-political work without further scrutiny. The Soviet government believed that a major cause of the League's diminishing impact on issues of security in the 1930s was a result of the organization's expansion into socio-economic work, and was also reluctant to accept any interference in its own affairs in the name of 'rootless cosmopolitanism'.[29] The second problem stemmed from the overwhelming desire of those responsible for founding the UN, especially in the United States, to brand the new organization as a departure from what had come before. The theory made sense: after the devastation of the recent past, the organizers of the UN realized any new body would need the complete faith and trust – or at least a willingness to try – of its membership. Thus, the unofficially agreed approach was to distance the UN from its predecessor: the League was branded a failure but the UN would be different. As a demonstration of how far the UN planners went in their efforts to publicly distance themselves from their predecessor, the League of Nations Sub-Committee of the Preparatory Commission spent a significant portion of its seven meetings discussing the correct terminology to use when mentioning the League. The word transfer in regard to activities was ultimately considered inappropriate – it implied a direct connection to the League – and was instead replaced with 'assumption of'.[30]

The various planning committees of the UN and its General Assembly had already agreed to transfer the Treaty Series function of the League – with a legal agreement already in place – as well as the Secretariat functions to the PCOB and the DSB, both of which were created by international conventions and therefore less tainted by the League's reputation. Nevertheless the UN planners did not suggest a process for transfer of these functions, no deadlines were earmarked and no roles or responsibilities were assigned to either the UN or the League.[31] Likewise, the General Assembly agreed to provisionally take on League activity in the fields of economics, employment, drug control, statistics, social welfare, and transport and communications but, as with the other functions, no concrete plans were put in place to realize this transfer beyond a request that the ECOSOC review the activities before the next meeting of the General Assembly in October.[32] Meanwhile, the health-related activities of the League were destined for a different institution: the new World Health Organization. Iris Borowy has written at much greater length about the League's health activity than can be covered here, but there was a post-war consensus among the Allies that they should create a separate and dedicated global health body into which the League's work, alongside the successes of UNRRA, could be funnelled.[33] League Secretariat officials like Yves Biraud and Raymond Gautier were involved in planning for a global conference on the subject from March 1946, but what this new institution would look like and any transfer of activity to it remained a lower-level priority until that conference was held over the summer.[34]

The uninterrupted continuation of the League's activities and functions was sacrosanct to the organization's leadership and members; Lester alone expressed this sentiment on a number of occasions in both correspondence and personal musings.[35] This is not to suggest that those in the UN did not feel the same way – behind the scenes the new UN Secretariat was eager to learn as much as they could from the League's example, including the commission of a 250-page review by former official Egon Ranshofen-Wertheimer – but the new organization needed to pursue transfer on its own terms.[36] In addition, returning to the transfer of the fixed assets, the immovable deadline of 1 August meant the League Secretariat's activities and functions – the organization's pride and joy – would have to wait while the less glamorous central services took precedence. These were the internal functions that facilitated the running of the building and the activities contained therein; they were, and are, the backbone of any organization. In the Secretariat's structure, this included the Supplies Branch, the Internal Service – which included technical, mailing, automobile and telephone services – the Stenographic Service, the Roneo and Multigraph Service, the Registry/Archives, and the Distribution Service, as well as the Library.[37]

The last of this group, the Library, was considered both an asset of the League as well as a central service and activity. It was home to a considerable collection of documentation and was built at the Palais with a gift from John D. Rockefeller Jr. In the report commissioned by the UN Secretariat on the possible continuation of League activities, Ranshofen-Wertheimer advised maintaining the Library in Geneva for the foreseeable future for several reasons.[38] Until the UN built its new permanent headquarters, there was little chance the Library could be accommodated in its temporary facilities in New York. Even if there were room, a move would undoubtedly cause disruption to services, and this would be felt most strongly in Europe which, having seen many of its major collections and libraries damaged during the war, would need the Library's resources.[39] Ranshofen-Wertheimer's experience with the subject matter – the reason he was asked to perform the review in the first place – was taken on-board by the UN; there was no disagreement with his proposal, and it was agreed that the Library should be maintained in Geneva until further notice.

The League's Archives meanwhile were also both a central service as well as an organizational asset, but their transfer to the UN had not yet been considered with any seriousness and Ranshofen-Wertheimer expressed concerns about the possibility of transferring all files to New York. Without knowing which activities and functions would be shifting to UN control, any move might prove redundant, and while some political archive material might be useful to the new organization, its leadership decided to wait and make a decision later.[40] Thus the Archives remained under League of Nations management when the Palais des Nations was handed over on 1 August 1946, but it was not the only central service to lag behind the rest. The Registry, Distribution Service, and Printing and Publications Department all remained under League control, for the very simple reason that the UN was not ready to take them on.[41]

All other general services, however, were transferred alongside the building as planned, following the preparation of agreements that set out terms for the relationship between the two organizations from August onwards. These culminated in a final Internal Circular to Palais staff of both secretariats on 31 July 1946, confirming that the League would continue to have access to the transferred general services, while the UN could continue to use those that had not, such as the Distribution Service and the Registry. The attached annex to that circular laid out, in detail, who was now responsible for what services, how they should be accessed by different staff and how the cost of these would be met. Clear and concise, it was a demonstration of how services could be transferred efficiently, given sufficient time and planning.[42]

While it was agreed that most League activities and functions would transfer to the ECOSOC, subject to subsequent review, this did not mean the new organization moved them either immediately or in toto. Despite majority support for a mass transfer, the Soviet opposition to this approach during the UN planning process resulted in the ECOSOC compromise and a piecemeal transfer whereby activities would move when the new Secretariat was ready, which had the added benefit of preventing any rushed decisions or unnecessary delays.[43] It was a sensible tactic and guaranteed that the new UN agencies responsible for these activities would be fully prepared for their transfer – helping to safeguard continuity – while also ensuring that no particular service would have to remain at the League if it was ready to move. In some ways this approach was good news for the League's management; the twenty-first Assembly had advocated the continuation of this work and explicitly granted Lester the authority to make sure transfer took place with as little interruption as possible. However, the Assembly also wanted the organization to liquidate rapidly, and the UN piecemeal method meant waiting for an as-yet-undefined period of time while the new institution organized itself. Lester wrote to Lie on several occasions in May 1946 to glean some kind of commitment or timetable from the new organization in relation to the activity transfer, but the new secretary general was too busy with his own problems to provide anything more than a vague response. Ensuring continuity of service meant there were no means by which the League could shut itself down before the UN was ready and the directive to liquidate as quickly as possible was effectively ignored until transfer was complete.[44]

If the UN assumption of the Palais's general services had already forced Lester and his colleagues to bend the parameters of their objectives, the attempts to transfer technical activities were even messier. The transfer of the EFO activity based at Princeton was agreed relatively early during this period, although this would cause its own set of problems in the months to come and is the subject of an in-depth case study later in this chapter.[45] The Communications and Transit Section, part of Department II alongside the EFO, was also earmarked early for transfer, no doubt thanks to Branko Lukac, the head of the service who was seconded to the UN Secretariat at the beginning of April.[46] This meant all of Department II, bar the Geneva-based component of the EFO, was scheduled to move to UN control on 1 August 1946, although Lester advocated early for transferring this last part of the department at the same time. He argued that splitting a department in half would undoubtedly lead to a disruption in services; however, he also accepted that this was not his decision to make and deferred to the UN's verdict.[47]

This chapter returns to the staffing situation of the League Secretariat in the next section, but here it is worth noting that all officials were given notice at the end of March that their contracts would be terminated on 31 July 1946. For those elements of the Secretariat expected to remain under League control after this date, short-term contracts would be offered to staff, as was the case with the Geneva section of the EFO.[48] On Monday 29 July, only three days before the League handed the Palais des Nations over to the UN, Lester received a message from Włodzimierz Moderow, by then the chief UN Secretariat official in Geneva, who explained that the UN had changed its mind and decided to transfer the remaining EFO personnel and activity in Geneva from 1 August. The new organization would keep the service at the Palais for at least three months and would offer contracts to the individuals in the course of 'the next few days'.[49] Although the service was effectively ready to move to new management, the decision came out of the blue – David Owen (assistant secretary general for Economic Affairs) only made the proposal internally at the UN on 24 July – and was just the first of many instances where the new organization's lack of foresight left the League picking up the pieces.[50] Lester in particular was left reeling by the request, especially as several officials had already signed temporary League contracts, and because there was no reassurance that their new UN contracts would be ready in time for 1 August.[51]

Lester's desire to see all of Department II transferred to the UN at the same time likely played a role in his decision to accept the new organization's last-minute proposal. However, similar events playing out at the same time in regard to Department III resulted in Lester attempting to exert some control over the situation for the first time in months. Department III of the Secretariat was made up of three separate activities: the Health Organisation, the Social Questions Section and the Drug Control Service, the last of which was separate from the Secretariat functions provided to the PCOB and the DSB.[52] League representatives were already involved in planning for a new global health institution, which would later become the World Health Organization but, following the world health conference in June 1946, no further progress in terms of transfer logistics was made during July.[53] Likewise there was no indication of when or how the ECOSOC Committee on Narcotic Drugs would be established and when the League's work in this area would transfer, and the same was true of the League's social welfare activity, which was heavily impacted by the war. Moderow and Lester exchanged communications in mid-July about the latter section, agreeing to discuss the matter further at some undefined point in the future, but the timing of these transfers remained a mystery to the League of Nations until 26 July.[54]

Adriaan Pelt, another former League official now working for the UN as the undersecretary general for Conferences and General Services, cabled Moderow on Friday 26 July, informing him that the UN intended to transfer all of Department III from 1 August, to coincide with the other transfers.[55] By the following Monday, as Lester was also dealing with the decision to move the EFO activity in Geneva, he became aware of this new instruction and, in a rare move for him, decided to push back. He did not refuse outright – despite noting in a letter to Moderow that 'It is so clearly impossible to carry out this "decision" at two days' notice that I should drop even the pretence that it can be done' – but he informed both Moderow and Pelt that he could not be held responsible for the disruption that would likely ensue from a rushed transfer.[56] Moderow agreed with him, also messaging Pelt and echoing Lester's suggestion that, if the UN Secretariat had now decided it was ready to take on these activities, a transfer date of 1 September would be much more appropriate.[57] Fortunately for Lester's sanity, Pelt agreed to the one-month postponement, but it demonstrated problems with two important elements of the UN–League relationship.

There was a clear lack of purposeful communication between the UN Secretariat in New York and the League in Geneva. That major decisions could be taken and communicated to Lester with less than a week's notice suggested either a clear lack of regard for the League's position and activity, or a lack of understanding regarding the impact of those decisions. The directive to move Department III with only three days' notice left no time to inform member states of the changes, prepare handover documentation or, perhaps most importantly, provide affected staff with sufficient notice of their termination or to draw up new UN work contracts. With former League officials like Pelt involved in the UN it was unlikely that the new organization's Secretariat lacked respect for its predecessor, especially considering the warm correspondence between Pelt, Lie and Lester, and it was therefore more likely that ignorance, presentism and the stress of building a new international civil service were the root causes. A letter sent by Trygve Lie to Lester on 6 August covered a wide range of issues, but not once did the UN secretary general mention or even make inference to the panic of one week earlier – he had already moved onto the next problem.[58] The UN was, and is, a more complex organization than the League, and the sometimes jumbled efforts at smooth transition demonstrated how difficult and time-consuming it was to establish its Secretariat. This is further evidenced by the second problem demonstrated by the end of July turmoil: the disconnect between the UN in New York and its officials in Geneva. Moderow was almost as taken aback by the last-minute decisions as Lester, and it revealed a level of disparity within the UN. Just as the League was not a homogenized collection of people who all felt and acted the same way, nor was its successor, especially as it was finding its feet. This confusion, with some elements of the UN not knowing what other parts were doing, would also rear its head when transferring the League's personnel.

People

At the start of April 1946, the Palais des Nations was busier than it had been in years, with regular Secretariat officials boosted by a growing number of UN personnel, as well as over two hundred individuals employed for the Assembly. The striking nature of the buildings in Ariana Park were impressive and inspiring, yet the setting – nestled in an estate away from the hustle and bustle of the city – could also intimidate. The sense of loneliness and isolation felt by those working there, especially during the war and in the run-up to the Assembly, was only exacerbated by the sweeping staircases, long corridors and high ceilings, so to many of those long-running members of staff it was a sweet relief to see the halls filled once again. To the casual observer it seemed as if business was booming, and while the grand farewell of the twenty-first Assembly was a long-awaited moment of catharsis for those who had been quite literally stuck in Geneva throughout the Second World War, it was also a bittersweet experience.[59]

In the months leading up to the Assembly, Seán Lester was under increasing pressure from Hambro to give notice to all remaining officials. The secretary general, concerned that dismissing staff with an arbitrary end date might leave the League of Nations shorthanded, was reluctant despite knowing it would have to be done at some point during the year. Hambro argued that the League must be seen to be dismantling, regardless of UN delays, suggesting key officials could be re-engaged on short-term contracts if needed.[60] Despite his protestations, both formal and informal, this was a battle Lester could not win and in late March 1946 all officials, regardless of contract type or rank, were given notice with a termination date of 31 July, chosen as the last day the Palais would be in League hands.[61] So as the League headed into its final Assembly, not only did Lester not know if he would have sufficient resources to actually liquidate the organization, its staff also had no idea if they would be employed beyond the summer. Loyalty to the League and to their colleagues, alongside the guarantee of work until at least the end of July, kept most officials with the Secretariat for the time being, but their long-term prospects were uncertain.

As the highs of the Assembly drifted away and the UN plans remained in development, the senior figures in the League Secretariat tried to occupy themselves with what they could control in relation to officials. This included calculating indemnities for staff, deciding the terms on which new temporary contracts would be offered from 1 August, who these contracts would be offered to and managing the expectations of its employees about their prospects. The Preparatory Commission and General Assembly had not guaranteed future roles for League employees and announced that no direct transfer of staff would take place. Offers might be made to League officials, and they were encouraged to apply for UN positions, but these would be based on new contracts with the UN Secretariat, and this was all the remit of the organization's secretary general, Trygve Lie.[62] Either way, it was unclear – to the League of Nations at least – if the UN would automatically re-employ the associated staff when assets and activities moved.[63] The UN held two interview boards in Geneva in the week following the end of the Assembly, where League officials interested in roles with the new Secretariat met with their prospective new employers to discuss their experience and skills but, more than anything, they were an opportunity for the UN to identify any officials it wanted to poach from the League's ranks.[64]

In the meantime, League officials were faced with uncertain circumstances. A total of 148 individuals met with the UN panels; however, the new Secretariat made it clear that these interviews were no guarantee of job offers, and individuals faced a tough decision regarding their League positions. They could stay, understanding that there was no promise they would be either offered temporary contracts to remain with the League for a few more months beyond July or moved to the UN in activity transfer. Even if they secured a temporary continuation of their role at the League, they risked missing out on opportunities with other organizations, and potentially finding themselves looking for work in six months when all the new positions created by the UN and its agencies were filled.[65] The alternative was to actively look for opportunities at the UN or other employers, leaving before 31 July and invalidating their chance at an indemnity payment.

Even when early offers of employment were made by the new organization, League officials were sometimes forced to make decisions with little time to consider their options. Phyllis van Ittersum, a twenty-six-year veteran of the EFO, wrote to a Princeton-based colleague in June 1946 explaining that she had transferred to the UN Secretariat as of that morning, in a new position as secretary to Alexander Elkin, the assistant director for Administration at the Palais des Nations. Disconcertingly she explained that 'the arrangement is quite temporary and very vague', and she was given only twenty minutes to make up her mind about the role.[66] Many of these officials had lived in Geneva for years, and some – like van Ittersum – had been with the League since its earliest days, and the change was a large upheaval whatever their decision.[67]

As officials made their choices, Lester's earlier concerns about resources started to come true. The UN, actively establishing its own Secretariat during this period, was starting to identify League officials – and their decades of experience – it wanted to join its ranks. Some individuals, such as Martin Hill – who would go on to have an illustrious career in the UN – and Léon Steinig left the League before the end of July, with the consent of Lester and the Administration.[68] Others, upon request from the UN and other agencies, were seconded to new positions for periods of time up to the termination of their League contracts at the end of July. These included two senior officials: Branko Lukac, head of the Communications and Transit Department, and Yves Biraud of the Health Organisation, who had been with the League of Nations for seventeen and twenty years respectively.[69]

These departures caused two different problems. The first centred on the management of the secondment requests, and this related back to the previously mentioned communication problems within the UN Secretariat. Despite Trygve Lie's early optimism that Lester and Adriaan Pelt would easily come to a 'suitable and convenient' arrangement on staffing, there was no standardized process by which UN officials were obliged to adhere until mid-June 1946; requests did not find their way to the League via a predetermined route or agreed point of contact.[70] Instead the League had to manage queries from a range of departments and, on more than one occasion, found itself fielding multiple requests for the same League official from different parts of the UN Secretariat. It was a burden on the administration of the League, and it was only when Pelt agreed to act as the channel for all future queries that the confusion started to recede.[71]

The second problem related to Lester's specific concern about a loss of resources. Some of the League's most experienced officials were desirable employees in the eyes of the UN, and Lester had to once again balance the Assembly's contradictory instructions to be as helpful to the new organization as possible, while also liquidating the League quickly and efficiently. The fewer officials he had at his disposal, the longer the liquidation would take, and losing the most senior and experienced officials increased the risk of mismanaging the process.[72] Despite the common misconception that liquidation was a quiet period for the organization, it was often the opposite, and the League needed its Secretariat's experience more than ever. This was especially true in the case of Seymour Jacklin, the League's treasurer, and subsequently a member of staff expected to stay with the organization until the end of the closure process. To Lester's surprise and consternation, Jacklin decided he would leave the organization on 31 July 1946, and instead nominated himself as a member of the Board of Liquidation, a position he was awarded during the twenty-first Assembly. Lester had his own personal difficulties with what he described as Jacklin's 'deep-seated inferiority complex' over the years – he privately suggested the treasurer had a 'long continued attack of persecution mania' and called him 'a stupid man' – but their professional relationship functioned adequately during the war and Jacklin's announcement was a surprise to many. The League of Nations would have to liquidate after the end of July without its chief financial officer.[73]

This pressure was further exacerbated by increased workloads for some members of the Secretariat. The dramatic decline in activity, brought about by the conflict in Europe and beyond, was rapidly reversing itself and requests for League assistance were on the rise. The levels of staffing, reduced to fit wartime demand, were now insufficient to handle even the routine work of the Secretariat. On numerous occasions, both the Publications Department and the Library requested increases in resources that fell on deaf ears.[74] Henri Vilatte, managing the Personnel Department, noted in a letter to assistant director of the UN European Office, Alexander Elkin, that his team would have to manage with only three members of staff after 31 July 1946.[75]

Lester was concerned about the staffing situation, but he was also motivated by a desire to look after his staff and wished to see his colleagues move onto new opportunities wherever possible. News of positions in the UN and other agencies was freely circulated among staff, and Lester raised concerns with his UN counterparts regarding the decision to only offer short-term contracts to staff transferred alongside services, activities and assets.[76] To what extent this was personal concern, or concern for his ability to continue running the League, is debatable, but it was most likely a little of both. Lester was closer to his officials than his predecessors, by virtue of the smaller number of staff under his control and the physical proximity of those who remained in Geneva during the war. For many of those who continued to work for the organization between 1940 and 1945, colleagues constituted their entire social circle. This was as true for Lester, a committed family man who suffered greatly while separated from his wife and daughters for several years, as it was for any other League official.[77]

However, Lester's personal concern for his staff was not without limitations and was significantly diminished on issues involving money. His relationship with the Administrative Tribunal, established in 1928 to address complaints from League and ILO officials, was fractious on occasion, especially following the latter body's ruling against the League in regard to staff dismissals in 1939 and 1940.[78] In short, the League of Nations leadership dismissed a large number of officials following the invasion of Poland in 1939 and then north-western Europe in 1940, often with a shorter notice period than the organization was contractually obliged to provide. The Administrative Tribunal ruled at the end of February 1946 that the League had acted unlawfully in this instance and should make financial restitution to the former officials in question. The League's leaders, however, proposed that they were not bound by the Tribunal's decision, eventually taking the issue to the twenty-first Assembly to justify their position. The real cause for concern for Lester and the Supervisory Commission – then acting as the Assembly's proxy – was the financial implication of the Tribunal's decision, especially as the ruling in February resulted in over a hundred former officials bringing cases against the organization – with more expected – by the time the twenty-first Assembly began. This worry was shared by member-governments wary of seeing their share of assets reduced and led to Assembly delegates voting to back the leadership's stance, effectively allowing the organization to ignore its own judicial body.[79]

The League's staff was not a unionized workforce, but staff were represented by a Staff Committee – a useful source of information about officials' concerns – and the relationship between the body and the leaders of the Secretariat could be combative during what was a difficult time for both officials and management. The Committee raised a number of issues that troubled employees, including the 31 July deadline set for officials based outside Geneva to remove their furniture from the Palais – which would prove to be a thorn in the side of the League Secretariat leadership throughout dissolution and is covered in greater depth in Chapter 3 – as well as the repatriation of officials recruited locally but not Swiss citizens.[80] They were also particularly vocal in regard to the calculation of indemnity payments for staff leaving the organization on 31 July.

The League of Nations Secretariat was comprised of a complex employee contract landscape by 1946. When the organization's future was particularly uncertain in 1939 and 1940, the Supervisory Commission instructed Lester's predecessor, Joseph Avenol, to keep staff contracts, where he could, in a state that allowed officials to be dismissed with minimal notice and obligations. This was designed to protect the League from excessive financial outlay while the organization was under great threat and, in theory, to allow officials to leave Switzerland quickly if needed. The practical result was a Secretariat made up of officials on a variety of different contract terms, some of which did not, from a legal perspective, reflect their length of service.[81] Although the organization's leadership made some allowances to ameliorate the unusual situation, they made little room for leeway when it came to financial recompense for employees. Not that this stopped the Staff Committee from continuing to press the issue however, continually pushing for the best possible deal for its members. This included lobbying for indemnity payments to be based on real salary values – including cost-of-living and other allowances – negotiating temporary diplomatic status in regard to Swiss taxation for those leaving the international civil service and ensuring any holiday leave not taken by 31 July would be remunerated upon termination of contract.[82]

The Staff Committee was not always successful in its efforts – usually on issues that involved asking the League's decision-makers for more money – and in this instance they had to wait until 30 July 1946 for their official response, just one day before most officials left the organization.[83] Nonetheless the Secretariat leadership, like Lester personally, was not averse to staff concerns and could work with representative groups in a positive way at times. An example of this related to the Staff Sickness Insurance Association, created in 1921 with a view to supporting officials in the case of illness or accident. With the UN unable to take over management of the fund, a solution needed to be identified that would remain true to the ideals of the Association, and specifically that it should only be used to provide remuneration to those who suffered accident or illness. Together, the Executive Board of the Association and the Secretariat leadership identified a solution whereby the Association could continue to function for former members now part of the UN Secretariat, while also remaining true to the principles on which the fund was founded. It was not a perfect solution, but was testament to the power of face-to-face negotiations, and demonstrated that while officials and the League's management did not always agree, they were able to work together in an industrious fashion when needed.[84]

The League of Nations had 397 employees on its books in April 1946, but within four months, as officials left for new opportunities or returned to their home countries, this figure shrank to just 73, and of that number, only 31 were expected to stay with the organization beyond the outstanding transfer of activities to the UN.[85] The Palais des Nations remained as busy as it was at the beginning of April, but the vast majority of those filling the halls were now UN officials. Some staffing issues were still to be resolved – the Staff Committee represented fewer individuals after July, but they remained a vocal force – but by the beginning of August 1946, at least some of the turbulence appeared to have passed.

The EFO at Princeton

The experience of the EFO office at Princeton between April and July 1946 was a microcosm of the wider League Secretariat experience during the same months. The group working there, nearly 4,000 miles from Geneva, had to contend with all the same aspects of transfer to the UN, including assets, activities and people, and their experiences demonstrated the full range of tribulations the organization had to contend with.

As already acknowledged, the League's technical activity was significantly more effective than its political endeavours in the 1930s, and this was especially true of the work around economics and global financial study.[86] When it became unclear if the Secretariat could continue working at full capacity in Switzerland in 1940, Arthur Sweetser, still technically employed by the League until 1942, worked with the Rockefeller Foundation and Princeton University's Institute for Advanced Study to invite several of the League's technical sections to continue their work in the safety of the United States. After some dithering by then secretary general Joseph Avenol, a contingent of eight officials from Department II, led by its director Alexander Loveday, relocated to Princeton on a mission to the United States. Away from a physically isolated and communications restricted Switzerland, the EFO flourished during the war, producing a range of publications on topics including the transition from war to peace-time economies, and commercial policy in the interwar period.[87]

By the beginning of April 1946, the number of people left in the Princeton office was twenty-eight – made up of eight Secretariat officials and twenty locally recruited staff – and they, following Loveday's departure in February 1946, were led by Ansgar Rosenborg, a Swedish member of Section who had been with the organization since 1921.[88] He was supported on a practical level by Percy Watterson, an accountant with the League's Treasury who would later become a critically important figure in the liquidation of the organization in 1947. While the group's prospects were in a healthier condition than some of their colleagues in Geneva – the ECOSOC had already agreed to the creation of an Economic and Employment Commission as well as a Statistical Commission – they were no more immune to the uncertainty enveloping the League. There was no timetable for transfer, no guarantee of roles in the new Commissions and, at the end of March, like the rest of the Secretariat, officials were given notice of the termination of their contracts effective 31 July 1946.[89]

The calculation of indemnities and benefits was complicated for officials based in Geneva, but there were added layers of complexity for those in the United States. On 8 April 1946, the day the final Assembly began in Geneva, Lester sent a five-page document to Rosenborg outlining the numerous rules and procedures to be followed regarding his charges in New Jersey, most of which were unsurprising. For example, the League of Nations would not pay indemnity to officials salaried by the Rockefeller Foundation grant issued in 1940; instead, this should be covered by the grant's remnants. Rosenborg was also asked, as soon as a transfer date was agreed, to issue local staff with one month's notice of the termination of their contracts. This did not affect the possibility of them moving to the UN and brought them in line with the circumstances of their colleagues.[90]

The more controversial of Lester's new rules, however, related to the Secretariat officials' entitlement to repatriation expenses and what were called leave journeys, that is, remuneration for travel to home countries as part of their holiday allowance. The League agreed to pay the costs of repatriation of any Princeton-based Secretariat official to either their country of recruitment or any other location they so wished, provided it was not more expensive than repatriation to the former. For example, an official recruited in France could not request repatriation to New Zealand. Crucially, however, these repatriation expenses came with an expiration date: all requests and journeys had to be taken within three months of leaving League of Nations employment, and these time limits were a worry for officials. Only two months earlier, Lester had also indicated that staff and their families would be entitled to the provisions outlined in the Staff Regulations, whereby the League would pay officials for the cost of travel to their home countries for holidays, as well as funding the cost of repatriation journeys upon termination of contracts. However, the decision to terminate contracts as of 31 July 1946 made the leadership change its mind: leave journeys would not be funded close to repatriation dates, nor would they be allowed at all if the Princeton office was too busy.[91]

Officials working in Princeton were not happy, and four of them wrote detailed breakdowns of Lester's updated guidelines in individual letters to Rosenborg, outlining their 'fresh anxiety' with the rules and the time restrictions now in place.[92] They felt punished for being based in the United States and were aggrieved that the League seemed to be putting economization above their contracted rights. There was a disparity in the expectations between the two groups: the officials in New Jersey and the Secretariat leadership in Geneva. The former felt let down by an organization they had dedicated themselves to, while the latter did not understand why those in Princeton were unwilling to accept the practical realities of liquidation procedures.[93] The lack of face-to-face interaction and reliance on slow postal communications meant the personal reassurance often needed in management of people, especially during times of great change, was missing. All of this was aggravated by the continued lack of news as to when this group might transfer to UN management. Worried for himself and his colleagues, Rosenborg tried to pursue the issue with the new organization directly in early May, but was instructed by Martin Hill, then a special adviser to Trygve Lie, to stay out of the discussions.[94] At the end of May 1946, with no news forthcoming, Valentin Stencek – director of Internal Administration and effectively Lester's second-in-command – suggested offering temporary contract extensions, to at least provide some reassurance to those based at Princeton that they would not be unemployed come 1 August.[95]

Despite the anxiety and concern about the future, the relationship between the Princeton mission and the leadership in Geneva was not irreparably damaged by the repatriation debate. When Adriaan Pelt privately informed the League's secretary general that the UN planned to transfer the EFO activity, assets and people at the end of July 1946, Lester pressed two issues on his counterparts in the UN. Firstly, that any new contracts offered to officials should not directly reflect those under which they were then subject. The war placed considerable financial constraints on the League and, as a result, officials' contracts were less favourable than they would otherwise expect or warrant; the Secretariat administration wanted to ensure these individuals were appropriately compensated for their work in the future.[96] Lester was also concerned that the UN was only offering temporary positions thus far, again relaying these worries to Pelt. He may have had little time for staff dissension on occasion, especially when it affected his budget, but Lester was not without concern for his Secretariat officials and their prospects.

The good news for the Princeton officials was that they now knew when they would be transferring – 31 July 1946 – with confirmation received at the end of June.[97] However the first contract offers did not arrive until 16 July, and an increasingly exasperated Ansgar Rosenborg was reduced to a direct appeal to David Owen, then in charge of the new UN Department of Economic Affairs, in order to chase the formal contract letters for his officials.[98] He was finally successful, but if the permanent Secretariat officials thought their situation was fraught with anxiety, this was nothing compared to their locally recruited colleagues.[99]

Rosenborg, understandably, had a stronger relationship with his local staff than the Secretariat leadership in Geneva did and was largely responsible for securing their future employment. In mid-July, Pelt cabled Lester to let him know that the UN hoped to 'clear [the local employees'] status one way or other within the next two weeks' – not particularly reassuring for individuals whose contracts were due to terminate in a fortnight – and while the League's leaders were supportive of Rosenborg's efforts to secure positions for his staff, it refused to temporarily prolong their employment while the UN made its arrangements.[100] Meanwhile, with only four days' notice, the UN invited the locally recruited staff to New York for interviews on 22 July, but informed them that as the new Department of Economic Affairs was undergoing 'a difficult organizational period' and Owen was away in Europe until mid-August, no offers of employment could be made for at least a month.[101]

The disarray in Princeton was further aggravated by the distance between Rosenborg and Geneva, in terms of both geography and the levels of priority attached to the problem. Like the frantic issues surrounding the transfer of the rest of the EFO activity in Geneva and the last-minute request to transfer all of Department III, detailed earlier in this chapter, much of the back-and-forth between the UN, Rosenborg and the League leadership took place over a matter of days. Queries and plans that might have been discussed weeks or even months earlier were hastily cobbled together in a disorganized fashion by both secretariats. David Owen, away in Europe, managed to exert some influence to have two-month contracts offered to local staff at the last minute, but the fortunate end to the issue did not negate the bedlam of the previous weeks.[102]

Of course the Princeton transfer was not just about people, it also included activities and assets, and the same last-minute approach extended to these as well. The UN proposed a takeover of the EFO at Princeton in early June, but the official confirmation was not forwarded to Ansgar Rosenborg for several weeks.[103] In many ways the proposed method of transfer was relatively straightforward from the League's perspective: all regular activity would continue as before, and officials would remain in the same office at Princeton until they could be relocated to New York. Very little would change on a day-to-day basis, except that Rosenborg and his staff would now report to UN Headquarters instead of Geneva. This was fortunate, as some of the more practical transfer issues were once again subject to a lack of forethought.

The major question surrounded EFO publications. At the proposed time of transfer, several publications were in different stages of preparation, and the issue centred on those reports completed by the EFO but at either the printers or with linguists for translation into French. The UN did not want to publish reports under a League masthead, but would it be right to publish them later under their own banner if they had been written by League officials? It may not have seemed like a vitally important issue during the relative commotion of May and June 1946 – hence the lack of urgency in addressing the questions – but the absence of prior consideration only made the matter more complicated as the weeks passed. Significant time was spent corresponding on the matter in July, and the dearth of preparation meant the problem was not resolved before the transfer date, leaving it to be dealt with in August and beyond, even though the EFO had supposedly been fully subsumed by the UN by that point.[104]

With the transfer of people and activity (mostly) dealt with, there was one remaining issue: the liquidation of the physical Princeton office. Percy Watterson, the one Princeton-based official not leaving the Secretariat with everyone else – he was a Treasury official rather than part of the EFO – was tasked with liquidating what was left of the office. Arrangements for the remaining fixed assets needed to be made and, as the future of the activity and staff remained uncertain until mid-July, neither Watterson nor the League administration had much time to consider the issue in advance. Additionally, while Watterson knew he would have one or two months after the EFO transfer to address any problems, he was still not entirely sure of his responsibilities. On 20 July 1946 he outlined what he thought were the outstanding questions in a letter to Seán Lester, suggesting: the disposal of publications left in the office; finding a home for the mission's library; removal of furniture and Treasury records to Geneva; the return of League items loaned to the New York World Fair in 1940, alongside the repatriation of the Peace Plow to Switzerland, created for the Centennial Exposition in Philadelphia in 1872 and gifted to the people of Geneva in 1878. Watterson had his list, but as an accountant his primary focus was the financial liquidation of the office; he had no instruction of what he was to do about any of these office assets.[105] It was not until 3 August, three days after the official transfer to the UN, that Lester informed Watterson that all these assets now belonged to the new organization. Although, as no costs had been agreed and negotiations with the UN had not yet happened, their transfer – like the publications issue – was distinctly more theoretical than practical.[106] Official records tell us that the EFO was fully transferred to the UN from 1 August; archive sources reveal that this is as much a pleasant fiction as the assumption that these months were without incident.[107]

Those officials working in Princeton saw the full consequences of a lack of transfer planning up close. The office's assets were a mystery to its liquidator, Rosenborg admitted he had no sense of the plans for their work and the personnel suffered some shabby treatment alleviated only by the persistence of their leader.[108] Despite the pandemonium of the previous weeks, Rosenborg was remarkably sanguine about the situation and his feelings towards his time at the League in a letter to Lester. The group was expected to stay in Princeton through August, and other than Watterson moving to a different office, life was expected to stay much the same.[109] Fortunately for all of those involved, the outstanding questions resolved themselves but that this was the case was a greater testament to the perseverance of the individuals involved than any strategic foresight on the part of either the UN or the League.

Conclusions

The concept of purgatory can be described as a period of interminable anticipation, waiting to learn of one's fate from a higher power; for the League of Nations that higher power was the UN, and by the end of July 1946 the wait was at least partly over. The process had been more reactive and tumultuous in nature than many in the organization had hoped, but a significant portion of the transfer work was complete. The number of Secretariat personnel was greatly reduced, and in little more than three months the League moved from the highs of the twenty-first Assembly to the lows of becoming lodgers in a palace they used to own.

During the months up to the end of July 1946 the League was forced to relinquish control over many of its affairs while also trying to maintain some dignity in the process. Lester had to swallow his pride on numerous occasions during those months, especially when faced with directives he genuinely believed would have a negative effect on services offered to not just League members but also members of the UN. The UN machine, by then in full flow if not fully formed, was able to dictate the terms on almost all matters by virtue of the power invested in it by governments. The League wielded little influence, and the areas where it was able to demonstrate some control were those where the UN allowed it. Constrained by the Assembly instruction to offer all possible assistance to the UN Secretariat in transfer, it effectively meant deferring to the new organization at all times. Lester had no recourse to a higher authority; the Board of Liquidation, as an entity, was ineffective in many of these instances. It would not intercede on issues relating to the UN and, as events often unfolded over mere days, its infrequent presence in Geneva meant it was absent when most needed. Lester often went to Carl Hambro and Cecil Kisch for advice but, conducted via post or sometimes cable, reaction times for urgent issues were just not fast enough to be of use.

The relationship forged between Lester, Hambro and, to a lesser extent, Kisch was, however, a welcome reprieve for the secretary general, as the Board chairman was especially able to provide counsel on issues that a subordinate member of the Secretariat could not. Lester's written updates to both men were an opportunity to not only inform the latter of progress but also a chance for the secretary general to express his more private concerns. Their connection was forged during the Second World War, which provided a strong foundation for their continued working relationship. When the League's existence was threatened in the summer of 1940, it was Lester and Hambro who arranged a Supervisory Commission meeting in Lisbon to pass a budget for 1941 and safeguard the organization's survival. The Commission was forced to meet outside Geneva for several years, but their strategic oversight from afar ensured the League lived long enough to pass on its responsibilities and experience to the UN.[110]

The link between Lester, Hambro and Kisch demonstrated the importance of productive professional relationships over both these early months and throughout the closure of the League, and the consequences when they were lacking. Existing associations were the most helpful to Lester, for example, with individuals like David Owen and Adriaan Pelt. The former served in the British Civil Service until he became Gladwyn Jebb's deputy at the Executive Committee of the UN Preparatory Commission, and while the length of his relationship with Lester and the Secretariat was not long, he was a key point of contact for the League during the UN's earliest days. He also had a particularly friendly relationship with Lester, the two often meeting for dinner when the latter was in London.[111] Their connection was important on a number of occasions, and never more so than when Owen intervened at the last minute to resolve the employment situation of the locally recruited staff at Princeton. Pelt meanwhile was previously a member of the Secretariat – for a significant number of years at the senior rank of director – and his understanding of the League as well as his willingness to engage with Lester and Stencek helped to ease the discomfort that accompanied their lack of control in regard to transfer. It is notable that the only occasion on which Lester felt able to contest the last-minute UN demands was when Pelt requested the transfer of Department III with only four days' notice.

Nevertheless the most important relationship during this period was that between Lester and Moderow. The latter was the most senior UN official in Geneva and while he and Lester had a fractious personal connection, their professional relationship was ostensibly satisfactory. It was, however, more distant than that between Lester and other members of the UN hierarchy, and there is no indication that the two spent significant time together, either personally or professionally. The discovery that the two interacted for the most part by letter, and often via intermediary, should have been of great concern to their superiors; the lack of personal contact guaranteed the relationship would never progress beyond the cordial. While a lukewarm connection between colleagues might not be out of the ordinary, and perhaps acceptable in many workplaces, as the two most senior representatives of their organizations in Geneva, Lester and Moderow needed to collaborate to address the complexity inherent in transfer. Even the frantic efforts of both men to protest the last-minute transfer of Department III activities in late July 1946 could not bring them together: they still primarily liaised in writing.[112] The disjointed interactions between the two, and between the League and UN Secretariats, only demonstrated how important robust rapport and the nurturing of collaborative relationships – or, at the very least, the willingness to exchange ideas face-to-face – were for the efficient transfer between organizations. Although the two men were not shouting at each other in the Palais corridors, one can only imagine what might have been achieved, and sooner, had they worked more closely.

Moderow was Lie's representative and should have been a useful resource for Lester when trying to fathom the new organization's motives and plans. The UN was, however, a very new institution, and the relationships within its own Secretariat were still forming. As demonstrated by Moderow's own difficulties in receiving information from New York, the UN was discovering the innate problems, or potential for problems, that came with a Secretariat divided by an ocean. Moderow was only as good a liaison for the two organizations as the directives he received from New York, and without frequent updates from his superiors, he was sometimes as out of the loop as Lester. The confusion surrounding the transfer of the Geneva-based activity of the EFO and Department III at the end of July was not the result of Moderow refusing to share information with Lester but rather poor communication from New York.

If the events of these months revealed anything, it was that careful and considered planning was vital to the smooth transfer between these two organizations, even if one of those organizations had all the power in the situation. The transfer of assets was a success because planning began over six months earlier and was given the time, space and resources required to make it happen. The agreed Common Plan between the League and the UN may not have had a lot of detail in the first instance, but it outlined the core elements of what would be included in asset transfer, as well as areas of responsibility for the interested parties. From this a more comprehensive and considered approach was defined and ensured that sufficient time was allocated.

With no clear timetable, and no indication from the UN when it would be ready to take on management of Secretariat functions and activities, it was almost impossible for the League to be proactive about other elements of transfer. Consideration of the many issues was left on the backburner until the last possible moment, leaving no opportunity for any of the strategic planning which helped the asset transition progress so meticulously. Sometimes the UN Secretariat seemed both blissfully unaware of and wilfully disinterested in the chaos its actions inflicted on the League, and it is likely this apparent indifference was the consequence of its own impending deadline; the second half of the first General Assembly, and the first to be held in New York, was scheduled for October 1946 and there was a frantic rush to ensure everything was ready for this heavily scrutinized event. To a large extent the League's attempt to control the transfer process during these months was a victim of the

UN's success; unable to properly consider the unknowable task ahead of it, the Secretariat was compelled to abandon its characteristically bureaucratic tactics. Nothing was dealt with until it was urgent, and this approach not only resulted in confusion but also risked the efficacy with which the transfer could take place. Furthermore, it disregarded the human cost of unplanned and disorganized change. The number of League employees affected was not huge, but this did not lessen the impact for those waiting to hear if they might need to move to another continent at short notice, or search for a new job with almost no warning.

In spite of the personal turmoil and frustration, most of the transfer to the new organization was realized on 1 August 1946; activities, functions and especially assets were assumed by the UN and by the beginning of August only a small collection of services remained under League control. As the second half of 1946 saw those remaining activities also become part of the new organization, the League was slowly becoming a shell of its former self, and yet the upcoming months would also allow its leadership to regain some of the control it had forsaken following the foundation of the UN. Instead, attention could now turn to the major task ahead: the liquidation of the League of Nations.

3

Geneva and New York, August–December 1946

When the League of Nations' Genevan estates were handed over to UN control on 1 August 1946, although some transfer and liquidation questions remained unanswered, a sense of relief emerged among the organization's Secretariat at the Palais des Nations. The months following the League's very public funeral in April 1946 were overshadowed by the rapid establishment of the UN Secretariat – a process the League of Nations was obliged to prioritize – and, with the majority of activities, assets and people successfully transferred to the new organization, a window of opportunity presented itself. Many inside the organization now felt that much of the outstanding work could be completed before the year ended, and it seemed that the stressful and reactive approach to liquidation that had dominated much of the summer would be replaced by something calmer and more structured. Seán Lester, the League's long-suffering secretary general, was particularly exasperated by the chaotic events of July, but even he felt relaxed enough about the coming months to take a ten-day holiday at the start of August. Yet by the end of 1946, the cautious positivity was gone, and the organization's Secretariat faced a lengthy list of unresolved issues with a severely depleted workforce.[1] This chapter reveals the continued impact of only focusing on the most urgent issues, what caused the dissolution to fall behind schedule and shows that the decisions taken, and crucially those not taken, in the latter half of 1946 were instrumental in pushing the League's closure into 1947 and beyond.

The final five months of 1946 rarely feature in the academic scholarship addressing the League's dissolution, which typically skips from the twenty-first Assembly to the division of assets among member states and the issuance of the Board of Liquidation's Final Report in September 1947. At a glance these months seem of little consequence to the League's story, and this has unquestionably played a part in the short shrift given to the period in historiography. No major decisions were made over these months: the Board of Liquidation was not in session, the first UN General Assembly in New York commanded the attention of governments and the dissolution work taking place in Geneva was superficially of a low-key nature. For instance, organizing repatriation expenses for Secretariat officials and purchasing glass cabinets for a new permanent exhibit at the Palais des Nations. To dismiss these months as inconsequential, however, would be a mistake. Looking beyond the superficial, the seemingly minor undertakings and lack of activity that defined the final third of 1946 demonstrate how and why the League's closure took as long as it did.

This was a time of shifting sands for the League, as the priorities of governments and other international organizations changed, and the previously unchecked momentum driving the closure process ground to a halt. Heretofore unknown or underestimated technical problems became apparent – including the taxation of League officials based in the United States, the transfer of Pensions Funds to the ILO and disagreement over the valuation of certain League assets – and the choice to address neither these nor any other issues deemed low priority served to lengthen the dissolution process. In addition, the institutional shortcomings of the closure mechanisms put in place by the twenty-first Assembly, especially the Board of Liquidation's relatively large membership and the lack of clarity regarding roles and responsibilities, combined to create barriers to timely decision-making. Furthermore, analysis of the events of the autumn of 1946 reinforces how the lack of precedent for the closure of IGOs led to the continued mischaracterization of the process as one that could be managed quickly and efficiently. This was made evident in the lack of an overarching approach to liquidation planning, and the willingness to accept the physical separation of the League's leaders from the Secretariat between New York and Geneva. The absence of leadership in the latter half of 1946 was a significant brake on progress, showing that without the presence and focus of decision-makers, the Secretariat officials left in Geneva could do little but wait for them to return in their ever-diminishing corner of the Palais des Nations.

The final five months of 1946 were a critical bridging period between the high levels of activity following the twenty-first Assembly and the drawn-out attempts to close the organization in 1947. The physical split of the Board of Liquidation – and parts of the Secretariat – between two continents was a significant challenge to overcome, both in terms of practicalities and logistics but also for the morale and motivation of those left behind. Without precedent to guide them, League members' representatives at the twenty-first Assembly created a framework for dissolution that was ill-equipped for this particular challenge. The lack of clarity around who was responsible for what also made it difficult to either adapt that framework to meet the change in circumstances or make any significant progress on liquidation. These issues were made worse by the lack of both operational and strategic planning for liquidation beyond a list of outstanding issues managed by the Board's secretary.[2] The presentism that focused only immediate issues and prevented in-depth consideration of closure over the summer was still a serious problem; however, by the autumn, it was no longer transfer issues that took precedence but instead New York and the UN General Assembly. There was no liquidation timetable, no prioritization of problems and no attempt to manage either the physical separation of Lester from the rest of the Secretariat or the nullification of the Board's decision-making powers. When the world's focus pivoted away from Geneva and towards New York, all momentum driving the League's closure was lost, leaving the Secretariat to face a difficult and unknown number of months of liquidation ahead.

Summer momentum

The weeks of August and early September saw much of the same rapid, pressurized change that characterized the earlier part of the summer, though with a little less of the poor inter-organization communication that also marred those same months. The end of July was a watershed moment for transfer between the League and the UN; the Palais des Nations and the rest of the Ariana Estate became part of the UN, alongside functions and activities including the Economic Intelligence Service, Communications and Transit, and the Library.[3] The UN was the key factor in driving this rapid change, which was negative for Lester and his colleagues in terms of the aforementioned stress, but also positive in providing the momentum necessary for much of the League's dissolution. The second half of the first UN General Assembly was scheduled to begin in October, and this deadline pushed the new organization to establish its own secretariat as quickly as possible, meaning the outside pressures that drove the changes before 1 August carried on into the rest of the month, ensuring almost all remaining areas of League Secretariat activity were moved to UN control by the end of the summer.[4]

The changes of the late summer were also facilitated by the fruitful relationship between the secretaries general of both organizations: Lester and Trygve Lie. While the two had communicated via correspondence previously, Lie's visit to Switzerland at the beginning of August brought the two men face-to-face, and they were almost immediately on good terms.⁵ This was of course in stark contrast to Lester's sometimes difficult relationship with Włodzimierz Moderow (director of the UN Office in Geneva), which reached its nadir in early August and was made all the more wearisome for the former as the UN officially took control of the Palais. At an official luncheon celebrating the handover and Lie's trip to Geneva at the start of the month, Lester took affront at a number of Moderow's jibes about the 'outsider position' he now occupied in Geneva and even belied his typically unassuming nature when Moderow suggested he had an emotional perspective on the issue of neutrality. In a diary entry recalling the luncheon, Lester wrote: 'I was flabbergasted and said: "rubbish, what do you mean by saying something like that?"' Lester's good relationship with Lie was all the more constructive by comparison and was most likely helped, as noted in the same diary note, by the UN secretary general's perceived shared dislike of his Geneva representative. Lester wrote: 'One thing to be said for Lie; I think he will not be easily deceived by time-servers and sycophants. His Geneva representatives have been feeling this.'⁶

The preceding eighteen months had been humbling ones for Lester as he experienced a number of professional slights – from the farcical events at the San Francisco Conference in April 1945 to the difficult and pressurized months working alongside Moderow – so his new friendship with Lie was a welcome reprieve and restored some of the prestige he felt his position was due. In letters exchanged following the handover of the Palais, Lie thanked Lester for his 'kind hospitality', 'constant helpfulness' and 'generosity and good feeling', to which the latter responded that Lie's 'spirit and personality inspire and encourage all who believe in the great work'.⁷ The nature of their relationship would later play into Lester's decision to attend the UN General Assembly as an honoured guest and, personal feelings aside, the new line of communication between the two men was a great improvement on the problems that dogged transfer practicalities during June and July.⁸

The major thrust of the late summer momentum was saved for those areas of Secretariat activity the UN had originally attempted to move to its control at the end of July: drug control, health and social questions. While that last-minute request provoked considerable consternation and stress in Geneva at that time – including Moderow – it meant the revised transfer date of 1 September was agreed early on, allowing for at least some advanced planning, even if it was only a matter of weeks instead of days.⁹ The new organization was not entirely prepared for the move – requesting somewhat basic information on the management of the PCOB and the DSB in late August – but the advanced agreement of a transfer date ensured the League's leadership could fulfil its obligations, providing a one-month notice period for officials and informing governments of the changes in advance.[10] The move of the Social Questions Section was the easiest of the three areas to manage – having no officials permanently attached to it since 1941 – but neither the Health Organisation nor the drug control mechanisms caused any unexpected issues from the League's perspective.[11]

These transfers meant a major portion of the League's Geneva activities were under UN control by the start of September and, despite the early confusion of Treasury official Percy Watterson in relation to the liquidation of the Princeton Office, the onward momentum meant he also effected the majority of his US-based transfers to the UN in a matter of weeks.[12] The remaining physical assets of the EFO office in New Jersey, including furniture, equipment and copies of League publications, all moved to the UN offices in New York on 29 August, alongside the former League staff working under EFO official Ansgar Rosenborg, who had been under UN management from the beginning of the month.[13] Meanwhile Watterson remained a member of the League Secretariat until the end of October in order to manage the financial liquidation of the organization's presence in the United States, moving to an office at Hunter College elsewhere in Princeton, where he continued to be assisted by Director Frank Aydelotte and the rest of the administration of the Institute for Advanced Study.[14] His work for the League was not over at the end of October, but his liaison with the UN was all but complete by the start of September.[15]

The remaining central services of the League's Secretariat also transferred to UN control quickly and, for the most part, quietly across August and September. The Registry and Distribution Service was the first to move on 1 September, followed by the Documentation and Printing Service a month later alongside the Publications Service.[16] Transferring the last of these, however, was not as straightforward a prospect as other areas of the Secretariat because, while it provided a central service role for the rest of the organization, it also held a considerable number of assets in the form of copies of League publications and their associated copyrights. While the theoretical transfer of these assets was agreed months earlier, the value of the publications and their inalienable rights, and thus the price to be remunerated to the League by the UN, became a point of contention.[17] An early figure provided by the League's Secretariat – 50,000 Swiss francs – was purposefully much lower than the publications were worth and was suggested only as a way of guaranteeing the UN's agreement to the transfer, with the belief that it could be re-negotiated in the future. The UN however understandably bristled when the League later suggested a new value of nearly 2,000,000 Swiss francs instead. Alexander Elkin, one of Moderow's assistant directors in Geneva, expressed his frustration with the League's unwillingness to negotiate in good faith, noting in a memo that while the UN had altered its position to talk of hundreds of thousands, 'the League talked – and still seem to be thinking – of millions'.[18] Elkin's frustrations aside, by late September, the new organization's attention was elsewhere, having moved onto the impending General Assembly, and haggling over the value of the League's publications was low on the list of priorities. The energy and momentum that so successfully propelled the other transfers of August and September did not dissipate but instead changed direction, and the question of publications value was deemed minor enough to be set aside for the foreseeable future, ultimately waiting until 1947 when it was negotiated alongside the rest of the League's fixed assets. The outstanding issue did not affect the Publications Service move to UN management on 1 October, but while this was reported as the official transfer date in reports to members, it was not the end of the affair. It was also not the last time the Board's formal reporting to members would obscure and obfuscate the difficulties of dissolution.[19]

Asset valuations aside, by the start of October, all the Secretariat's technical activities had moved to UN management. The vast majority of the League's fixed assets – or, at least, those the UN was immediately concerned with – had also been transferred to UN control, but once these had been effected the pressure to deliver the outstanding elements of closure waned quickly, and the first signs of a slowdown were visible. Despite the UN taking over the Palais des Nations on 1 August, they still had not taken responsibility for the associated utilities by mid-October and did not seem to be in a rush to do so.[20] Other League assets, including a number of funds the UN had tentatively agreed to manage in future, were shelved for later consideration, presaging a wider trend that would characterize the following months and ultimately thwart efforts to close the organization as quickly as possible.[21] Without the external pressures driving progress, the once unmanageable momentum that had enthusiastically realized the decisions of both the UN General Assembly and the League Assembly during the summer had slowed to a crawl.

4,000 miles away

At its tenth meeting in late July, the Board of Liquidation – the oversight group responsible for dissolution and the League's only remaining decision-making body – noted for the record that it would not be in session again for some time due to the scheduled UN General Assembly in the coming autumn.[22] While it was not the first time representatives to the new organization would gather in person, it was the second half of the first General Assembly, the first meeting to take place in its new home of New York and the first since the UN Secretariat had been established. With this in mind, almost half of the Board of Liquidation's members – now counting former League Treasurer Seymour Jacklin who, having left the Secretariat on 31 July, officially became a member of the group from 1 August – left Europe to attend the Assembly, including both Carl Hambro and Cecil Kisch, the chair and vice-chair respectively.[23] The opportunity to travel to New York also proved an irresistible lure for Lester, who was invited by Trygve Lie when they met at the beginning of August, leaving behind Valentin Stencek – director of Personnel and Internal Administration – and the rest of what remained of the Secretariat at an increasingly lonely Palais.[24]

New York is almost 4,000 miles from Geneva, and the geographical separation between the League's Secretariat and its most senior leaders created a number of obstacles to the organization's dissolution. The first was the time and energy spent organizing the logistics for Lester's trip, and while the UN assisted in regard to the secretary general's accommodation, Percy Watterson – still working from Hunter College in Princeton – spent a not-insignificant portion of his time in September and October making preparations for Lester's trip.[25] He opened several bank accounts in New York, arranged for League publications to be available should Lester need them and generally acted as a central liaison point for Lester and Cosette Nonin – Lester's secretary – during their stay in the United States. Even after Watterson left the Secretariat at the end of October, having taken up a new role in the Food and Agriculture Organization in Washington, DC, he continued in this liaison role until the secretary general returned to Geneva in December.[26] Nonetheless, even though Lester and Nonin's trip diverted dwindling resources away from closure work, the Secretariat in Geneva was at least able to maintain contact with the two once they arrived in the United States.

Members of the Board of Liquidation meanwhile, although granted international civil servant status via their positions, were not Secretariat officials and were under no obligation to keep the League informed of their whereabouts. Carl Hambro, the Board chairman, spent nearly four months away from Europe in the latter half of 1946, leaving Norway in mid-September and not returning until the final days of the year.[27] He also neglected to leave his New York address with officials before his departure, leaving Chester Purves – the Board of Liquidation secretary – with no means of contacting the chair until he was able to glean the information from Lester when the latter arrived in the United States almost a month later.[28] Government representatives at the twenty-first Assembly in April 1946 could not have anticipated the logistical impact of a UN General Assembly held in North America on its part-time Geneva-based Board, but the same was not true for the League leadership. Both the Secretariat and Board members were aware at least two months in advance that some of the latter would be away from Europe during the autumn, but the potentially negative impact of this absence was not given any further consideration beyond a vague commitment to liaise via correspondence if needed.[29] Intergovernmental governance, even during the time of the UN Preparatory Commission, had traditionally been administered from Europe, and the League had simply not encountered a transatlantic split in its leadership before. There was a genuine underestimation of the effect this would have which, combined with the lack of liquidation precedent, left the League unprepared for the challenges ahead.

Naturally the major problems brought about by the physical distance between New York and Geneva were the travel and communication delays. Passage across the Atlantic took an average of seven days, although this could of course be lengthened by weather problems and did not factor in the time taken to journey to and from European ports.[30] For instance, Lester left Geneva on 14 October 1946, spending just under ten days travelling westwards across the Atlantic to New York, and embarked on his return voyage on 29 November, this time passing nearly two weeks on his journey.[31] Approximately twenty days of travelling might not, at a glance, have seemed a great deal of time, but in addition to the ten days of holiday already taken by Lester in August, this meant he was physically away from his office and uncontactable for a full month during the latter half of 1946.[32]

Wary of the physical separation, Lester and Stencek took great pains to keep each other updated as much as possible while the former was in New York, usually in the form of ad hoc lengthy letters every week or ten days, but conducting business via correspondence naturally added delays to proceedings.[33] Although cables could be used to send urgent information, they were intrinsically limited in terms of the amount of detail that could be included, and longer documents and letters had to be sent via more conventional means. By illustration, Board members Hambro, Seymour Jacklin, Adolfo Costa du Rels and Lester were able to meet in-person for an unofficial meeting only once while they were all in New York on 29 October, but the minutes of the session were not issued to the rest of the group for another five weeks while draft versions made their way back and forth across the ocean before the document could be distributed.[34]

Furthermore, communicating via letter or cable was simply not as productive as meeting face-to-face, which allowed for the exchange of information on a much more rapid basis, as well as the generation of ideas that comes from being in a room with people working on the same problem. And the League was not alone in underestimating the perils of this ocean-sized obstacle: the UN was having its own issues with communications between New York and Geneva. In September 1946, Moderow took the unusual step of bringing his concerns to Adriaan Pelt, UN undersecretary general and based at headquarters in the United States, noting that the system 'would not, at the moment, appear to be working as smoothly as might be hoped'. Documents were somehow going missing in transit, and even cables – which should have been more reliable – seemed to be subject to delay, with a lag of up to a week in some cases.[35]

The lack of face-to-face interaction also impacted the functionality of the Board of Liquidation, as the physical division of the group meant they were unable to hold an official meeting for the rest of 1946. Across the first set of Board meetings in April and May, the group agreed terms of reference which defined the quorum for decision-making as five members.[36] With four of the Board – including both the chair and vice-chair – in North America, and the other five scattered across Europe, holding a full meeting was almost impossible. One early suggestion proposed sending one of the Europe-based Board members to the United States to reach quorum, but the diversion of resources required to put the logistics in place, and an estimated cost of almost 67,000 Swiss francs, meant the possibility was dismissed early on.[37] The closest the group came to a meeting during these months was the informal gathering, held at the end of October with Hambro, Jacklin and Costa du Rels, but without quorum, authoritative decision-making was impossible, and it was the only time they met as a group during their respective months in the United States.[38] Correspondence held in the League's Archives suggests that members based in Europe were slightly more concerned by the lack of Board meetings – Jaromír Kopecky wrote to both Lester and Stencek on several occasions to query the date of the next session, not realizing that many of his colleagues were still in North America – but their discomfiture was never serious enough to warrant more than gentle reassurance from Stencek or Purves that the group would meet again as soon as possible.[39] Ultimately, no Board of Liquidation meetings for over six months meant no decision-making or high-level direction at a time when, dealing with unanticipated issues, the Secretariat needed its input.

The physical distance between the League's decision-makers and the organization's Secretariat was a serious barrier to the timely completion of the closure process, diverting resources to activities unrelated to the dissolution, and causing delays in both everyday business and major decision-making. A key illustration of this centred on the production of the Board's Second Interim Report for members, which was supposed to be issued to governments on 1 December 1946 as per the Resolution for the Dissolution of the League of Nations approved by the twenty-first Assembly.[40] Although the final document was released with this official publication date, the League's Archives reveal it was heavily delayed due to both a lack of progress in liquidation and its forced completion via correspondence across the Atlantic, ensuring it was still in draft stages throughout December and not actually distributed to members until late January 1947.[41] The 1 December publication date stayed on the document only because the Board of Liquidation – and historically the League as an institution – was intrinsically concerned with its performance and reputation with governments, and it was easier to change the date on a report than openly admit the dispersion of leadership had caused delays.[42] However, the 4,000 miles of ocean represented more than just a physical obstacle to be overcome, it also signified an overall shift in the international community's gaze, which was no longer fixed on Europe.

Shifting priorities

Most of the League's work between the end of the twenty-first Assembly and the handover of the Palais des Nations to the UN was driven by the latter organization, resulting in a harried effort to transfer numerous Secretariat activities over a brief period of time. The 1 August handover and transfers of August and September was not however the end of the UN's influence on the dismantling process. The new organization's agenda remained as relevant as ever, although this time the impact was less direct, as the UN Secretariat's focus moved away from the League, taking with it the attention of those who might otherwise have been engaged with the liquidation in Geneva. The physical distance between the Secretariat and its leadership caused obvious problems for the closure process, but the mental distance between the same groups had just as much, if not more, of a negative impact.

Seán Lester made the decision to travel to New York after he returned from holiday in August 1946, but we can only speculate about why he chose to accept the invitation. He had a good working relationship with Trygve Lie and noted to Carl Hambro that the offer was also 'of a certain semi-political interest in the history of the two organizations', yet he also claimed to be disinclined towards public ceremony and ultimately spent very little time at General Assembly proceedings while in the United States. In a personal letter to Arthur Sweetser, Lester admitted to avoiding Lake Success – the temporary home of the UN until 1951 – wherever possible, explaining: 'I do not like hanging around there.'[43] We might surmise that he wished to remain physically close to the Board chairman to ensure efficient management of the closure process, but there is little evidence for this other than a passing mention in an August letter to Hambro when he wrote: 'I do not know how long I really can stay but it may be possible for us to do something there in relation to the Liquidation Board.'[44] There was likely also an appeal to spending time away from the claustrophobia of Geneva for Lester; it was an opportunity to work with the UN on something new, as well as a chance to see friends and colleagues after a long separation. His personal and professional struggles during the war are well-documented, but the immediate post-war period meanwhile was exhausting in a different way, as governments' attention returned to the League and planning for the new organization reached fever pitch. His decision therefore to accept Lie's proposal immediately after returning from his August holiday indicated a desire to take a break from the pressures of Geneva for a few more months. Lester certainly remarked in a letter to Valentin Stencek in November that he was preferring to spend his time working on matters with their mutual friend and former Secretariat colleague, Egon Ranshofen-Wertheimer – by then working as chief of the UN Overseas Offices Division – and he enjoyed the opportunity to socialize with old friends such as Manley Hudson and Arthur Sweetser.[45]

Despite some early concerns that Lester might experience the same disregard he endured at the San Francisco Conference, the League's secretary general was invited to New York as a respected dignitary which, having risen to the position during wartime, came with a standing and profile he had rarely experienced before.[46] While he had occupied the most senior position in the Secretariat for over six years, his experience of the post had been as either the beleaguered leader of a small wartime staff or as the junior partner in negotiations with the UN. While his absence was a hindrance to his Geneva colleagues, travelling to New York was an opportunity for the former journalist, politician and diplomat to be at the centre of building something positive, away from the increasingly thankless job of dissolution.

Still, Lester was not the only senior League figure to have his attention drawn away from the organization after the summer of 1946. As previously mentioned, the twenty-first Assembly did not specify that – like members of the League's

Supervisory Commission before it – acting as a Board of Liquidation member should be considered a full-time position, and most members managed their Board responsibilities in addition to their everyday roles. Take, for example, the four members attendant in New York for the UN General Assembly – Carl Hambro, Cecil Kisch, Seymour Jacklin and Adolfo Costa du Rels – all of whom were present as representatives, either in an official or unofficial capacity, of their respective governments. They were not there to formally speak for the League or its interests and were almost exclusively occupied with their governmental engagements while the General Assembly was in session.[47] Geneva was 'out of sight, out of mind', and while the League's closure remained of concern to the group, it was simply not as important, nor as urgent, as the successful launch of the UN. Resultantly, although it is not possible to state with conviction that Lester travelled to New York to remind Board members of their commitments to the League, the secretary general's presence did ensure they could not entirely forget the list of outstanding tasks awaiting them in Geneva.

Lester was particularly concerned about the focus of Seymour Jacklin, with whom he had had a particularly fractious relationship over the past twelve months.[48] The former League treasurer and deputy secretary general had only become a Board member at the start of August 1946, but Lester found it almost impossible to get Jacklin to respond to letters, let alone speak to in person. In a letter to Cecil Kisch in early November, Lester wrote of his impression of Jacklin during a recent meeting: 'His attitude struck me as uninterested, critical and still resentful.'[49] The secretary general had not supported the plan to add Jacklin to the Board in the first place – the move left the League's Treasury without a treasurer during liquidation – and his busy schedule only made achieving quorum all the more difficult for a group that Lester already felt was too large to work effectively.[50]

It was to be expected then that Lester noted, in a letter to Arthur Sweetser, that he was having trouble getting the Board to focus on League issues.[51] Unfortunately for the secretary general and those trying to resolve some of the challenges arising from closure, even when they were able to draw the attention of Board members to the dissolution, the latter wanted to focus on lower-priority issues. An ongoing US income tax case involving former Permanent Court of International Justice Judge Manley Hudson continued to take up valuable resource, despite the matter having been discussed, and supposedly resolved, at previous Board meetings, as did a disagreement with Alexander Loveday, the former director of the EFO and ranking member of the Secretariat in the United States during the war.[52] The problem stemmed from the long-awaited removal of Loveday's furniture – still stored at the Palais des Nations – and while similar arrangements for other former officials were rightly managed by more junior Secretariat colleagues, Board members involved themselves in Loveday's case. The more important the figure, such as a former PCIJ judge or a former Secretariat director, and the closer the personal friendships between them and Board members, the more likely it was the latter would spend valuable time on the case.[53] Perhaps it is not surprising that more powerful individuals would receive preferential treatment from the Board, but with half of its members so busy in New York, the more time spent on relatively inconsequential questions was less time spent on the more serious issues.

All this exposed a fundamental problem at the heart of the Board: the misconception of what the liquidation of an IGO would involve, and the commitment and resources required to realize it. The group was made aware of the prevailing problems in the autumn of 1946, but no action was taken to address them. The Secretariat in Geneva continued to produce Board of Liquidation documents and fortnightly progress reports while members were away from Switzerland, yet there is little evidence these were acted upon or followed up.[54] With no past examples to draw upon for guidance, there was a fundamental misunderstanding of how long some issues would take to resolve, leading to recurrent dismissals of their urgency. The recurrent choice to delay discussions until the next Board meeting – unlikely to take place until February 1947 – reflected the genuine belief that matters could be dealt with in a small collection of meetings, despite all the evidence from the liquidation thus far that suggested this was an overly ambitious objective.

Several major problems surfaced during the autumn, none of which were addressed. The transfer of the Palais des Nations and its associated assets was settled in an agreement dated 31 July, but a key component of the move to UN ownership remained outstanding: the price the new organization would pay the League and its members for the privilege.[55] An outline schedule was included in the Common Plan agreed at the start of the year, but whether this total was final and, if not, what the value should reflect was a source of disagreement between the two secretariats.[56] Lester argued the final figure should represent the full cost price of the buildings, taking improvement works and the result of as-yet-unresolved arbitration cases into account. The UN meanwhile wanted to use the value outlined in the Common Plan, although this figure, as was discovered by Stencek some months after it was first documented, was never accurate. Erroneously, the original total used in the Common Plan was produced for the end of 1944 as opposed to 1945 and, crucially for talks with the UN, a footnote to the agreement – which would have noted that the figures were subject to further discussion – was accidentally omitted, leaving the League at a disadvantage before negotiations even started.[57] Meanwhile Board members, occupying more senior diplomatic roles that would have allowed them to intervene in the differences of opinion, continued with their unexplained decision to remain outside negotiations with the UN. The same was true for the transfer of the Staff Pensions Fund from the League to the ILO, which was initially considered a *fait accompli* at the proceedings of the twenty-first Assembly. The ILO, however, had not yet approved the transfer and, along with problems relating to the Fund's holdings, it became increasingly clear the organization was in no hurry to take on the responsibility.[58] In practice at least, the ILO was no longer subject to League control, and it had no reason to submit to conditions it found unfavourable.[59] Early pressure to initiate negotiations from the League's Board would have been useful during the autumn months, but its absence relegated what would become a contentious topic to 1947.

Rumbling in the background during these months was another overlooked problem that would ultimately push the completion of League business into 1948: an ongoing debate with the US Treasury Department over the taxation of League officials based in the United States during the Second World War. A legal test case, separate from that of Manley Hudson and instead involving former EFO official John Henry Chapman, was in the process of being initiated on the League's behalf in the States. Although there was little action or acknowledgement of the lawsuit in late 1946, some League officials began to express doubts upon learning more about the proceedings. Émile Giraud, the League's legal advisor and a member of the Secretariat for nearly twenty years, explicitly stated that the case was a lost cause and should not be pursued, but his advice was ignored.[60] Seymour Jacklin felt the same way but Lester, hearing the former treasurer's opinion, did not reconsider the Secretariat's approach to the issue or inform other Board members, ensuring any opposition to pursuance of the case was quietly brushed aside.[61]

As mentioned earlier in this chapter, the European-based members of the Board were marginally more proactive in pushing for a meeting in the latter half of 1946, but they brought their concerns in this regard to Lester or Chester Purves rather than Hambro, and this raised important questions about the relationship between, and respective responsibilities of, the secretary general and the Board.[62] The relationship between the Board and the Secretariat was ambiguous; there was a distinct lack of definition as to who was ultimately responsible for delivering liquidation, and what power Lester had, if any, to force the Board into action. The dissolution resolution agreed at the twenty-first Assembly was explicit as to the power of the Board to replace the secretary general should the latter be unable or unwilling to carry out his duties, but not vice versa. The Board of Liquidation was initially designed to function much as the Supervisory Commission had done from 1938 – as a proxy for the League Assembly – but how the Secretariat, and specifically the secretary general, was supposed to liaise with the group was unclear.[63] Ultimately Lester chose to take a more subservient position, meaning he felt unable to make strategic decisions independently, nor press the Board to make those decisions in his stead. Yet, despite knowing this approach to decision-making would suffer while the General Assembly was in session, neither the Board nor the Secretariat believed the situation required a remedy, either in advance or during the New York-based proceedings. This created a void of oversight and decision-making for several months during the closure, made all the more frustrating for some officials who felt, following the transfer of activities and functions to the UN, that there was an opportunity to progress liquidation in this period of relative calm.

While the spring and summer months of 1946 were dominated by a frantic effort to enact dissolution as quickly as possible, the autumn months exposed a significant problem at the heart of the whole endeavour: there was no plan. The UN, as an organization, was unprepared for the speed at which it was forced to establish its Secretariat, but it otherwise knew what it wanted to achieve and when.[64] So while the external impetus of the UN helped drive the first elements of the League's dismantling, when the transfers were complete – when the new organization had secured what it needed from its predecessor – it became all too obvious that the overwhelming pressure on the League's Secretariat during the spring and summer meant it was unable to think strategically about its own objectives or schedule. Unfortunately, however, even after the UN demands on League Secretariat time dissipated in September and October 1946, the urgency of the General Assembly and its demands on many of the League's leaders – Hambro, Kisch, Lester, Jacklin – meant the organization's closure continued to be the victim of UN's establishment schedule.

Without the driving force of the Board of Liquidation's strategic guidance or any associated deadlines, there was a complete lack of internal momentum in the Secretariat. Only the most pressing of issues were advanced during these months, and these were only considered as such because they were matters concerning external stakeholders. The Board's Second Interim Report was cobbled together in a rapid and perfunctory fashion through correspondence between Chester Purves and other Board members. The group acknowledged there was little to report in the way of progress and, as already noted, the geographical distance and lack of Board input meant the document was still issued over a month behind schedule.[65] The only other matter settled by the Board over these months was driven by a deadline set by members: the production of a budget for 1947. However, like the interim report, it was drawn up at the last minute, was one page in length and only made provision for January to March 1947 in order to appease both governments and the members of the Board who continued to believe that a budget beyond that would not be required.[66]

By the end of 1946, over eight months after the twenty-first Assembly, the League's Secretariat still had no agreed plan for delivering dissolution beyond Purves's list of outstanding Board agenda items, no deadlines other than an arbitrary completion date of the end of March 1947 and no means of making any decisions or managing progress without the Board of Liquidation.[67] Over the summer the Secretariat had been drowning in last-minute requests for assistance from the UN, but by the time the leaves were falling in Geneva, the League's own ill-preparedness was at the forefront. With its leadership absent, those officials remaining in the Swiss city found themselves in an unenviable position.

Empty spaces

While Lester was away from Geneva, Valentin Stencek, director of Internal Administration, was effectively left in charge of the Secretariat on a day-to-day basis, as well as continuing to carry out his responsibilities as the unofficial operations chief for the organization.[68] He was overwhelmingly busy throughout this period, not because the League was making great progress with dissolution but because there were fewer and fewer resources available to him, and there was ample work to be done at both a strategic and operational level. For instance, a large portion of Stencek's time over these months was consumed by efforts to remove furniture from the Palais des Nations belonging to Secretariat officials, both former and current. Staff had been allowed to store personal belongings at the Palais in the early 1940s as a result of the logistical problems caused by wartime. Upon termination of officials' contracts, Secretariat regulations granted them reimbursement for the cost of removing their items back to their home countries but, while the League was more than happy to pay, the physical removal arrangements had to be made by the former staff member in question. By October 1946 there were 122 removal cases outstanding, over 60 of which still had furniture on site at the Palais. Deadlines for their removal were regularly pushed back, despite the fact that the buildings were no longer under League management, and Stencek bore the brunt of organizing new procedures, contacting officials and breaking the news of further delays to the UN Secretariat.[69] Indeed there were very few matters he was not involved in to some degree or another, from liaising with Moderow on outstanding issues relating to transfer of the Palais, organizing repatriation benefits for former officials and even approving the purchase of a garden hose for the New Delhi Office, which was still under League management until the end of 1946.[70]

The former Austro-Hungarian civil servant was not known for personal candour or small talk in his correspondence – if anything, he was somewhat formal – but he also obviously cared about those in his charge. When planning the transfer of the drug control functions in August, Stencek went out of his way to ensure a new position in the League Treasury for Evelyn Curry, then an official with the Opium Section. Curry had previously been part of the Secretariat contingent based in Washington, DC, but personal clashes with Léon Steinig, the secretary to the PCOB, forced her return to Geneva. It is unclear exactly what caused the professional relationship between Curry and Steinig to break down from 1943 onwards, but from letters exchanged in early 1945 it was clear that Curry's position in the United States had become untenable, and that this was the result of Steinig's attitude or behaviour rather than Curry herself. The situation was so bad in fact that Curry requested either a transfer back to Europe or for the acceptance of her resignation, the former of which was granted. Not wanting to lose an individual as talented and experienced as Curry – who had been with the Secretariat since 1924 – Stencek suggested the lateral move to the Treasury to help the League's resource issues, as well as keeping Curry employed until she received an offer of a new position from the UN, away from Steinig. Stencek was under no obligation to make any such arrangements but did so out of the duty of care he felt for his colleagues, especially one who had already been compelled to work in difficult circumstances.[71]

Stencek was devoutly committed to his work, but he was not immune to the frustration growing in the League offices. He took the rare step of complaining to Lester in a letter in November regarding the lack of communication on the US income tax issues, describing the situation as 'rather embarrassing' and that he felt 'quite incompetent to give any advice as to what should be done'.[72] Chester Purves, managing his increasingly long list of issues for the Board to address upon its reconvening, also expressed his disappointment at the lack of headway in letters to both Lester and Kisch, telling the latter that there was 'very little progress to report', and that the Board's second report to members would be 'even more jejune' than the previous one as a result, adding that the whole endeavour was 'rather disconcerting'.[73] Both men and their colleagues had, in effect, been temporarily forsaken by their senior leadership, and not even the famous Geneva espirit de corps was immune to disillusionment.

Those left in Geneva were not a homogeneous group, and like any workforce they were a collection of individuals with individual concerns. There was an obvious bond and professional camaraderie between them, most evident in their commitment to the shrinking organization, but they were not without their disagreements or conflicts. Many of the Secretariat's female officials – who constituted a third of its numbers at the start of August 1946 but over half by the following January – had, as their more senior male colleagues left the organization, taken on more responsibilities and work beyond their typically junior ranks.[74] A notable example was Constance (Connie) Harris, officially the longest-serving Secretariat official, who joined the League in 1919 as a stenographer, acted as the secretary of the Central Section from 1933, was then entrusted with the work of the Social Questions Section from 1941, before becoming the acting head of the Personnel Office following Henri Vilatte's departure in 1946.[75] When she finally left the Secretariat in August 1947, the high regard in which she was held and her varied career were reflected in a letter from Lester: 'That you are entitled to feel satisfaction at the way in which you have always performed your duties is amply attested by your record, from which it is evident that the excellence of the work you have done is matched only by the variety of its character.'[76]

The increased workload and responsibilities of officials during liquidation were acknowledged by the League's leadership, and much appreciated as resources became thin on the ground, but requests for promotions and salary increases were refused time and time again. Evelyn Curry, so well-respected by Stencek that he acquired a new role for her in August 1946, was recommended for promotion to the Intermediate Class on a number of occasions by her former manager Bertil Renborg, but was denied each time in spite of her recognized 'excellent service'.[77] Cecily Babington, part of the Board of Liquidation's Secretariat, wrote to Stencek at the end of July 1946 to request an increase in salary and threatened to resign if her appeal was not met: 'I find that I am considerably out of pocket, therefore to my great regret I feel my best course would be to return to England and look for other employment.'[78] Stencek turned down her request and Babington, 'reluctant to leave the Secretariat before the completion of the work of the Board of Liquidation', ultimately stayed with the organization until the end of August 1947.[79] In addition to the repeated promotion and increased salary rejections, all officials were on temporary contracts, as per the mass notice issued to staff in March 1946, and these were only renewed for two months at a time, leaving people unsure when they would be dismissed.[80] This, of course, was only exacerbated by the lack of deadlines or plan for dissolution that might have, at least, given them some indication of when their service would be terminated.

Staff also had to suffer the ignominy of no longer controlling their own buildings, and this loss of control led, on occasion, to pettifoggery. Just days after the Palais was handed over to UN management, the UNRRA held its fifth Council meeting in the former League buildings, making use of the services and facilities on hand. As the session took place less than a week after the Ariana Estate transfer, League officials were heavily involved in the advanced planning, provided support throughout the Council sessions themselves and worked closely with the UN Secretariat to assess the expenses owed, seemingly charging UNRRA for every possible item. A schedule of monies, agreed between the three organizations after the Conference, listed the expected charges for telephony, heating and services of particular individuals, alongside reimbursement for more surprising items including eighty-six pieces of broken china and glassware, eighty-two articles of missing office supplies, and two missing cleaners' smocks, coming to a total of more than 30,000 Swiss francs.[81] The Palais des Nations was an extraordinarily grand collection of buildings and grounds, and it had lent the League of Nations – and its staff – a sense of authority, even as the organization was becoming increasingly insignificant on the world stage. Ilaria Scaglia has explained that the League's purpose-built home was designed to reflect the resilience and majesty of the Alps it faced, and it was certainly easier for Secretariat officials to feel better about their position and global standing when they occupied such a palatial home, but the transfer of ownership to the UN took this comfort from them.[82] This was made all the more galling by the diminishing number of League officials, as although Secretariat numbers had already reduced dramatically since the start of 1946, people continued to leave between August and December. Slowly but surely most officials either transferred to the UN or moved on to new roles entirely, including senior officials who had been with the League for decades, such as Émile Giraud, Percy Watterson and Henri Vilatte (head of the Personnel Office).[83]

By the time 1947 began only twenty League officials remained in post.[84] The autumnal months of 1946 had not been kind to those that remained: their most senior colleagues had taken the opportunity to travel across the Atlantic for the glamour of New York, refused their applications for remuneration or recognition for having repeatedly gone above and beyond the call of duty, ignored their requests for assistance with the most difficult of liquidation issues, and declined to provide them any kind of indication of their job security. They had lost control of the little they had left and come to the unfortunate realization that without the organization's assets and services, the wider world did not really seem to care about the League anymore.

Conclusions

The months of August to December 1946 represented a period of great change for the League and its Secretariat, in terms of its functions, its resources and its position on the global stage. It was by no means the first time the organization had found itself relegated to the lower echelons of public consciousness, but its brief renaissance following the war was at an end, and the UN's direct involvement with the League was greatly diminished once the majority of transfer questions had been answered. This might have represented, in other circumstances, a chance for the League to finally take control of its fate and enact the closure it wanted. The pace of change following the twenty-first Assembly was rapid and driven by the UN's timetable but, while this pressure lessened once the majority of transfer was effected, presentism and unfamiliarity with the challenges of liquidation continued to scupper proceedings. Progress on issues surrounding closure, both great and small, was minimal at best, and at worst a great source of frustration for those Secretariat officials in the thick of things. Unlike those earlier months in the year, much of the direct external pressure on the organization had dissipated but the League was not ready for either the change in international focus or the freedom it had been granted to take charge of its own death.

There is no doubting the negative impact caused by the physical separation of the Secretariat from many of its senior leaders – on morale, on efficiency and on decision-making. Communication delays were an obvious inconvenience but the lack of face-to-face interaction and support from leadership were even more challenging to overcome, and the experience of those based in Geneva suffered as a result. The latter half of 1946 was a time of great change for the Secretariat as an institution – in terms of numbers, responsibilities, and prestige – and being left behind by its most senior figures was yet another test of officials' commitment both to each other and to the League's brand of internationalism. The glamour and glitz of New York, where every hotel room was booked and the world's diplomats were gathered, was – figuratively speaking – a million miles away from the war-damaged corridors of Europe, and the experiences of those working in these two places could not have been more different.

The UN, its General Assembly and New York were, to everyone other than the handful of League officials in the Palais des Nations, more important than anything else in the realm of international governance in the second half of 1946. The inherent urgency in the UN's work in 1946 was an impossible challenge for the League Secretariat to overcome and realistically officials could do little to change this global shift in attitudes, something recognized by Valentin Stencek in a letter to Lester in October 1946:

> Judging by the papers here it [New York] seems to have become one of the centres of world politics, all the most prominent people staying there and even the Conference of Foreign Ministers being held there ... Things are pretty quiet here, although I have plenty to do.[85]

The League of Nations was no longer the home or centre of intergovernmental relations – but it was also ill-prepared for the impact of that change. If these months reveal anything, it was that the League was not truly ready for the trials it might expect to face during liquidation. This shortfall in preparation extended from the specific, such as the insufficient mitigation for the Board's impotence during the General Assembly, to the wide-ranging, that is, the complete absence of a liquidation timetable. The lack of precedent from which to look for guidance meant problems could not be anticipated in advance, and there was a constant sense of 'fire-fighting' across the Secretariat. The League leaned heavily on bureaucracy throughout its lifetime but, in closure, rigour and design were replaced by confusion and disorder.

During the high summer of 1946, as transfers to the UN progressed rapidly, if haphazardly, it might have been hard to believe that the League of Nations Secretariat would still be working to close the organization's doors almost eighteen months later. The key to understanding why this was the case can be found in the autumn of 1946, as the world's attention turned away from Europe, leaving the Secretariat without decision-makers and exposing serious deficiencies in the organization's machinery and planning for closure. The external pressures that were once a source of stress and anxiety for the officials in Geneva had gone, but with them went the motivation and impetus so desperately needed to make dissolution a reality. Distance, both physical and psychological, was not conducive to momentum, and only served to highlight the fundamental difficulties with the organization's liquidation: no one understood the scale of the task, and it was hard to find anyone willing to focus on the closure of a defunct institution when more urgent matters called for attention. When the League's leadership slowly returned to Europe as 1946 came to an end, the organization was no closer to liquidation than it was months earlier, and many of its officials recognized that 1947 would likely prove as challenging a year as any other in its history.

4

(Un)Avoidable delays, January–July 1947

The first half of 1947 marked the final push of both the League of Nations' Secretariat and the Board of Liquidation to close the organization in as dignified and orderly a fashion as possible. The late spring and summer of 1946 were dominated by the rapid transfer of many of the League's activities, functions and officials in order to support the establishment of the UN Secretariat, while the UN General Assembly in New York in the autumn had placed the League's liquidation on the metaphorical backburner for several more months. The first General Assembly had diverted the focus and physical presence of individuals crucial to the League's closure, including the Board's chair and vice-chair – Carl Hambro and Cecil Kisch respectively – as well as the secretary general Seán Lester. By January 1947, however, they were all back in Europe and ready to concentrate on the liquidation process. The mood among these leadership figures was bright after their time in New York, and they anticipated the resolution of the outstanding dissolution issues by the end of March or April at the latest. Their confidence was however misplaced: the first Board of Liquidation session was not scheduled to begin until February, the agenda for those meetings contained over thirty separate items and it would ultimately take over eight months to issue the Final Report on liquidation to members.

The Board of Liquidation was the League Assembly's proxy in closure questions – it represented both the concerns and interests of members, who had otherwise dispensed of their decision-making powers in relation to the organization – and was the strategic driving force behind closure; they effectively decided what would happen and when. The group, made up of nine representatives from different member countries, met ten times in 1946, but needed thirty-two separate meetings in 1947, across sessions in February, April, June and July, to conclude the League's outstanding business. A large part of the delay was brought about by the Board's intense focus on its financial commitments to members, which manifested itself in the pursuit of outstanding contributions, protracted negotiations with the ILO and the continued 'entertainment' of a much-disliked income tax lawsuit in the United States, but the preoccupation with money was merely a symptom of a different affliction. The senior leadership of the League, especially the Board of Liquidation, was gripped by the need to protect the organization's reputation in both the short and long term, and this chapter shows how this fixation on legacy motivated so many of its choices through 1947.

The chapter examines three crucial elements of this time period and demonstrates, through them, how feelings of pride and fear compelled both decision-makers and officials during a time of high activity and frustration.[1] Firstly, this chapter looks at the Board of Liquidation's pride in the League of Nations – in terms of satisfaction with what it had achieved and the prestige it thought the institution was owed – as well as how this was realized in the group's efforts to protect its legacy, and how those decisions have had an impact on our contemporary study of the organization. More specifically, this section outlines how the Board's concerns about its reputation and performance during liquidation materialized in a number of ways, but most extravagantly in its increasingly grand plans for the permanent League exhibit in the Palais Library building, even at the expense of its other central tenet: providing a good return on investment for members.

The second component of the chapter reflects on the League's relationship with its partner organization, the ILO, as a demonstration of the Board of Liquidation's wider preoccupation with its reputation and how this manifested itself in the group's efforts to bolster the institution's funds before closure. As the ILO was financially tied to the League from its inception, the relationship between the organizations has always been a critical element of their respective histories, and this remained true during the League's dissolution and especially during the first half of 1947. This chapter reveals how a breakdown in the working relationship between the two organizations' leadership in 1947 – ostensibly over money – and a change in power dynamic were the major causes of the delay to the League's liquidation, and how pride and obstinance on both sides contributed to the setbacks.

The third and final section looks at the Secretariat officials still working for the League during 1947, their own pride in the organization and the relationship they shared with the Board of Liquidation. Those who remained in 1947 were often unusually committed to the League, towards both their colleagues and the organization's ethos, but that dedication was not always rewarded or recognized by the institution's leadership, and even in cases where it was, the officials in question sometimes found their loyalty taken advantage of. They were also rarely allowed to take part in the Board's attempts to safeguard a long-lasting legacy for the organization, excluded from the deliberations over what should be included and discovered that the Secretariat, arguably the first international civil service, was not considered worthy of celebration.

This chapter ultimately shows how pride in one's work, efforts to preserve an organization's dignity and an inherent emphasis on public relations came to affect the League's final months, in both positive and negative ways. Many of the Board of Liquidation's decisions during 1947 were guided by the overarching refrain: what will people think? The preoccupation with maintaining standards of practice, constructing an official view of the dissolution process and appointing itself guardian of the League's memory were all results of the leadership's attempts to safeguard the legacy of both their own performance since April 1946 and the organization as a whole. The League of Nations was not what it once had been, and the Board frequently struggled to come to grips with that reality. Nevertheless, the decisions made by this small group of men in 1947 not only affected the way in which the League closed but continue to have long-term repercussions for our own examination of the organization.

Controlling the narrative

The League's reputation was at the forefront of the organization's consciousness from its inception; the institution's founders knew public support was vital for its survival. In his study on the Secretariat written during the Second World War, Egon Ranshofen-Wertheimer described the organization's focus on public relations as groundbreaking: 'In no other respect did the creation of the League mark a more complete break with habits of the past than in the new kind of relationship between a diplomatic body and public opinion.' This early form of public relations was managed by the Information Section, which was created to ensure consideration was always given to both publicity and opinion in the organization's work. The Section was consistently one of the largest elements of the League Secretariat, and Emil Eiby Seidenfaden calculated that, between the late 1920s and 1932, almost 20 per cent of all Secretariat salaries went to officials working within it.[2] By the time the Board of Liquidation came into existence in 1946, public relations had been a fundamental tenet of the League for over twenty-five years, and the organization's leadership was accustomed to considering wider opinion and the institution's reputation when making decisions. And, as a consequence of the international community's desire to distance the UN from its predecessor, senior figures within the League had been focused on the need to rehabilitate the organization's legacy for some time. Despite governmental pressure to withdraw from the public sphere quietly, the League's leadership held a full ceremonial Assembly in April 1946 to officially begin the liquidation process, not only because it believed the correct procedures should be followed but also because it was an opportunity to correct the negative trend in public opinion. Former Information Section official and constant League devotee Arthur Sweetser wrote to Hambro following a meeting in February 1946 that he believed the organization was being blamed for the shortcomings of governments:

> It is alarming what a perversion of history is being perpetrated today, partly consciously by those who want to find a scapegoat for their own failures and partly unconsciously by those who did not live the past and do not know any better. In any event, the League is all too often being held responsible for the shortcomings of governments and the really guilty parties are being allowed to go scot-free.[3]

This concern and preoccupation with how people would reflect upon both the Board of Liquidation and the League as a whole dictated much of the former's decision-making during the dissolution period. In some cases, this influence was indirect – to be explored in the later sections of this chapter – but at other times it was unequivocal. This section looks at how the Board tried not only to control the story of liquidation but how it also claimed ownership of the League's long-term legacy in the process.

Throughout the closure process the Board attempted to control the narrative surrounding the League's dissolution through the contents and backdated publication dates of its four Interim Reports to members, but its Final Report to members was the pinnacle of the group's efforts.[4] Although these documents were all relatively similar in structure – covering the progress of transfers, financial questions and liquidation of non-transferable services – the Board was determined that this, the League's last word, would take on a mantle greater than the sum of its parts. Hambro made the importance of this document clear to his colleagues in the group's twenty-eighth meeting: 'The CHAIRMAN felt that the Final Report should be a dignified document. It would, after all, be the last word heard from the League – a kind of epilogue.'[5] While the Interim Reports were pulled together by the Secretariat and a small drafting committee led by Cecil Kisch, the Final Report had significantly more input from the rest of the

Board, and the group spent considerable portions of its time during 1947 on the text. As early as February, the Board's deliberations on outstanding member contributions were predicated on how the group would be able to present their decision-making to members and how the use of certain wording would justify the choice to vigorously pursue debts in some cases, and forgive them in others.[6] These discussions became increasingly prevalent in meetings as 1947 progressed, and by the final sessions in June and July, the composition and editing of the report became the primary subject of the Board's meetings.[7]

In private the Board had committed itself to a 31 July publication date for the Final Report, and it hinted as much to members in the opening remarks of the fourth Interim Report published at the start of May.[8] In order to meet the self-imposed schedule, Board members were expected to continue working on the subject between the June and July sessions, reviewing drafts and sending comments to the Secretariat.[9] Introducing this deadline meant the group was trying to compile a full and coherent report of the dissolution while simultaneously still trying to make that dissolution a reality, so it was not surprising that the Report's finer detail was still the primary topic of conversation at the Board's last meeting – its forty-second – in late July.[10]

The Board was deliberately meticulous over the report and its contents because it had a clear sense of what it wanted to achieve with its publication. This was the last testament for the organization, but the Board also saw it as a mark sheet for its own performance as the arbiters of the League's dissolution. As a consequence the report was not a complete or wholly accurate depiction of the previous fifteen months, but instead a carefully selected highlight reel of the Board's accomplishments which downplayed problems, emphasized achievements and obfuscated several dates of transfer. The group did not want to be blamed for problems it felt were beyond its remit – for example, noting that it held no responsibility for the problems arising from the dissolution of the International Institute of Intellectual Cooperation – and the supposed dates of transfer for the Staff and Judges' Pensions Funds were listed in the report as having taken place earlier than they actually had.[11] The document outlined the measures taken to manage the long-running income tax dispute in the United States and the decision to continue pursuing a lawsuit, but neglected to mention that the said decision had been made in spite of the low chances of success and the negative attitude of many Board members towards it.[12] No explanation was offered for the delay in dissolving the organization, and the ill-tempered nature of the negotiations between the Board and the ILO was left out of both the Final Report and the discussions at the ILO Governing Body session in June and July, perhaps an indication of both sides' discomfiture at the whole endeavour and an effort to keep up appearances.[13] The Board wanted the narrative put forward in its Final Report to be accepted as both the official and only version of the organization's closure, and in this regard its efforts were a success. The later response from members was almost non-existent, suggesting acquiescence, and the long-term impact has been a similar willingness from scholars to accept this quiet and unremarkable version of events.[14]

The Board was highly conscious of the contemporaneous opinions of members and the wider international community, but the group was serious about its self-appointed role as protector of the organization's memory and was therefore also concerned with the League's longer-term reputation and how it might be viewed in the future, using the time left before liquidation to plan accordingly. This cognizance was evident in the Board's planning for the organization's Archives which, it believed, occupied an important place in not only shedding light on the League experience from within the institution but also rehabilitating its image and legacy in the decades to come.

The Archives were officially moved to UN control in 1946 but plans for the future practical management and use of the League's files were left for later discussion. Although the UN now effectively owned the Archives and employed the League's former Registry officials, the files remained on-site in Geneva, documents created by the Secretariat continued to be deposited as before and the outstanding issues were put aside due to the perceived lack of urgency in their address.[15] What needed to be agreed between the two organizations before the League liquidated, however, included questions such as how the UN would manage these files in the future, where they would be kept and what kind of rules would the new organization's officials be bound by when using them.

Lester and the Board had two central goals regarding the Archives' future usage. Firstly, they wanted the files to be physically safe, a concern that tied in with their wider anxieties around the UN and its respect for the League's property. This had materialized elsewhere as fears that the new organization would neglect or abandon the Palais des Nations, and although that fear was later allayed, the Board was worried that the collections would be broken up or moved to New York.[16] They were also anxious about the security of the Archives, and specifically the confidentiality of some Board documents, which were not easy to delineate from less sensitive papers.[17] The Board's documentation was, for the most part, deposited in existing Registry files alongside other items not related to the liquidation; few Board-exclusive files or jackets were created for its documents. For example, proceedings of the Board's sub-committee on missing member contributions – which included details of sensitive negotiations with governments – could be found in a box with a range of other Financial Administration files and documents from the previous ten to fifteen years, and this filing system remains in place today.[18] While the League's recent past and actions remained fresh in the mind of governments, the Board did not want its confidential discussions and decision-making to cause controversy or reflect poorly on the group's performance.[19]

Ultimately its fears in both these instances – in terms of the future safekeeping of the files and the careful management of any confidentiality issues – were unfounded, and the UN proved more than amenable to League requests. This was partly a result of the UN's willingness to accommodate the League leadership on said requests, its agreement that the Archives represented a valuable resource and also the work of the UN Chief of the Communications and Records Service, Bertil Renborg, a former head of the League's Drug Control Service who left the Secretariat less than a year earlier, as well as Włodzimierz Moderow.[20] In early November 1946, the latter wrote to Adriaan Pelt in New York to raise concerns about the files, noting that they were 'of considerable historical interest and we should take every precaution to preserve them as a whole'.[21] During in-person negotiations in February 1947, the UN agreed to keep the Archives at the Palais and created strict guidelines for the request and usage of League files from officials in both Geneva and New York. The outcome was as positive as could have been hoped for from the Board's perspective.[22]

The Board's concerns about safety and security emanated from its desire to preserve the League's Archives for the future. Lester and the group repeatedly stressed their wish – in both Board meetings and correspondence with the UN during 1946 and 1947 – that the organization be studied for decades to come as a means of restoring its reputation, as exemplified in a letter from Sweetser to Hambro: 'What seems to me more important by far is that, if history is allowed to be misread in this way, we will have lost the principal lesson of the past quarter century and run the risk of making the same mistake all over again.'[23] In a February 1947 letter to Moderow thanking him for his work guaranteeing the future of the Archives, Lester wrote that he hoped the organization's files be made available so 'serious students of international affairs during the period would be enabled … to make use of them'.[24] In a memorandum covering disposal of the Board's papers, drafted by Chester Purves and Lester in June, the men maintained that while there was sensitive information contained within these files, removing any documents or sections of minutes 'which may be considered unsuitable for preservation' would be time-consuming and difficult, and that doing so 'would certainly destroy their value as historical records'.[25] The Board agreed with them, prioritizing long-term legacy over the short-term risk of controversy, and ensuring that both the League and its dissolution could be studied many decades later.[26] The group's choice to preserve the Archives in as open and accessible a fashion as possible was a prescient one; in 2009 the collection was added to UNESCO's Memory of the World Register in light of its value to global heritage.[27]

The Board did not pass up even the smallest opportunity to make its mark on the League's legacy. At the end of 1946 Frank Walters, a former assistant secretary general and twenty-year Secretariat veteran, was granted access to the League Archives long before they were made public to facilitate his research for a comprehensive history of the organization.[28] Although Walters left the Secretariat in 1940 and his book was neither funded nor officially endorsed by the League, he was considered enough of an ally to the organization that his research would not pose a threat to its legacy. If anything, senior figures both within the League and supporters outside it were happy that an old friend was working on the matter before anyone else, knowing that he would likely provide a comprehensive but kind evaluation. Arthur Sweetser, unswervingly faithful to the League cause, wrote to Lester in early August 1947, expressing his happiness with Walters's new role and noted that he would have a 'big contribution' to make in his book, which he believed would 'set the record right' on the organization.[29]

With Walters's independent, but welcome, book research underway, Cecil Kisch suggested to Lester at the end of April 1947 that perhaps the League might use some of its remaining money to finance an official history of the Nansen office. Despite similar background musings from Hambro in the past, the timing of the suggestion was surprising for its tardiness in the dismantling process and was undoubtedly predicated on the idea that it would be another opportunity for the League to present its version of events. Both Fridtjof Nansen and the Nansen International Office for Refugees were extraordinarily popular in the 1930s – the latter winning the Nobel Peace Prize in 1938 – and funding an official history of its work was likely seen as a safe way of capitalizing on its popularity. Lester, however, was less than enthused in his responses to both Kisch and the Board chairman, explaining that there was no room in the budget for such an endeavour, that it would be hard to justify – its public popularity aside – why they had chosen the Nansen work above other areas and, with only a few months of liquidation work left, there would be no one left in the Secretariat to supervise its completion. In short, the idea was a last-minute pipe dream from Board members that was otherwise an entirely impractical notion and, thankfully for Lester, the discussions went no further.[30]

Less impractical, but also completed at the last minute, were the League's preparations for its permanent exhibit at the Palais des Nations. An exhibition hall was part of the original plans for the Palais in the early 1930s and designed to house pieces from the League collections, but the organization's leadership at the time never seemed entirely sure what they were trying to create, with different names used in both correspondence and official documents to describe it: museum, permanent historical collection, exhibit, portrait gallery. Conceived as a space within the wider Library building, early sketches in the League Archives show a long, gallery-like room with copious amounts of southerly natural light. Naturally the plans were set aside up to, and during, the Second World War, as uncertainty about the future and a limited workforce made it both pointless and almost impossible to achieve anything tangible. As soon as the war was over however and the League's impending fate was decided, the idea came to prominence once again.[31]

In the early stages of its existence, the Board of Liquidation seemed to have as few concrete ideas about the exhibit as its pre-war forebears. Discussed at the first set of meetings in late April and early May, the collection was referred to only as 'artistic and photographic material illustrating the history of the League', but the group agreed that it should take the time to design a permanent display of these items and put them in place before the organization went out of existence.[32] The planning process began in a common-sense fashion, creating a sub-committee made up of senior Secretariat figures Willem van Asch van Wijck and Tevfik Erim (both members of Section in Department I), as well as Arthur Breycha-Vauthier (assistant librarian), who would deliberate and then report back to the Board with a list of figures they might want to feature in the exhibit, how prominent they should be and any other proposals for the space.[33] The three men produced a lengthy list made up of diplomats and statesmen they believed should be highlighted – only Stencek took the time to note that no women featured in the sub-committee's suggestions – and the Board quickly seized the opportunity to become involved, using its contacts to request items from foreign dignitaries and governments, weighing in on the respective portraiture sizes for different statesmen and even approving cabinet purchases.[34]

As senior figures in the services of governments, the members of the Board were better placed than most other League officials to receive successful responses when requesting photos and paintings and were able to exert pressure on foreign administrations in a way the Secretariat was not. Daniel Secrétan, board member and Minister Plenipotentiary on the Swiss Federal Council, pressed his Government for a bronze bust of Giuseppe Motta, and Arthur Sweetser – not a Board member but once again supporting the League in his free time – was able to procure a photograph of John D. Rockefeller Jr. directly from the latter's son.[35] The Board's responsibilities were almost exclusively focused on closing things down, but the exhibit was about building something new, and as Biltoft has noted in their work on the concept of 'goodwill value', the group was especially encouraged about a project designed to cement the organization's legacy for many years to come.[36]

As 1947 began the Board continued to use its influence to obtain portraits of figures from the sub-committee's list, but as more time passed the scope for the exhibit started to creep beyond the original vision of a portrait gallery. Despite the early progress in agreeing to a list of names and their respective prominence, there was not a great deal of coordination of either the Board or Secretariat activity. Theoretically Secrétan was overseeing the project from the Board's perspective, but with members scattered across North America and Europe in the latter half of 1946, there was little chance to review progress of the increasingly disparate activity. From a Secretariat point of view, van Asch van Wijck, Stencek and Lester were all involved, but no single individual had control of the project or was responsible for coordinating the work.

The most involved figure was an international official, but by 1947 he no longer worked for the League of Nations. Arthur Breycha-Vauthier joined the organization's Secretariat in 1928 as an assistant librarian and had, therefore, been closely involved with the earliest plans for the exhibition space. He sat on the Secretariat sub-committee in late spring 1946 and suggested a much wider remit for what he called 'the Museum', noting that it ought to not only show records of the League's activities but also demonstrate how the organization was a unique venture in international relations. In a letter to Stencek in May 1946 he proposed a number of exhibits, including overviews of the practical working of an international conference, the League's work on drug control – including some drug paraphernalia – and caricatures of the organization.[37] His general vigour and enthusiasm for his work had been praised by Lester in the past, but his primary involvement in planning for the exhibit diminished when he was transferred to the UN alongside the rest of the Library staff in the early autumn of 1946.[38] Although he was forced to take a back seat while he settled into his new position, he remained involved in the project – albeit now from the perspective of a UN official – coordinating the receipt and removals of collection items, and even chasing portraits for inclusion.[39] The Board of Liquidation and the

Secretariat took advantage of the librarian's enthusiasm for an endeavour that he had helped design, but Breycha-Vauthier did not seem to mind too much. If anything, he used the situation to his benefit, continuing to make suggestions for the exhibit during 1947 and frequently volunteered himself as a resource for his former employers. He suggested the addition of some bronze signage welcoming visitors to the exhibit and a guidebook-type pamphlet providing further details on the displays; both ideas were taken on by the Board at the League's expense.[40] Breycha-Vauthier was free labour for the League's project, but he used the Board's preoccupation with the organization's legacy to support an endeavour he was not only personally invested in but also one he would soon take over management of in his role at the UN.

Breycha-Vauthier and the Board were both able to keep adding to the design of the permanent exhibit as a result of the continuing delays to liquidation. More time meant the collection was able to expand beyond what it might have been limited to, had the League dissolved as intended in March 1947. 'Six rather nice modern tapestries made by some French women' for the League's Pavilion at the New York World's Fair in 1939–40 – on the themes of Clan, Medieval State, Village, Family, Nation and Federation – which were moved to Haverford College during the war for safekeeping were shipped back to Geneva by Percy Watterson so they too could be included.[41] The extra time also allowed the Secretariat to find alternatives for figures for whom official portraits were proving difficult to source. A portrait of Aristide Briand was finally acquired after months of chasing the French Government – even if it was one of the statesman on his deathbed – and more ideas for new exhibits kept coming.[42] Another item added to the displays was a Woodrow Wilson Foundation medal awarded in 1930, although it is worth noting that the medal that eventually went on display was a replica, as the original was lost somewhere in the Palais in the intervening years, and the Secretariat had a copy made rather than admit the error and ask for a replacement.[43] The collection also expanded to incorporate exhibits about the 'lesser lights' of the League – an idea originally proposed by the sub-committee in 1946 – meaning there was an increased focus on the work of committees and the organization's technical achievements. Just a few of the suggestions made by the Board included features on the Disarmament Conference, the Leticia and Chaco Commissions, and extraordinary figures like Countess Apponyi, the only female delegate to preside over an Assembly Committee in the League's history.[44]

The overall effect of this extra time and input from figures such as Breycha-Vauthier was a historical collection that became increasingly ostentatious and eye-catching throughout the year. It was no longer just a means of displaying a few portraits and memorabilia from the League's lifetime, but instead – at least for the organization's leadership – came to represent something greater. At a Board meeting in early July 1947, Cecil Kisch expressed his anxiety that the collection might become 'a mausoleum' and instead encouraged his colleagues to think of the exhibition as a living, breathing space within the (now UN) Library.[45] And so the plans for the collection quickly spread to include films on the activities of the League and the use of audio recordings of famous speeches produced by the Information Section in the 1930s, as well as Breycha-Vauthier's bronze signage and guidebook.[46] In line with the Board's thinking about the future study of the League's Archives, Kisch also suggested the inclusion of a reading room space within the exhibit, hoping to encourage visitors to sit and engage with organizational material.[47]

This was the Board's chance to tell the League's story from its own perspective, uncorrupted by the subjective voices of outsiders. The irony was sadly lost on the group that while this was indeed an opportunity for the Board to put forward its account of the institution's history, it had a vested interest in portraying the League as positively as possible, and it also represented just one pillar of the organization. An early suggestion from Stencek in May 1946 to consult Secretariat members on the exhibit and what could be included was never followed up on.[48] The Secretariat, as a central pillar of the League and the facilitator of the strategic achievements heralded by the Board, was conspicuous by its absence from the collection. Beyond the secretaries general, officials had no presence in the exhibits, nor did they have a voice in identifying what should become part of the League's legacy. The Board of Liquidation was appointed as the Assembly's proxy in closure proceedings, and this meant it claimed the monopoly on both the dissolution process and on the League's memory.

The culmination of the increasingly ambitious plans was a ceremony on 17 July 1947 to mark the handover of the collection from the League to the UN. Prominent League figures including Lester were present, as well as representatives from the Norwegian and Swedish Governments who were there to officially present portraits of Fridtjof Nansen, Carl Hambro and Hjalmar Branting.[49] The idea was first suggested in May 1947 and, while it was a low-key affair with a handful of brief speeches from guests, local press were invited for what would actually be a more public display of the passing of the torch than anything that had come before it.[50] In his speech accepting the 'precious gift' of the permanent exhibit on behalf of the UN, Moderow assured the attendees that the new world organization would strive to maintain the collection as the

League would have done and paid tribute to his institution's predecessor: 'By their work and their deeds these men had left deep marks in the history of peace and reconciliation, and would be considered by future generations as craftsmen in international cooperation.'[51] Following the pomp and circumstance of the twenty-first Assembly for the League, and the first General Assembly of the UN later in the same year, the backstage wrangling and transfer between the two organizations was kept firmly behind closed doors, even including the handover of the Palais in the summer of 1946. The ceremony on 17 July, simple but proud, was as much an indicator of the League's 'quiet death' as anything else that took place during the dissolution period.

The ILO and keeping up appearances

While the Board of Liquidation's pride in the League's history helped build a long-term legacy for the organization, that same pride led to some intransigent decision-making in the first half of 1947, especially in regard to the ILO. The ILO was created in 1919 alongside the League and was designed to contribute to a peaceful world through a tripartite system – made up of labour representatives alongside those from employers and governments – and focused on social justice.[52] It was not, however, an entirely independent organization, relying on the League Assembly to approve its budget on an annual basis, and on the League Secretariat to gather the contributions from members that made up that same budget, creating what David Morse, director general of the ILO from 1948 to 1970, later called a natural conflict between the two organizations.[53] Emmet O'Connor, in his preface to Edward Phelan's memoirs, even went as far as to suggest that the ILO had enemies within the League's membership who resented the former's creation as a special concession to labour concerns.[54] This tie to the League of Nations meant the ILO, despite having the freedom to pursue policy set by its own membership – which included states not part of the League – was never truly in control of its own fate while that link remained in place. The two organizations were entwined from birth – a big brother and a little brother – and their twenty-five-year history played a not insignificant part in the closure of the League, especially the delays in its realization. This section examines the tricky nature of the relationship and disagreements between the League and the ILO in 1947, and how the Board of Liquidation's seemingly dogged focus on propriety and financial questions was, in reality, a side effect of decision-making based on apprehension and fear of condemnation.

The ILO moved almost all its operations from Geneva to Montréal during the Second World War and, unlike the League, was able to assemble full organizational meetings during this period. The most important of these was the International Labour Conference held at Philadelphia in 1944, the hosting of which was not only an achievement in itself during wartime but the ensuing Philadelphia Declaration was a crucial development in gathering international support for the organization's future. The Declaration restated the ILO's mission for a post-war world and grounded the organization in an affirmed commitment to the equality of human beings and their right to pursue their well-being and all economic opportunities. Its contents did not necessarily change the outlook or aims of the institution, but instead, as outlined by David A. Morse, took the ILO's original mandate and reformed it 'in more comprehensive and positive terms'.[55]

The ILO was desperate to avoid the League's doomed fate, but its survival was by no means a foregone conclusion, even in the face of its success in Philadelphia. Despite assurances that it would continue post-war, the ILO was not invited to take part in the negotiations at Dumbarton Oaks and suffered the same fate as the League's representatives at the San Francisco Conference in 1945, with accommodation issues, no official accreditation for the delegation and Edward Phelan, the Irish director general, forced to leave by the Soviet delegates due to his citizenship of a neutral state – something Lester also struggled with but ultimately managed to avoid.[56] Nevertheless Phelan was determined to guarantee the organization's survival, publicly trying to distance it from the League, and, although full independence was not possible, the ILO succeeded where its big brother failed and endured into the post-war world as the first UN agency.[57]

By the start of 1947, the two organizations were in very different positions than just one year earlier. The ILO had made official its relationship to the UN and was ready to begin a new chapter in its history, while the League was getting to grips with its dissolution to-do list. In the eyes of the Board of Liquidation, the organization's position had not changed to that degree; it was no longer the leader in international governance that it once was – that honour now fell to the UN – but the League name still, as far as the Board was concerned, commanded respect and the group felt the need, as it did with the organization's Archives and the Museum, to protect its reputation as a bastion of decorum and procedure. The ILO, meanwhile, assured of its place in the new international system, embraced the self-assurance that inevitably collided with the League leadership's long-standing pride to cause all manner of problems for the liquidation.

Although the relationship between the ILO and League leaderships turned somewhat fraught in 1947, the two organizations were not always at loggerheads. The two Secretariats worked alongside each other in Geneva for two decades at a time when their very existence was an experiment for international organizations, and the relationship between Phelan and Lester was an example of the friendships that could grow between international civil servants. Their connection began when Lester became Ireland's representative to the League in 1929, and the two men and their wives played bridge on a weekly basis when they were in Geneva together.[58] The greatest obstacles to the smooth running of the ILO–League relationship in 1946 and 1947 were related to financial questions, but when money was not involved, the long-standing relationship between the two Secretariats could usually bring about a reasoned conclusion to any issues.

For example, the persistent problem relating to the removal of officials' furniture and belongings from the Palais was eventually resolved with a little help from the ILO. The League Secretariat had previously found it difficult to compel officials, both former and current, to remove their belongings, and the deadline for doing so was put further and further back, effectively extending dissolution. With no resolution in sight by the start of 1947 it was becoming an increasing problem, so the Board approved a plan whereby all officials with outstanding belongings at the Palais were given an option: remove items and submit claims by 31 October 1947, or provide a verified estimate by June and have 75 per cent of the total granted immediately. The latter option was overwhelmingly popular, especially with those officials still working for the Secretariat, as it guaranteed reimbursement for the majority of any removal costs without a worrisome deadline to contend with. Lester knew, however, especially in those cases where officials chose the former route – albeit at a risk if they did not do so before the deadline – that this committed the organization to administrative work up to the end of October, months after he expected the Secretariat to leave the Palais. Instead he turned to the ILO at the start of the year, asking Phelan if his Secretariat would be amenable to taking on this work after dissolution, dependent on the League providing funds to cover the expected costs of the removals and throwing in a small clerical fee.[59] The ILO accepted, and a niggling problem that had bothered the League's administration for almost a year was resolved with relative ease by demonstrating a willingness to work together.

Not all financial questions were necessarily problematic either, as there were minimal issues regarding the transfer of what remained of the League's Working Capital Fund. Part of the Final Assembly's resolution to dissolve the League included stipulations for the Fund to be transferred to the ILO as soon as possible, meaning the transfer of over 2.5m Swiss francs was quickly agreed and carried out in under two weeks in April 1947.[60] The specific nature of the instruction from a higher authority, in this case the League Assembly, was undoubtedly helpful as it reduced the likelihood of the leaderships becoming bogged down in drawn-out negotiations, but where guidance was less forthcoming, arguments about money tested the relationship between the two organizations. Major disagreements arose from four issues in the first half of 1947 and the detailed nature of these disputes not only reveals why the League's liquidation took longer than expected but also how the most ardent champions of objective decision-making and procedure could become blinded by pride and worries about their reputation.

The first of the disagreements between the two organizations related to the Staff Pensions Fund for officials of both the League and the ILO, which was established by the eleventh Assembly in 1930, and was overseen by an Administrative Board made up of representatives appointed by both organizations' leadership, as well as those nominated by members of the Fund.[61] The Resolution to Dissolve the League of Nations, agreed at the twenty-first Assembly in April 1946, called for the administration of the Fund to be transferred to the ILO, which was later agreed by that organization – on the condition that another actuarial review confirm the Fund's fiscal health – at the International Labour Conference in Montréal in September and October of the same year. All seemed well as far as the League's leadership was aware; the Pensions Fund Administrative Board raised no concerns when it met in December 1946, a paper to the Board of Liquidation at the end of January 1947 outlined the previous steps taken by the League to bolster the Fund, and the Actuary's report showed the Fund held a surplus of over 5m Swiss francs at the end of 1946.[62] Satisfied that all the necessary conditions had been met, Lester telegrammed Phelan to begin the transfer on 28 January, but the transfer had already started to falter without the League secretary general's knowledge.[63]

The League leadership made a mistake in assuming the ILO did not have its own interests to consider. Phelan replied, over a week after Lester's message, with a telegram of his own which stunned both the Board of Liquidation and the Secretariat. The ILO disagreed with the League's use of an actuarial yield rate of 4.5 per cent; instead it preferred a more realistic 2.5 per cent rate in line with that used by the UN.[64] At this lower rate, the Pensions Fund's surplus would be wiped out and the ILO wanted the League to cover the deficit before transfer, which translated into an additional 2.5m Swiss francs from the organization's coffers.[65] If this proposal was rejected, the ILO leadership argued that its Governing Body would never agree to transfer the Fund. All the arguments that followed stemmed from an impasse arising from the Final Assembly's decree that the League was responsible for handing the Fund over to the ILO in good financial order: it was never made clear which party was responsible for deciding what 'good financial order' actually meant.[66]

Lester and other Board members were initially both surprised and disappointed by the ILO's entrenched position; at the start of February, the leadership was still working towards the end of April as a final closing date for the League and the new state of affairs posed a risk to the schedule.[67] Nevertheless, the group trusted that the upcoming Board of Liquidation session – the first time the group had all met in-person since July 1946 – would give it the opportunity to produce a counter offer, negotiate a final settlement with Phelan and his colleagues and still meet the expected deadline. Their first counter proposal suggested taking the necessary 2.5m Swiss francs from government contributions collected during 1947 – whether they were for that year or for years previous – thereby bolstering the Fund and providing 'a windfall' for the ILO. This was despite the Board's own concerns that doing so, that is, propping up the Fund with monies from League members, would unfairly benefit the members of the ILO who did not fall into that category, and the group was intrinsically wary of doing anything that might be contrary to its commitment to regulations or unpalatable to its membership.[68] Yet in spite of the Board's confidence that its counter offer would be both agreeable and readily accepted by the ILO, it falsely assumed that the latter organization held the weaker negotiating position, and that it was not busy with its own work and efforts to settle its relationship with the UN.

The relationship between the League and the ILO was not, historically at least, one of equals, and the former's leadership struggled to realize or accept that this was no longer the case, finding it difficult to comprehend that the latter was no longer bound to acquiesce to either the Board of Liquidation's assumptions or timetable. The ILO executive group responsible for high-level decision-making and offering recommendations to the International Labour Conference was its Governing Body. Made up of a rotating group of representatives from members, it met three times a year and was scheduled to hold the first of its 1947 sessions in March, at which point the Board of Liquidation expected its counter offer to be put to the group for discussion and approval.[69] Lester and his officials waited for a response each day the Body was in session and, not hearing anything to the contrary, assumed – once again – that all was proceeding well. It was only after the session closed that Lester discovered Guildhaume Myrddin-Evans, the chair of the Governing Body, was opposed to the Board's counter offer from the start and had not put the issue on the meeting agenda. The secretary general was shocked and frustrated, Myrddin-Evans's decision effectively extending the League's liquidation to at least June, when the Governing Body was next scheduled to meet.[70] However, progress in the intervening months was also slow while negotiations between the two leaderships were forced to take place via correspondence, neither body being present in Geneva at the same time as the other.[71] The Board of Liquidation expressed a willingness in its April meetings to come to some kind of compromise with the ILO, but the need to hold these negotiations at an executive level – beyond the remit of Lester and Phelan, both of whom were consistently present in Geneva – meant in-person discussions with ILO representatives could not start until both bodies were in the same place at the same time: June 1947.[72]

So a date for the negotiations was set, but administration of the Staff Pensions Fund was not the only outstanding problem; there were three other issues creating friction between the Board of Liquidation and the ILO Governing Body. The first concerned another Pension Fund, this one established for the Judges of the Permanent Court of International Justice. The Court was superseded by the new International Court of Justice in 1946, but the administration of the Pension Fund was not transferred alongside the other assets, and instead the ILO had provisionally agreed to take on its management. While the Fund itself was nowhere near the size of the Staff Fund, the yield rate percentage was once again a point of contention, and there were outstanding questions for the Board regarding the number of judges eligible to receive a pension and how much additional funding was required to make it fiscally unassailable.[73] The Board, as with the Staff Pensions issues, was reluctant to swallow its pride and decided to take a course of action that would protect the organization – and its members – financially while also, hopefully, reducing the likelihood of ILO objections. Sensing the matter might be best resolved by consulting an outside authority, the League sought the opinion of a Dutch Insurance Company, which provided a quote based on a rate of 2.5 per cent.[74] Feeling safe that the transfer of this Fund was the most straightforward of the outstanding issues, Lester put the Company's proposal to Phelan and Myrddin-Evans in early May, but was disheartened to find that the ILO, while not necessarily opposed to the idea, was not willing to agree just yet either.[75]

The second outstanding issue with the ILO related to the distribution of certain members' shares of the Working Capital Fund, which had been removed from the Fund in 1946 and placed into a suspense account to safeguard against non-payment of contributions before liquidation. These were known as contributions in suspense and totalled 1.4m gold francs, but the Board had not yet decided how, or if, this money would be distributed. The ILO, first raising the question in April 1947, argued that the funds should be split between the two organizations as they had been during a similar situation when Chile withdrew from the League in 1940.[76] Lester, however, still bruised by Myrddin-Evans's unwillingness to compromise in other areas, admitted to Hambro that, while the Board was likely to agree to Phelan's request, he was disinclined to concede any ground to the ILO while the rest of the negotiations remained so turbulent.[77]

The third outstanding issue centred on the Board of Liquidation's decision to not distribute to the ILO any contributions' arrears older than two years, and instead retain these funds for the League alone which was, according to Lester, 'the really sore point' for Myrddin-Evans and the ILO, and they harboured 'a violent resentment' as a result.[78] The League's Supervisory Commission had waived Article 33(b) of the Financial Regulations between the two organizations during the war and distributed contributions in arrears to the ILO, but the Board reasserted its former authority by reinstating the Article in 1947 without consulting or informing the other organization, letting Phelan and his colleagues believe they would receive the funds as before. In a letter to Lester at the start of June, the ILO's director general attempted to articulate his anger in as polite a fashion as possible, noting that 'it would appear appropriate that the Board should follow the procedure under which those Regulations were always applied in the past', but behind the scenes the ILO was furious that the Board of Liquidation had unilaterally made the decision without consulting them.[79] Receiving no concessions on the matter from the League, the ILO leadership used its new position of authority and refused to resolve any of the four aforementioned disputes in isolation – even where a resolution seemed relatively straightforward as with the Judges' Pensions Fund – instead insisting on negotiating all four issues in one package deal.[80]

All the animosity, ill-feeling and wounded pride culminated in face-to-face negotiations when Myrddin-Evans, Hans Oersted and Joseph Hallsworth – representing the Governing Body – visited the Board of Liquidation during its thirtieth meeting on 13 June 1947. The goodwill that Phelan believed was necessary for the financial relationship between the two organizations to work was nowhere to be found, and the meeting was unusually bad-tempered.[81] The session was dominated by lengthy diatribes from Hambro on the League side, and Myrddin-Evans for the ILO, with both men increasingly frustrated with the other's perceived intransigence. Myrddin-Evans had to apologize at one point in the meeting for his 'facetious remarks', while Hambro, a consummate diplomat with years of experience, became so tired of proceedings that he suggested they abandon negotiations for the day.[82] Yet as ill-tempered and prideful as it was, the meeting was not a waste of time. With the benefit of meeting face-to-face – thus recognizing the ILO's unwillingness to compromise its stance – and aware of the need to expedite the League's dissolution, the Board of Liquidation finally accepted that it had little choice but to accede to the ILO position. The final deal ultimately accepted the Governing Body's suggestions on all the issues bar the original demand for a bolstered Staff Pensions Fund to the tune of 2.5 per cent yield rate – the Board having managed to negotiate a 2.75 per cent rate instead and a consequent injection of just over 2m Swiss francs before the Fund was transferred.[83]

Over four months of posturing and arguing on the side of the League, and the result was almost exactly the same as it would have been had the Board accepted the ILO position at the start of February. Superficially these clashes looked like a spat over money, each side wanting a greater slice of the proverbial pie, and the League's actions in other areas seemingly provide further evidence for this argument. By way of illustration, the pursuit of outstanding contributions from members was a major part of the Board's focus throughout the dismantling process, and rarely did a Board meeting pass without contributions featuring on the agenda. Hambro even explained to the group in February 1947 that he did not want governments to know that the League had been so successful in retrieving contributions long-since-forgotten by members both past and present; he did not want states with outstanding debts to have an excuse not to pay.[84] Taking this approach, threatening members with both non-participation in the distribution of the League's assets and receiving a black mark in the new UN copybook, meant the Board was able to recoup over 28m Swiss francs through 1946 and 1947, from an original outstanding total of almost 44m.[85] This left only six countries – Albania, Bulgaria, Ethiopia, Liberia, Paraguay and Spain – with their combined 6.2m Swiss francs debt to both the League and the ILO unpaid at the end of the organization's liquidation.[86]

The Board was equally ardent with its recoup of other debts, including those owed by former sales agents for League publications. The outstanding figure in April 1946 stood at almost 100,000 Swiss francs, but the Secretariat's relentless pursuit saw this reduced to 38,000 by the end of June 1947 – a reduction of over 60 per cent.[87] No debt was too insignificant to chase, including a small debt owed by a Tokyo sales agent named San-Yo-Sha. The decision to do so involved Percy Watterson – working full-time for the FAO since November 1946 and supposedly only helping the League to close its US financial accounts – pursuing the case with the US Custodian of Alien Property in his spare evenings and weekends, all for an amount of only 3,000 Swiss francs.[88]

This dogged pursuit of even the smallest amounts of money, especially when compared with the millions of contributions owed by governments, shows that it was not always the money that made a difference to the Board of Liquidation: it was a matter of principle. The recoup of funds was naturally of concern, representing as it did the interests of members, but the concept of legality and procedure was important to a group that had little else to motivate it in its final months other than a job well done. Neither the Board nor Secretariat officials were under the impression that their work over the institution's final months would be met with immediate renown or fanfare; the best reward they could hope to receive was acknowledgement from members that it had liquidated the organization as well as possible and, for the Board, that meant executing its responsibilities in a meticulous manner and upholding the standards to which the League had held itself for the past twenty-five years.

This self-regard and commitment to a set of standards established at the end of the previous world war was the Board's central cause of anguish when dealing with the ILO approach to negotiations. The Board believed the ILO was trying to cheat its way to a better deal, and this offended its sense of fair play. Much of its grievance stemmed from a separate ILO decision to withhold 1945 and 1946 budget surpluses from the League, a stance the Board believed was against the rules and, coupled with the ILO outrage regarding 1947 contributions in suspense, highly hypocritical.[89] All of this was further exacerbated by the unofficial liquidation deadline the Board had set itself of March or April 1947; it knew the ILO leadership was aware of the timings and genuinely believed they were wilfully delaying proceedings in order to obtain a better deal. The Board assumed, and events would prove, that the longer the negotiations continued, the more likely they would be forced to accept the ILO position. The group felt it was being taken advantage of, and perhaps this rankled the League's leadership more than anything else, leaving it blind to the negative effects of its unwillingness to cede ground from the start.

The long-held power dynamics of big brother and little brother had shifted. The League was a defunct international organization, largely forgotten even by its membership, while the ILO was now an official UN agency and had been given a new lease of life and energy as a result. After decades of subservience to the League's agenda, it now had the ability to control its own fate – relatively speaking – and provide its membership with the best possible return on investment. This meant pushing the League to bolster the Staff Pensions Fund as much as possible before taking on its administration, negotiating all the contentious issues concurrently and even trying – albeit unsuccessfully – to push for a larger slice of the League's Renovation Fund to pay for upkeep of the ILO property lake frontage.[90]

The Board did not like it, but with time it became clear they had little option but to acquiesce to the ILO position. Kisch warned Lester in the spring that the dynamics between the League and the ILO had changed, and they ought to avoid a row with the latter, especially in light of the long-standing relationship between the two organizations. Referring to Guildhaume Myrddin-Evans, Kisch said: 'I think you were right not to be too violent with him. We don't want to end up with a row with the ILO which we have done so much to help.'[91] The Board's commitment to rules and regulations meant it was never happy with the final arrangement – although that blow was softened by the better-than-expected results in chasing members' outstanding debts – and feared that its concessions to the ILO would be discovered by members.[92] In an effort to avoid events reflecting poorly upon the group, no mention of the controversy and bitter recriminations made it into the Board's Final Report to members, references to the release of contributions in arrears were removed and for the benefit of members, the transfer of the Judges' Pensions Fund and the Staff Pensions Fund was presented as having taken place on 1 April and 31 May respectively, several weeks earlier than in reality.[93]

The Board of Liquidation believed that acquiring a large financial windfall for members was one of the markers of a successful liquidation, and the group's desire to protect the legacy of both the League and of its own performance led it to make decisions that ultimately proved counter-intuitive to the speedy deliverance of closure. In its meetings and in relation to the arguments with the ILO, the Board referred to its negotiating position as being 'morally right', but as the outcome of the wrangling with the Governing Body showed, taking the moral high ground did not achieve very much. It did not matter if one of the organizations was more 'right' than the other. The idea that the disputes would be resolved in the manner they had always been, following the same rules and procedures, with the same power dynamics as had existed before the war, was wishful thinking. The Board of Liquidation did not appreciate that negotiating with the ILO in 1946–7 was not the same as doing so ten years earlier. The relationship between the two organizations had changed, and the ILO's priorities were no longer the same as the League's. The presentism that compelled the Secretariat to adhere to the UN timetable in 1946 was just as much a factor in the negotiations with the Governing Body in 1947 and, once more, there was little the League of Nations could do but acquiesce to the uncertainty. The organization's leadership took great pride in its twenty-five-year history, but that same pride often made it blind to the realities of the impotent position in which it found itself. Both the League and the ILO acted with stubbornness and bad faith during their prolonged negotiations, but by 1947 only one of these organizations had the agency and influence with which to support its posturing.

The rearguard

During closure, the Board of Liquidation was effectively free to do what it wanted, for better or worse, with little to no oversight. As this chapter has shown thus far, many of the decisions it made in 1947 were affected by a desire to pursue what it believed member governments wanted, that is, money, alongside the attempts to build a positive legacy for the organization, sometimes at the expense of speed and, as this section reveals, the League's staff. When the Secretariat returned to work in 1947, it was made up of just twenty officials – twelve women and eight men. Fifteen of them were still in post by July, but two months later only three remained.[94] This section looks more closely at this 1947 cohort and the League leadership's relationship with them, revealing the different attitudes towards them from the Board and the Secretariat's senior figures, and why these officials were not allowed to claim ownership of even a small part of the legacy the Board was trying to build, despite their own long-running commitment to, and pride in, the League of Nations.

As a group the 1947 officials were at the older end of their working lives – their average age was almost fifty – and the vast majority had worked for, and been loyal to, the Secretariat for many years. Eight of the officials left in 1947 had over twenty years each under their belts, the longest serving of whom was Constance (Connie) Harris. She joined the Secretariat in 1919 at the age of twenty-two and stayed with the League for over twenty-eight years before leaving in mid-August 1947 at the age of fifty. She held the longest tenure of not just those remaining in 1947, but of any other League Secretariat official in its history.[95] A number of the group also had more than one appointment with the League, and several of them had four or more separate appointments across the Secretariat's lifetime, suggesting a level of commitment both from these individuals to the League and from the League to them.[96] Some of their appointments only lasted for short periods, but overall they added up to considerable service. Kathleen Harrison, a shorthand-typist, held four separate appointments spanning from 1924 through to 1947 for a total of 12.75 years – the shortest of the group – while Winifred Oberdorff also had four appointments working as a copyist and stenographer, but this time adding up to almost twenty years of service.

There are numerous examples among these officials of individuals wanting to return to the Secretariat again and again, and senior figures endeavouring to accommodate them. Oberdorff joined the Secretariat as a copyist in 1919, serving for thirteen years before leaving to get married. Unfortunately, after fewer than two years of marriage and aged only thirty-one years, she was widowed in 1934. With no means to support herself she wrote to the Secretariat asking to return and, as she was well-regarded during her previous tenure, it was agreed to re-engage her. Oberdorff left again in 1940 when the Second World War forced a mass exit of officials, but came back to the League in 1946 as a stenographer when Valentin Stencek facilitated her return once again, who later went as far as to convince Oberdorff to stay with the Secretariat in April 1947 when she tried to leave the organization for a better paid role with the new UN Refugee Organisation.[97] A very similar case was that of Alma Raisin (later Schibli), who joined the Secretariat in 1920 and left to marry in 1926. Also widowed at a young age, she wrote to the Palais during the Second World War as she was finding it difficult to financially support herself and her son following her husband's death, and she was subsequently offered a position as a shorthand-typist. These women obviously felt some degree of confidence that the leaders of the Secretariat would be amenable to their requests and, judging by the positive responses they received, their faith was justified.[98]

There are other instances among the group of officials remaining in 1947 of the Secretariat's leadership choosing to not only respond positively to pleas for employment, like those from Oberdorff and Schibli, but to also actively seek out and recruit former staff for new positions. Cecily Babington, hired to support the Board of Liquidation in early 1946, had previously worked for the Secretariat as a shorthand-typist between 1922 and 1935. Chester Purves was also directly re-engaged to take on the role of secretary to the same Board, having previously worked as a member of Section in the Internal Service for eighteen years, several of which were spent as a direct assistant to Valentin Stencek.[99] His return was lobbied for by both the latter and other figures in the leadership, so much so that he was allowed to bring his niece Ann with him – and temporarily find work for her with the Secretariat – when he returned to Geneva in 1946.[100]

One of the most notable examples of officials' dedication to the League came in the case of Percy Watterson. Born in Leeds in 1887, he joined the Secretariat at its inception in July 1919 as an accountant. He stayed in the Treasury throughout its lifetime and relocated to Princeton alongside the EFO in 1940 to support its work. When the final EFO staff in the United States transferred to the UN at the end of July 1946, Watterson – despite having already found a new position with the FAO – stayed in New Jersey on a part-time basis in order to close the Princeton office and wrap up the League's financial matters in the United States, while simultaneously working in his new role.[101] It was originally anticipated that this split of roles between the League and the FAO would only last for two months while Watterson wrapped up loose ends, but by the start of October it became clear that finalizing the League's US-based business would take longer than planned. Nevertheless Watterson was totally committed to both the League and its Secretariat, and felt he was indebted to the institution he had worked for the majority of his career to complete the work he had started. In a later letter to Stencek in June 1947, he reflected on his relationship with the organization: 'despite the fact that my heavy duties here have meant confining my work for the League to week ends, I have felt that I owed it to the League'.[102] He officially left the League's employ and joined the FAO as expected, full-time, at the start of November 1946, but that was not where his relationship with the Secretariat ended.

Instead, Watterson agreed to use his weekends and evenings on the League's behalf, while working a full-time job for the newly established FAO – his new employers having agreed to the arrangement.[103] The topic of financial restitution was discussed between Watterson, Lester and Stencek, but no decision was ever reached and ultimately the Englishman, assuming the work would take a matter of a few weeks to conclude, agreed to volunteer his time without salary. However the work was still not complete by the end of 1946 and, despite outsourcing the publication of the EFO's final work – titled *Europe's Population in the Interwar Years* and written by Princeton academic Dudley Kirk – to his former colleague Ansgar Rosenborg at the UN, Watterson found himself toiling on League-related problems throughout 1947.[104] Originally his responsibilities were confined to the closure of the League's accounts in the United States, but as liquidation proceedings dragged on he became the default liaison for any outstanding problems the League had in North America, and his workload was much greater than he could have originally anticipated. As already mentioned, he chased debts for the League and acted as a point of contact for Lester while he was in New York in the autumn of 1946, but he also dealt with forgotten insurance accounts and even spent time arranging the shipment of the celebratory tapestries belonging to the League which had been on display at Haverford College during the war.[105] Despite these numerous additional tasks, Watterson managed to close the

League's US-based accounts in May 1947 – the delays to Ansgar Rosenborg's EFO publication notwithstanding – and his commitment to the organization remained steadfast despite the lack of restitution, but even he became frustrated at times.[106] He was most exasperated by the lack of communication about his activities, occasionally expressing annoyance that one-half of the Secretariat did not seem to know what the other half was doing, and having to remind his Genevan colleagues of updates he had already provided.[107] However there was one additional matter that devoured Watterson's time more than any other in 1947, and it tested his dedication to the League to its limit: the organization's legal case against the US Internal Revenue Service.

Secretariat officials based in the United States during the Second World War were obliged to pay income tax as non-resident aliens during their time there. Ordinarily officials were exempt from paying such taxes in Switzerland so the League decided to pay lump sums to these individuals to cover the income lost until an appeal against the taxation could be launched. The League believed it had solid legal grounds to reclaim the money, hoping to provide a better financial deal for its members in the process, and thus launched a test case using John Henry Chapman, a New Zealander who worked for the EFO in Princeton, and had been with the League as a member of Section since 1921. Should the case be successful, the outcome would set precedent for other officials, and the Internal Revenue would be forced to reimburse these individuals who would, in turn, repay the League.[108] A law firm in New York, Edwards & Smith, was pursuing the case on the League's behalf but the physical and mental distance between New York and Geneva meant that the League's leadership was not always particularly well-informed or knowledgeable about the process. This was especially true after the departure of Secretariat legal advisor Émile Giraud in late 1946, which led to misconceptions as to what the case would involve from the League's perspective and how long it would take to resolve. The League's leadership laboured under the assumption that the case would be settled before the organization dissolved itself, despite repeated warnings from Harold Edwards, of Edwards & Smith, that any court decision would be unlikely before September or October 1947 at the earliest.[109]

In the autumn of 1946, Giraud and several members of the Board of Liquidation expressed serious concerns about the case's likelihood of success, the increasing legal costs and the lack of definite timeline. The Board made the decision to push on regardless, but as time passed the case started to represent more of a burden than an opportunity.[110] Carl Hambro called the lawsuit 'disgusting' in a letter to Lester in March 1947, and once again suggested they 'cut our losses' and abandon the case.¹¹¹ At its twentieth meeting on 12 April, several members of the Board echoed Hambro's concerns, but Kisch convinced the group that $5,000 – the outstanding fees quoted by Edwards & Smith – was a worthy price to pay for a possible pay-out of almost $80,000.¹¹² So, despite his misgivings, Hambro wrote to Edwards again to confirm that the League would be going ahead with the case, explaining that members would be more likely to forgive an unsuccessful verdict than having spent $25,000 on a case they then decided to drop.¹¹³

The decision to pursue the costly lawsuit despite everyone's misgivings may have seemed foolhardy, but the Board's discussion in its twentieth meeting and Hambro's consequent letter to Edwards reveal why the group would take such a risk. Once again the decision to continue seemed to be about money – the League did not want to be seen wasting any – but the Board's preoccupation with propriety was also responsible. Pursuit of the lawsuit, like the pursuit of outstanding debts, was the 'right' course of action. League officials had never paid income taxes while they were part of the Secretariat and, from the Board's perspective, although the League decided to reimburse those US-based officials as a matter of staff welfare in the interim, they should never have been taxed in the first place. Even though the United States was not a member of the League and had never agreed to an arrangement whereby officials would be exempt, the organization's leadership believed it had the right to demand its $80,000. As far as the Board of Liquidation was concerned, it was a matter of principle and, as echoed in meeting records, it did not want to explain to members why the League had spent $25,000 to initiate the case, only for it to be abandoned before its conclusion.¹¹⁴

Nonetheless the decision to continue, borne out of the Board's apprehension about its reputation, resulted in difficulties that were centred not just on the schedule and the costs but also on what was involved in pursuing it and who was responsible. With Edwards & Smith based in New York, and many of the former officials to which the lawsuit applied still living in the United States, Percy Watterson was, as far as the League's leadership was concerned, conveniently placed to coordinate the work. This included obtaining financial details and power of attorney forms from his former colleagues, as well as liaising with Edwards & Smith lawyers, despite not being made fully aware of the details of the case by the leadership or other officials in Geneva – another cause of frustration on his part.¹¹⁵ When Watterson left the League in October 1946, he could not have imagined that he would still be using his weekends and evenings to settle the organization's business many months later, and still without salary.

Yet he never complained – at least not in official correspondence – and never refused a request for help, which would once again prove fortuitous for the League's leadership when it became apparent the case could not be resolved before the organization dissolved. In a letter to Valentin Stencek, dated 4 June 1947, Watterson summed up his feelings about going above and beyond for his former employers:

> Despite the fact that my heavy duties here have meant confining my work for the League to week ends, I have felt that I owed it to the League and the Board of Liquidation to satisfactorily wind up matters as a fitting termination to the many years of service I enjoyed with the Organisation.[116]

The Board's choice to pursue the case despite the League's impending closure raised an important question: how could an organization pursue a lawsuit if the said organization no longer existed? The answer proposed by Edwards & Smith was to appoint a trustee to act as a final executor of the League's estate: someone who could tie up the last financial loose ends once the organization was otherwise dissolved. Initial discussions suggested either Hambro or Lester as suitable candidates, but attention soon turned to Watterson, once again conveniently located in Washington, DC. Stencek had the unenviable job of conveying yet another appeal for assistance to his former colleague, taking great care to note that costs would be covered, the work would likely be complete by 'October at the latest' and that Watterson must clear the proposal with the FAO first.[117] Including the time it took for Stencek's letter to cross the Atlantic, only six days passed before Watterson confirmed via telegram that he was happy to take on the trustee role – provided it did not take up too much of his time – and that the FAO had agreed.[118] Unfortunately for Watterson the work would once again take up a significantly greater portion of his time than expected, but the Board concluded, consciously or not, that it could take advantage of, and benefit from, his continued willingness to go above and beyond for the organization.

The Board of Liquidation had both a physically and emotionally distant relationship with the officials of the Secretariat. Most of the Board members had very little contact with staff beyond Lester, Stencek and Purves, as well as possibly Cecily Babington and Dagny Gran – both of whom worked alongside Purves supporting the administration of meetings. As a consequence this meant the group did not have the same loyalty to officials, past and present, that Lester did as secretary general; it tended to view the Secretariat as separate from the rest of the League of Nations it was trying to build a legacy for. The Board felt a responsibility to protect its version of the organization's history and essentially claimed a monopoly on what was, and what was not, to be preserved; the Secretariat was not part of the process.

The commitment to acting as legal adjudicator for the League's closure and its allegiance to rules and procedure meant the Board could be less than benevolent when it came to decisions involving officials, and especially requests from staff for leeway or flexibility surrounding said rules. One of the Board's most unsympathetic rulings came in relation to the (supposedly) voluntary contributions paid by officials during the war. These contributions were purportedly for staff welfare purposes and pooled into a central fund, but in reality it became another strand of general funding for the organization, with Stencek calculating that of the 1,025,982 Swiss francs collected from officials between 1940 and 1946, only 41,220 Swiss francs, just over 4 per cent, had been used for officials' benefit.[119] In June 1947, Yves Biraud – former president of the League Staff Committee and by then a WHO official – wrote to Hambro on behalf of another ninety-one co-signees asking him to return the contributions to staff.[120] Biraud argued that they had not been used as originally intended, the scheme had not been truly voluntary – noting that the funds had been listed in official budgets as income before Secretariat officials even agreed to the arrangement – and that the League was now in sufficiently good financial health to warrant the reimbursement, which was calculated in a Board of Liquidation document at just under 1m Swiss francs.[121] No current official signed the letter, but Stencek noted that a number of them – although not specifically named – were sympathetic to their former colleagues' proposal.[122] This was a request of an ethical nature, signed by officials who had worked hard for the League – on reduced pay – during the most dangerous time in the organization's history, and submitted to a group of men who enjoyed privileged positions in the diplomatic world. The Board often spoke of its moral duty and commitment to doing what was right in its meetings, especially in regard to the ILO Staff Pensions debacle, but in this instance the request was only discussed in brief at the group's thirty-second meeting before being dismissed without argument. Carl Hambro even went as far as to suggest the only reason the claim had been made was because the former officials in question had heard 'the rumours concerning the large sums at the Board's disposal'.[123]

The Board was not entirely without sympathy for former officials. Percy Watterson travelled to Vichy in June 1940 on League business, but following the invasion of north-western Europe, he was forced to abandon his car and flee to England via boat. Almost six years later he submitted a claim for 2,500

Swiss francs to cover the loss, and while the Board was not happy about the delay in his request, decided to grant him a partial indemnity of 1,000 Swiss francs.[124] Another example in which the Board granted some leeway was that of Doctors Park and Dakshinamurthi, both of whom worked for the League at the Epidemiological Bureau in Singapore and had lost personal effects during the Japanese bombardment and invasion of the city in 1942.[125] The Board did not believe it had a legal case to answer, but Kisch pointedly noted that, as the two men had shown loyalty to the League, the organization may have a 'moral liability' to uphold. Confident that making payments of £1,250 to Park and 1,000 rupees to Dakshinamurthi would not set a precedent for similar war-damage claims, the Board agreed to grant these indemnities on the proviso that no legal liability should be accepted.[126]

One particular request for assistance came to the Board on several occasions in 1947 regarding Lucie Courtault, a Frenchwoman who served as a clerk in the League's Paris office between 1920 and 1940. Now over sixty years old and partially infirm, the devaluation of the French franc meant that her League pension was no longer sufficient to live on, and while Courtault received some financial respite as a result of an earlier claim in the spring of 1946, she requested assistance again in 1947. The Board discussed the matter in its twenty-second and twenty-fourth meetings in April and, while the group was deeply sympathetic to Courtault's plight, it was concerned that granting funds directly from the Board could create a dangerous precedent. Committed as it was to conducting its affairs in line with regulations, the Board did not want an influx of requests from former officials to deal with, so it engineered an indirect means of assistance. The Board granted 15,000 Swiss francs from League funds to the Administrative Board of the Staff Pensions Fund, to be distributed by the latter at its discretion, but on the proviso it be used only to relieve the case of Courtault and others like her suffering financial hardship. This allowed the Board of Liquidation, and the League, to help those in the direst need of assistance, while shifting responsibility for it to an arguably more appropriate source and keeping its staunch principles intact.[127]

Nevertheless Courtault's request for assistance was just one of many dealt with by the Board and unfortunately for the Frenchwoman's former colleagues, the group was often much less sympathetic to their claims. Emile Henneberger appealed for compensation following his contraction of emphysema, a condition he claimed was brought about by working in unheated parts of the Palais during the war.[128] Similarly, Tatiana de Peganow appealed for disability compensation following her dismissal from the Secretariat in 1929 due to ill-health.[129] Léon

Steinig, a former US-based official, requested a rebate on further taxes he had been forced to pay as a result of the League's decision to refund his income tax in the United States as a lump sum.[130] All of these requests were denied by the Board of Liquidation.

Lester was party to Board decisions – he sat in on all its meetings even if he was not a member – but outside of sessions his instinct tended towards protecting his officials, especially those still working at the Palais. After years of reduced salaries and stagnant benefits caused by the League's diminished wartime budget, many officials – especially those in more junior roles – were finally granted long-overdue increases in both salary and benefits at the start of 1947.[131] He also pushed for other international organizations in Geneva to recognize its newly employed former League officials as international civil servants. As these individuals were already in Switzerland when they were recruited, they were often categorized as locally recruited employees – which did not provide the same protections and benefits as an international official – despite most of them having originally moved there to work for the League from their home countries.[132] He also tried to secure future employment for those left working at the Palais. He provided references for individuals, and in June 1947 he sent letters advocating for his officials to the UN – both in New York and Geneva – the ILO, the Preparatory Commission for the International Refugee Organisation and UNESCO, alongside mini-biographies of each member of staff.[133] Unfortunately he was not particularly successful in this endeavour – most of the new institutions had already filled their ranks by the summer of 1947 – but the lack of success did not diminish his efforts on their behalf.

Lester's working relationships were, for the most part, strictly serious and professional, but on occasion he let down his guard with those with whom he worked closely. His secretary since he became deputy secretary general in 1937, Cosette Nonin, left for a new position with the UN Geneva Office at the end of January 1947, and Lester wrote a kind and thankful letter to her upon her departure:

> I have had no work in which you did not participate and I have never felt either the need or inclination to conceal from you any element, political or personal, touching upon our Secretariat life … It is no wonder that this has developed a relationship which I will always look back upon with pleasure and satisfaction.[134]

He was also particularly grateful to Stencek, writing, 'I never shall be able to say enough' in a note celebrating the latter's twenty-five years of service in 1946, and showered his right-hand man with uncharacteristically effusive praise in a farewell letter in August 1947:

> During a career of more than 26 years' duration in which you have been called upon to fulfil duties of a most varied nature, you have shown yourself to be an excellent international official. Your deep sense of responsibility, tireless industry, thoroughness and impartiality have been remarkable. Your imperturbable efficiency, calmness in every emergency, your good judgment, common sense and sense of proportion, always most estimable qualities, have proved invaluable in the difficult days of war and liquidation.[135]

The Final Report to members, issued by the Board of Liquidation, claimed that approximately two hundred former League officials moved to the UN, or its agencies, following the former's dissolution. Despite the consistent repetition of this number in scholarship since the Report was released, it has not been verified and this seemingly rosy figure did not always reflect the experience of those Secretariat staff that stayed with the League through 1947. Although some of the officials mentioned above were able to find other roles as international civil servants following their departure, it was not as easy as it was for their colleagues who transferred directly into positions at the UN or elsewhere in 1946. Connie Harris left the League without another position lined up, as did Evelyn Curry and Marie Boiteux, despite the latter's expressed wish to move to another international organization.[136] Between them, these three women had over seventy-five years of experience as international officials, but aside from Lester's efforts, they were let down by a lack of interest from both the new organizations and their most senior leaders.

The Board of Liquidation was not impervious to officials' concerns, but the Secretariat simply did not feature in its legacy-focused priorities. When discussing requests from current and former officials, Board members would often note that they felt empathy for the people concerned and that the appeals were sometimes justified but, in contrast to the group's maintained belief that the moral high ground was important in the negotiations with the ILO, in these instances rules and procedures were more important.[137] The leadership's commitment was to the League as an institution rather than the League as a workforce of Secretariat officials, and this approach influenced the Board's policy in all areas of decision-making. It meant the group could take advantage of Watterson's commitment and refuse legitimate requests for financial compensation, while prioritizing issues that would reflect well upon the organization as a whole.

Conclusions

Reading the Board of Liquidation's Final Report to members, one might be forgiven for assuming the months leading up to its publication were relatively quiet and without controversy. It contained no mention of delays to closure, or long-running disagreements with the ILO; it was a carefully crafted message designed to reassure governments that the process was over and that the Board had safely delivered on its responsibilities as an impartial arbiter. Behind its meticulous message, however, was a Board of Liquidation motivated by both pridefulness and apprehension, an official legacy designed by only a handful of men and a Secretariat barred from sharing in the ownership of the League's memory.

The League's founders rightly understood that public and member support were vital for its survival – hence the groundbreaking early emphasis on public relations – but the endemic desire to prove itself worthy remained a part of the organization's psyche long after its fate was sealed. Pride in the League experiment and the longing to be seen as a credible part of the international community, by those both in 1947 and in the future, guided almost every course of action taken by the Board in its final months. They aimed to preserve the organization's legacy via a double-pronged approach: keeping governments happy by providing a good return on investment and using all possible means to ensure the League story was not further maligned or erased after it was gone.

There were both positive and negative repercussions, depending on one's interests, to the Board's approach to liquidation in 1947. The group was undoubtedly successful at recouping debts owed to the organization, and its pursuit of such monies was of benefit not only to members but also occasionally to officials – current and former – who received long-overdue increases in salary and, where they were successful, compensation claims. The League's well-endowed coffers also allowed the Board to pursue its increasingly grand plans for the permanent exhibit. Without the additional available funds, it is unlikely the Board and Arthur Breycha-Vauthier would have had the means with which to make the League Museum a reality, at least on the scale to which they aspired. The Board was in no way obliged to continue with the 1930s plans for a permanent exhibit – it was not part of the Assembly's resolution to liquidate the organization – but the tenacity of its members, and of Secretariat officials, saw the establishment of a museum which remains in the Palais des Nations today as a continuing testament to an organization that many in the international arena in 1947 would have happily seen removed from collective memory.

In many respects the Board of Liquidation had reconciled itself to the nature of the organization's reputation in the post-war world. It knew that the efforts to please governments and other international organizations with a proper liquidation would not change the way many felt about the League's past, and the endeavour to provide members with a good return on their financial investment would not save the institution's reputation in the short term. The League's ingrained focus on public relations and prestige, however, meant that the Board was unusually aware of the power of narrative and how control of it could be used to influence people long after the organization was buried. The actions taken to keep the League's Archives together and accessible to researchers have had many of the long-term implications the Board wished for, even if academia's reassessment of the organization took a little longer than it would have liked, and said reassessment has not resulted in a complete turnaround on how we think about the League's relative merits. Nevertheless, without the leadership's pioneering recognition of the importance of archives, it is unlikely we would understand, and be able to study, the League with the ease to which we have become accustomed.

Yet the Board's pride and fear of reproach also proved self-defeating. The efforts to pursue debts, while advantageous for the organization's finances and the perception that the leadership was taking its role seriously, caused significant delays to the liquidation process. While the choice was never made explicit in correspondence or official minutes of Board meetings, the group decided appearance was more important than expediency. It was an approach that was representative of the League's approach to the management of outside opinion throughout its lifetime; as described by Ilaria Scaglia, the organization's decision-making was frequently driven by fear of outside feelings and opinions.[138] The League needed, and wanted, to be liked, and this outlook did not disappear because the organization was in liquidation. This manifested itself in the ongoing pursuance of contributions, the decision to continue with the income tax lawsuit and the tumultuous negotiations with the ILO, which might have been settled months earlier had the Board addressed the situation sooner. The same events were further negatively affected by the perceived injury to the leadership's ego, brought about by the ILO's entrenched negotiating position. Edward Phelan and Guildhaume Myrddin-Evans were no longer obliged to kowtow to the League's suggestions, but the Board was not ready to accept the new power dynamics of 1947.

The Board of Liquidation had a tendency to act like it owned the League which, in some respects and as already mentioned, meant it acted fervently to protect the organization's memory. However, this sense of entitlement did not include, and also resulted in sometimes shabby treatment for, the League's most dedicated officials. Sadly for these individuals, the Board's efforts to please – the targets of which included governments, the general public and even unknown future researchers – did not include those who had worked for the organization for decades. Board members were not wilfully malicious, but the group took the view that it was not responsible for the Secretariat and instead acted first and foremost with the interests of members in mind. The positive rulings made in favour of officials only tended to occur if said decisions did not impact negatively on the organization's financial situation, and if actions could be taken quietly without setting a precedent for others. Officials were dedicated both to each other and to the idea of the League, but 'the League' was not always loyal to them in return. Despite the efforts of Lester and Stencek, a number of individuals who wished to remain in international civil service were unable to find new positions upon leaving the League, and the willingness of those like Percy Watterson and Arthur Breycha-Vauthier to go above and beyond the call of duty was taken advantage of. The Board was fixated on preserving the League's memory, but the legacy it was trying to build did not necessarily reflect the whole organization. The Secretariat, arguably the backbone of the institution and the one constant throughout its lifetime, was not part of the image the Board was trying to preserve and was cast aside as a result.

July 1947 marked the end of the Board of Liquidation's work. The organization itself was still lingering on its deathbed, but the leadership decided strategic oversight was no longer needed and Hambro's group parted ways for the last time on the 23rd of that month. There were no official celebrations of its work at that meeting or even a few words of commemoration or thanks. After six months of inactivity, the group endured thirty-two meetings across four separate sessions in 1947, doing its utmost to protect the League's reputation both then and in the future. In many ways it succeeded in what it set out to achieve: financial recompense for members was better than expected, it enabled the future study of the organization and built a physical memorial that continues to stand at the heart of the Palais des Nations. Nonetheless that same commitment also resulted in a liquidation that was months overdue, an abandoned and unappreciated workforce, and an inability to recognize that prideful posturing was not an advantageous approach to negotiations. The Board spent so much of its time either looking back at the organization's glory days or forward to the desired reassessment of its legacy in the years to come that it often forgot to manage the practicalities of 1947.

5

Many endings, August 1947 and beyond

At what point did the League of Nations cease to exist? On the surface this might seem like a straightforward question with a clearly identifiable answer, but the institution's closure was elaborate and is not easily simplified. The organization was made up of various facets, some more palpable or physical than others, and all were legitimate aspects of what Arthur Sweetser described as 'this first Great Experiment', but few of the League's elements drew to a close at the same time.[1] This chapter examines the weeks and months following the Board of Liquidation's dissolution in July 1947, the challenges faced by those officials still working in the League's name and the elements of the organization that outlived it. And, most importantly, this chapter asks if it is possible to, and if we should, declare one of the League's many endings more valid than the others.

The mood among the League's leadership was once again relatively high at the end of July 1947. The Board of Liquidation departed Geneva for the last time following its final meeting on 23rd of that month and, having taken action to establish the permanent exhibit and the long-term protection of the organization's Archives, the group felt satisfied with its achievements. Board members identified only the Final Report as outstanding business and 'agreed that unless anything unexpected should occur requiring a meeting in the meantime, the Board would not need to hold another formal meeting and would be regarded as dissolved on 31st July, 1947'.[2] As far as the group was concerned, their work – as well as that of the League of Nations – was over, and this chapter scrutinizes what followed, highlighting a number of problems that prevented the organization concluding its business, and further challenging misconceptions about the timing of the League of Nations' death.

Compared to the high levels of activity in 1946 and the first half of 1947, the League's last months were not particularly hectic or tumultuous. Instead this chapter covers a period in which the organization was experiencing a long, drawn-out demise, a spectre of its former self but still labouring to turn off the lights. Closer examination of these months transforms our understanding of when and how the League actually closed, demolishing the long-held belief that the organization disappeared from the world in the spring of 1946, or even the summer of 1947, and instead suggests that elements of both the organization and its institutional memory continued into 1948 and beyond. This chapter also forces us to consider what we mean when we talk about the end of an organization; what markers need to be in place to make the end a reality, and does it matter if we are unable to identify this moment in time for the League?

This chapter is structured around the League's many endings, with five sections focused on key points at which different aspects of the League concluded. The first examines August 1947, the month following the Board of Liquidation's dissolution and leading up to the dispatch of its Final Report to members at the start of September. The second covers a further eight weeks up to 25 October 1947, when the League officially disbanded the Secretariat and seemingly closed its financial accounts. The third section then features the months up to the end of January 1948, wherein the last official communication from the League was sent to members, and the fourth covers February 1948 and beyond, during which a handful of former Secretariat officials continued to manage organizational business and field requests from outside parties. The final section of this chapter focuses on the fortunes of those Secretariat officials who remained with the organization through 1947, and how these individuals were specifically recruited by the new post-war global institutions to take advantage of their collective knowledge and keep the League's memory and experience of international civil service alive.

An international organization's last tasks are a long way from the glamour and excitement of assembly meetings and conferences; instead they are often tedious, repetitive and thankless in nature. The League of Nations was predisposed to publicly touting its work – the organization had depended on support from governments for its survival – but its wearisome final duties were completed behind closed doors. Endings are inherently messy; the League's last officials discovered that even the most well-organized liquidation could not envisage or plan for every scenario. No matter how hard they tried, there was always something else to be done, and they knew there would be no notoriety or thanks for their efforts at the end. At least six months passed between the Board's dissolution and what might be considered the termination of League business; this chapter reveals why this was a laborious process for those overseeing it and suggests that trying to attribute a single definitive ending to the League is just as thorny an endeavour. The Board of Liquidation, Secretariat officials and state members of the organization all had different perspectives on the League, and these viewpoints were accompanied by opinions on when the institution came to an end, potentially varying by months or even years. The date of an organization's death, without a pre-agreed definition of what that means, is inherently subjective; this chapter not only suggests that this quandary cannot be remedied for the League but also proposes accepting the uncertainty that comes with it.

The public end: August 1947

By the end of July, much of the League's liquidation was complete and the end was finally in sight for both the Secretariat and those outside the organization. The Board had dissolved itself, having drawn the conclusion – after forty-two meetings – that oversight was no longer required, meaning the last steps to symbolically shutter the League could now be made. The weeks up to the end of August became the public end of the organization, the point at which the leadership exhorted to the rest of the world that the work was over, and they could all be congratulated on a job well done.

The one remaining major task, from the perspective of the Board of Liquidation at least, was the completion and publication of the Final Report to members. At the twenty-first Assembly back in April 1946, the agreed resolution to dissolve the League explicitly stated that the Board 'shall make and publish a report' to members, and 'declare itself to be dissolved', after which 'the liquidation shall be deemed to be complete', hence the Board's focus on its publication as the conclusive marker of closure.[3] This was its indicator of success; once completed, its members could be satisfied their work was done. Despite the rush of activity in June and July, however, the Report was not finished by the time the Board dissolved itself at the end of the latter month. The greater part of the document was ready, but the French version of the text was not yet finalized – for which the French-speaking members of the Board, specifically Émile Charvériat, Daniel Secrétan and Jaromír Kopecky, were relied upon – and Carl Hambro was slow to give his final sign-off on a document he knew needed to be beyond reproach.[4] He continued to send small changes to Chester Purves, secretary of the Board of Liquidation and the person responsible for finishing and arranging the publication of the Report, some of which identified inconsistencies in the text while others highlighted minor formatting issues.[5] Nonetheless, even when these changes were made, Purves was still unable to finalize the Report, noting in a letter to Cecil Kisch in mid-August that while the second proof had since been sent to the printers, Hambro wanted yet another chance to review the document and its appendices before sign-off, a task prolonged by the former Board chairman's return to Norway.[6]

Furthermore Hambro also spent a week in Sweden on a diplomatic mission – a trip of which Purves was unaware – meaning the latter became increasingly frustrated by the delays, writing what he described as 'a rather desperate telegram' to the chairman in an effort to hurry him along and complaining to Lester that he was 'at a loss to explain the delay' just days before he was scheduled to permanently leave Geneva.[7] The Board secretary's contract was due to expire at the end of August and, with personal business to attend to in London, Purves was committed to meeting his deadline, even writing to Hambro on his final day as an official to inform the Board chairman that his latest set of corrections and changes was sent too late to be incorporated into the Report.[8] However the end of Purves's Secretariat tenure was not the only reason to hurry along the completion of the document. The UN Secretariat placed an order for 1,500 copies of the Report back in early August, hoping the document could be used as a basis for discussion at the upcoming Second General Assembly starting in September. Meanwhile the Board had already agreed to release the Report with an official backdated publication date of 31 July, and the longer the period between this and the actual publication, the more likely the time discrepancy would be noticed. Despite work on both the Report and liquidation continuing throughout August, this earlier date was the end point the League's leadership wanted the rest of the world to focus on.[9]

The official communication sent to members alongside the Report in the first week of September explicitly stated that the Board's work was completed at the end of July, and a press communique issued at the same time backed up this version of events, specifically noting that all claims had been settled and affairs terminated in good order.[10] Representatives of the press were also invited into Seán Lester's office in the first week of August to hear a summary of the Final Report – mostly a recap of the Board's work transferring activities and assets to both the UN and the ILO – to reinforce the idea to outside observers that the League's work was complete. An unnamed reporter from the *Tribune de Genève* reported as such in their article summing up the meeting, noting that while a few officials would remain with the organization for a month to deal with minor matters, the League itself ceased to exist on 31 July.[11] Similar, albeit shorter, articles appeared in both *The Times of London* and *The New York Times* within twenty-four hours of each other, reporting the same official story, with the London paper noting that 'The League's existence was formally terminated on July 31'. Meanwhile *The New York Times* write-up was only six sentences long and buried on page 12 of the August 5 edition between an article on coal output in the Ruhr valley and a large advertisement for a sale at Famous Wines and Liquors Inc.[12] Neither the press at the time nor its readers were particularly interested in the end of the League of Nations. No letters to the editor made it into editions following these latest reports, not even from Arthur Sweetser, who had previously written to *The New York Times* on several occasions in support of the organization.[13] By the summer of 1947 wider audiences had simply stopped caring about an institution long gone from public consciousness, and newspaper editors were more than happy to accept the sanctioned story put forth by the League's leadership. Even governments, the major stakeholders in the dissolution and the primary beneficiaries of the Board's focus on bolstering the organization's finances, barely responded to the League's conclusion.[14]

The official narrative was more than just a convenient story concocted for the outside world; the organization's leaders treated August as the month in which the League ended. The value of the organization's material assets to be transferred to the UN was finally settled at 46,194,569.29 Swiss francs – converted to US $10,809,529.21 – and congratulatory letters passed between figures such as Lester, Trygve Lie and long-time League stalwart Sweetser.[15] Lie wrote to Lester towards the end of the month, his thank you reflecting a relationship predicated on their shared understanding of what it took to be the secretary general of an IGO. Lie also took pains to note how grateful he was for Lester's work in not only facilitating the transfer process but also ensuring the UN did not need to start from scratch due to his safeguarding of the League's activities during the war; he acknowledged that it could not have been an easy task:

> It has been of the greatest importance to me personally to have, as it were, as my predecessor someone like yourself who has so willingly given his very best efforts at all times in what must have been a very disheartening and depressing task.[16]

Sweetser's celebratory letter was written earlier in the month, following the publication of *The New York Times* article which, as Sweetser noted in his correspondence 'brought the grand news that you are at the end of your long vigil in Geneva and I want to send you this line of warmest congratulations on a grand job grandly done!!!'. The letter was a typically lengthy three-page missive on the struggles of managing international organizations, written specifically in response to the publicly declared end of the League; Sweetser, like Lester, Lie and

Hambro, acted as if the work was done: 'It is gratifying indeed to think that the organization which meant so much to so many kept its flag flying to very end and passed out of the picture with all its details cared for and cleared up.'[17]

August was likewise marked by the departure of the majority of the League's officials, including Lester himself. The secretary general officially remained in his post until the end of the month, but he permanently returned to Ireland on the morning of 8 August 1947. Lester had no intention of remaining on the organization's payroll beyond that point, but Valentin Stencek successfully persuaded Hambro – in light of the secretary general's continued counsel via airmail until the end of August – to extend his contract until the last day of the month.[18] If managing the League during the Second World War proved stressful for Lester, overseeing the organization's liquidation was just as, if not even more, taxing. By the time he left Geneva he had spent seven years in a role he originally held no ambition for, presiding over an increasingly maligned and abandoned organization. His was a difficult and unappreciated task, and he had little interest in staying in Geneva until the bitter end; after many years separated from his family, and satisfied that he was finally free to leave his post, he slipped away to County Wicklow with neither fanfare nor recognition.[19]

Lester was far from the only member of the Secretariat to depart following the Board of Liquidation's dissolution. Between the Board's last meeting on 23 July and 31 August, twelve of the fifteen officials still employed by the League left the organization, including stalwarts such as Otto Jenny, Evelyn Curry, Willem van Asch van Wijck and Connie Harris.[20] All of the League's officials had been employed on temporary contracts since August 1946, renewed on a short-term basis every two to three months as needed.[21] The leadership's decision in July and August 1947 that the work of the League was over, alongside the public assertions supporting that position, meant officials' contracts were allowed to expire and the vast majority of what remained of the Secretariat fizzled away over a few weeks. As with Lester's departure, there were no official festivities, no celebration to mark the passing of the milestone; instead members of the Secretariat quietly drifted away across the month. The only recorded acknowledgement of their partings came in official letters sent to the individuals in question by either Lester and Stencek, thanking them for their service, and while the letters were wholly affable, they seemed scant recognition for often decades of commitment.[22]

Many of those leaving in the summer of 1947 had been part of the Secretariat for decades, but many of them had only worked together closely in recent months and years. This meant these farewell letters were often impersonal by virtue of the fact that the officials who would have been best placed to write them had already left. For instance, Evelyn Curry served in the Secretariat as a shorthand-typist for over 22 years, and while Stencek took the time to add a sentence giving his personal thanks for her work as his secretary over the past year – 'I have had occasion personally to appreciate the excellent quality of your work, your intelligence and reliability' – his letter to her was otherwise a dispassionate summary of her career history. Perhaps a clinical thank you was better than nothing, but even the most devoted of officials like Curry might have found statements such as 'Your excellent health has made your services uninterruptedly valuable' less than inspiring after two decades of commitment.[23] These were long careers coming to an end, but as the last officials standing, there was no one left to commemorate with.

There is good reason to think that the end of August 1947 effectively marked the end of the League. The little white lies of the Final Report were finally agreed, the press reported on the end of the organization at the start of the month and all but three Secretariat officials had flown the nest. Valentin Stencek, the most senior figure remaining, wrote to Uno Brunskog, the League's auditor, on 20 August explaining that he hoped to officially close the League's financial accounts on 1 September and consequently complete the League's business just a few days later. Looking beyond the public announcements, however, to the work taking place in August reveals this was an overly ambitious goal.[24] Although much of the League's more substantive activity was over by the end of July, and despite the public assertions to the contrary, the Secretariat was not occupied with only liquidation activity during August 1947.

The Museum, handed over to the management of the UN at the end of July, still continued to occupy officials' time. Van Asch van Wijck provided framing and colour guidelines to the South African Government, Stencek took over writing thank you letters for donations and even Hambro continued to act as a liaison during the month.[25] There were small administrative issues relating to a money transfer to the former Indian Office of the League – by then part of the UN – that needed to be resolved with a London bank, and bills to settle with the UN apropos League officials seconded to the new organization in 1946.[26] Stencek was also forced to write to Hambro in the latter half of August, asking for the chairman's counsel; in the efforts to resolve the problems plaguing the reimbursement of furniture removals and repatriation costs for officials, the Board of Liquidation had overlooked what would happen to the funds transferred to the ILO for the administration of these refunds, should the remaining individuals neglect to submit their claim by the October deadline. This was in addition to the work involved in transferring the funds across to the ILO because, despite the agreement between the organizations having been made over two months earlier, the financial transfer was effectively forgotten until the very end of August, forcing Stencek to fast-track both the transfer of the 31,000 Swiss francs in question and the instructions for how it should be managed.[27]

Despite all the public pronouncements to the contrary, towards the end of August both Lester and Stencek realized that there were still elements of work to be completed before the Secretariat could truly close its doors. Some bank accounts had been closed up to this point, but there were still a number of financial issues to resolve, including the settling of more bills with the UN, transferring various funds to other organizations and of course the finalization and audit of the accounts.[28] These were alongside a number of trivial but necessary tasks still outstanding – Lester euphemistically called them 'several other points requiring treatment' – forcing the secretary general to write to Stencek on 23 August and instruct him to extend his own contract through to the end of September, alongside that of Peter Welps – a twenty-year veteran of the Internal Control service – and 'any secretarial assistance you may need'.[29] Lester's instruction proved especially providential just a few days later when, responding to Stencek's query regarding the audit of the final accounts, Uno Brunskog – based in Stockholm – explained that the financial review would have to wait until he was next able to come to Geneva in October.[30]

The staff and leadership were all-but gone, the Final Report was with governments and the world's press had announced the liquidation work complete. This was the public end of the organization: the point at which the League told both members and the wider world that liquidation was over. It was certainly an ending – with the Board's last tasks complete and Lester back home in Ireland, strategic oversight was effectively over – but it was not the end. Sat quietly in a corner of the Palais des Nations, Stencek, Welps and Marie Boiteux – the 'secretarial assistance' and shorthand-typist with over twenty-six years of League experience – continued to labour in an effort to truly dissolve the organization and bring the Secretariat's work to a close.

The end of the Secretariat: 25 October 1947

The League's next ending occurred on 25 October 1947, the day on which the organization's Secretariat ceased operations. As an institution, the Secretariat was the scaffolding that supported all League activity, and it is unsurprising therefore that this framework outlived almost every other element of the organization. The group was reduced to only three people at the start of September 1947 but there was still work to be done, and while the termination of any organization is naturally dominated by financial activities – settling outstanding obligations, arranging audits – the dissolution of the League in September and October 1947 reveals that the organization's liquidation was more complex than simply signing-off a set of accounts. Stencek, Welps and Boiteux soon came to understand that there was a reason the organization's most senior leaders were unconcerned with seeing the work through until the bitter end: tying up the loose ends of any endeavour, especially one as ambitious as the League, was often uninspiring and tedious.

With all but two of his colleagues gone, Stencek frequently found himself working on tasks that would otherwise have been dealt with by more junior officials. The jobs he was called upon to do during these weeks ranged from the small – such as paying for the League's subscription to *The Times of London* – to the more involved, for example, the continued oversight of the removal of items belonging to former officials of the Permanent Court of International Justice at The Hague.[31] The period might have laid the groundwork for the financial closure of the League, but the eight weeks in September and October also acted as a clearing house for all those tasks left until the last minute, either mistakenly overlooked in the past or neglected due to their wearisome nature.

In 1933, the French Government loaned three Sèvres porcelain vases to the League and, having seemingly been overlooked in the earlier activity of 1947, they needed to be repatriated to Paris before liquidation was complete. It was not a quick task; the French Government had effectively forgotten about the vases during the Second World War and not responded to previous enquiries made on the League's behalf, and thus Stencek had to first convince the French Foreign Ministry to grant their approval to make arrangements for their return.[32] Once their repatriation was approved, attention turned to finding a reliable removals firm, acquiring sufficient insurance – the vases were valued at 25,000 Swiss francs – and supervising the physical removal process, from packing to transportation. The administration of the procedure took weeks – confirmation that the vases had been received by the French Government was only sent on 24 October – and at a cost of over 2,000 Swiss francs, a total higher than originally anticipated due to both the insurance costs and, because of air traffic delays forcing the vases to travel by land rather than via aeroplane, increased transportation fees.[33]

Some of Stencek's tasks were not that different from those he might have had to complete normally, such as writing letters of recommendation for former colleagues, while others were unique to the situation. Lester's swift departure at the beginning of August meant the secretary general was unable to complete some of the personal administrative work that accompanies an international relocation, leaving Stencek to take on these tasks on his behalf. The assignment perhaps most tangential to his Secretariat role involved trying to sell Lester's car via a dealer in Geneva, which was made more onerous due to the type of car. Archival correspondence between the two men does not mention the model, but Stencek was forced to explain to Lester that the vehicle's powerful engine meant there had thus far been little interest from buyers: 'I was told that had it been a 7-seater they would have already found a purchaser, but for a 5-seater everybody finds that being rather powerful, the running expenses are too high.'[34] A buyer was eventually found in late October 1947, albeit at a lower-than-hoped price, but Stencek was still required to complete the necessary paperwork around the sale, including returning the number plates to the appropriate Swiss agency and claiming a reimbursement on the insurance.[35]

The sale of Lester's car was hardly a pressing matter in relation to the closure of the League, although it was emblematic of some of the issues that arise when an international civil service disintegrates and many of its constituent parts return home. Much of Stencek, Welps and Boiteux's work over September and October could be categorized as tedious or unspectacular, but it was almost always necessary, and one such example related to a missing Judges' Pensions payment of 14,000 Swiss francs. The money was meant to be paid to Judge Willem van Eysinga in January 1945 and the said amount was transferred to the Société de Banque Suisse, with an order to pay van Eysinga the equivalent amount in Dutch florins. Unfortunately the funds never arrived in the Netherlands, instead becoming held up at Dresdnerbank in Berlin, whose assets were frozen at the end of the war. Previous attempts to gain restitution from the Société de Banque Suisse proved unsuccessful, and so in July 1947, the League retained a Geneva lawyer to pursue the matter. Needless to say, the last-minute efforts proved ineffective over such a short time period, and the issue was one of very few that the Secretariat was unable to successfully resolve before the end of October. Unwilling to write off the 14,000 Swiss francs, and as the ILO had agreed to administer the Judges' Pensions Fund in the future, the debt was transferred to the Staff Pensions Administrative Council at that organization for resolution. Available archival material does not make it clear why the affair was left so late in the liquidation process, especially as the money had effectively been in limbo for over two-and-a-half years, but the delays stopped Stencek and his colleagues from closing this part of the League's business. Chasing down the money was a tiresome task, especially considering it might have been settled months earlier, but it was a necessary one; despite the prevarication the issue would not, and did not, resolve itself.[36]

Like the missing pension payment, many of Welps's and Stencek's final tasks in September and October focused on money, as one might expect when closing an organization. This included settling more debts with the UN – coming from intermittent profits from the sale of publications, administrative costs such as officials' telephone calls and stamps – and continuing to close the organization's many bank accounts both in Switzerland and overseas.[37] Many of these account closures were accompanied by transfer requests, moving the remaining financial assets in these accounts to successor organizations. The 31,000 Swiss francs earmarked for the outstanding staff removals' claims was finally transferred to the ILO in early September, while the remnants of the Library Building Fund – a little under 2,000 Swiss francs – were moved to the UN in Geneva with the explicit disclaimer that the money would be used to continue development of the permanent exhibit in the Library building, and that the League's auditor would verify the veracity of the expenditure.[38] The remnants of the Rockefeller Grant were also transferred to the UN, although this time to the New York headquarters, to be used towards the publication of the last remaining report financed by the EFO during its time in Princeton.[39] The League's liquid assets could also be definitively calculated, with a total of just over 15m Swiss francs returned to members, either as credits in members' accounts with the UN or directly to governments not yet part of the new organization.[40] Brunskog was also a man of his word, returning to Geneva in mid-October as promised. He verified the organization's accounts and issued a report to members explaining his conclusions on 25 October 1947.[41]

This date, 25 October, became the new end point publicized to both members and other outside parties, and even before Brunskog's audit, it was the end point Stencek started to work towards. In the middle of October, Stencek began writing letters to a range of different institutions – some local, others international – to both inform them that the League of Nations would cease to exist from 25 October 1947 and to thank them for any cooperation their institution shared with the organization throughout its history. A small number of them were sent in Lester's name – although he did not write them or sign-off on their contents – but the majority were sent by Stencek, and the recipients varied from the Swiss Federal Council and the president of the Geneva State Council to the chief of the Geneva Police and the Geneva Postal Service. Most of the letters followed a similar template – some even used the exact same wording – but the occasional letter took on a more personal tone, especially as some of the recipients worked closely with Stencek in his long-term role as Director of Personnel and Internal Administration.[42]

Stencek had not just worked alongside his League colleagues for over twenty years, but also those figures in Geneva he liaised with on a regular basis, and while he had already taken the opportunity to say goodbye to his colleagues, as Stencek's final weeks passed by he used the official thank you letters as a chance to bid adieu to these other friendly faces. His letter to Louis Casaï, for example, the director of Geneva Public Works, went beyond the formulaic and veered into the personal, thanking the latter for his amiable and welcoming attitude. It was a sentiment reciprocated by Casaï in his response, who wrote 'vous avez eu l'art d'accomplir, avec un sang-froid et un égalité d'âme tout-à-fait remarquables' – a great compliment for a man who prided himself on his self-discipline. Stencek's letter to Gallois at the ILO similarly felt less like a formality and more like a personal choice – an official letter had already been sent to Edward Phelan – as he rued the loss of their working relationship and expressed hopes that they would stay in contact: 'C'est avec un bien grand regret que je vois cette collaboration se terminer prochainement, mais j'espère rester en contact avec vous car je ne quitterai pas Genève.'[43] Yet even when the letters were more formal, it is not to suggest that this formality always came at the expense of genuine thanks. For instance Stencek's letter to John Lachavanne, Directeur-conservateur du Registre foncier in Geneva, was shorter than some of his other notes, but he still took the time to thank the latter for his good-natured responses to requests from the Palais: 'vous avez toujours répondu aux demandes de l'administration avec le plus grand bon vouloir'.[44] Stencek was skilled at adapting his style, writing in more personal terms when he held a closer working relationship with the individual in question, and taking a more conventional, if nonetheless earnest, approach when contacting those with whom he had only a passing acquaintance.

Valentin Stencek was somewhat forsaken by Lester in September and October. When Lester left for Ireland in early August 1947, it was done with the belief that the 'few matters of secondary importance' would only take a further two to three weeks to complete.[45] While Brunskog's absence from Geneva meant a delay to the final audit, it was still expected that the eight weeks of September and October would be straightforward, or at least relatively quiet. Stencek even hoped to spend the first twelve days of October on some much-earned leave, but the aforementioned collection of both mind-numbing and financial tasks prevented the realization of that wish, and Lester's absence did not help.[46] While Lester officially left the League's employ at the end of August, there was an expectation – at least on Stencek's part – that he would make himself available via correspondence to help complete the final few tasks of liquidation. However Stencek found Lester hard to pin down in September and early October, sending written updates on progress that often featured reminders noting that he had not yet heard from the secretary general on a number of issues. In an update letter to Lester at the end of September he wrote 'I have been waiting for some news from you', followed by another request for guidance just a few days later: 'I hope the letter has reached you as I am beginning to wonder why I have received no news from you since the beginning of September, although I have written to you on several occasions in the meantime.'[47] After years of keeping the League's sinking ship afloat, Lester had, in effect, mentally 'checked out' of the institution, choosing to mark his return to Ireland as a clean break from a challenging time in his life. There is no record in the League's Archives that he was involved in any liquidation matters after his departure – bar the instruction to extend Stencek and Welps's contracts – effectively leaving those in Geneva to manage the outstanding questions alone. Fortunately Stencek did not seem to mind too greatly, or at least not so much as to officially record any grievances. When he wrote to Lester on his last full day at the Palais in October, he did so with warmth and affection, thanking the secretary general for treating him as a 'trusted collaborator and friend' rather than a subordinate, and expressed a desire to keep in touch in the future. If he felt at all aggrieved by the lack of communication from Lester in the previous weeks, he hid it well.[48]

Instead it was Stencek, with support from both Welps and Boiteux, who was obliged to manage the remaining tasks. Their work in September and October was unexciting but also inescapable and served as a reminder of the realities of closing a complex organization like the League. It was not declarations at the twenty-first Assembly or Board pronouncements that dissolved the League, but the quiet labouring of officials. The Secretariat, once made up of a peak of 707 individuals in 1931, was down to just three souls by September 1947, and when Boiteux left at the end of that month, only Welps and Stencek remained.[49] Like the colleagues who departed during August, the two men's oft-extended contracts were finally allowed to expire and, with their departure on 25 October, the Secretariat was no more. With no employees, no bank accounts and its assets either liquidated or transferred to other bodies, the institution known as the League of Nations quietly ceased to exist.

The final 'final report': 31 January 1948

To outside eyes the League looked closed, and the Secretariat was no more, but the organization's business was not done. Stencek might have sent out the official thank you letters and closed the accounts, but work did not stop on 25 October 1947. Even if all the archival evidence to the contrary is ignored, the League itself contradicted its closure narrative when it issued a final official communication to members at the end of January 1948. The League's declarations of closure, dated either in August or October 1947, proved resilient over time; the official narrative put forth by the organization has been accepted at face value in the years since but it must now be recognized that this officially sanctioned version of events was provided by an unreliable narrator. In light of the organization's leadership tendency to alter the truth of liquidation in its formal reporting, it is perhaps not surprising that the supposedly authoritative end of the League was not quite the definitive full stop it appeared to be.

When Stencek sent his final liquidation update to Lester on 23 October, he noted that he would probably still come into the Palais des Nations to check on affairs, and his prediction proved correct.[50] Every day the sixty-three-year-old – the oldest member of the 1947 Secretariat cohort – travelled up the hill to the Ariana Estate and, even though Geneva was enjoying 'a beautiful autumn' – Stencek's own words – it could not have been an easy task to continue labouring on an experiment long since abandoned by almost everyone else. Nevertheless his commitment persisted, and in a November letter to Percy Watterson, Stencek noted that there was always something for him to manage: 'Although the Secretariat has been closed down since 25th October, I still come every day to the Palais des Nations as there is always some business to be attended to.'[51] Whether this was liaising with Watterson or dealing with the correspondence received from governments in response to the official closure, Stencek's work, despite him no longer being employed by the League, continued intermittently into 1948.

Just as the eyes of governments and diplomats turned towards New York and the UN in the autumn of 1946, one year later the majority of the League's ongoing business was also taking place on the western side of the Atlantic. Watterson, by then officially the League's trustee and liquidating agent, had been granted a small fund for his work expenses and was continuing the informal role he had played for the past year: the League of Nations' American liaison. Just as the League's financial affairs were being closed in Geneva, this small financial package – $7,359.81, including $5,000 of legal fees for Edwards & Smith, the firm handling the Income Tax lawsuit – meant a new bank account cropped up in the organization's name, albeit as part of the longer 'P. G. Watterson, Trustee and Liquidating Agent, League of Nations', at the Princeton Bank and Trust Company.[52] Despite the official story, the League of Nations still had financial assets in its name, and its business in North America continued with Watterson at the helm. The FAO official found himself dealing with a collection of small tasks in his new side role as the League's executor: using his newly minted funds to send EFO material from a former League official to the UN in Geneva, responding to more queries about the previously mentioned World's Fair tapestries and trying to locate the missing publications debts held by San Yo-Sha in Japan.[53] None of these tasks were particularly onerous or time-consuming, but like those that occupied Stencek and Welps in Geneva, they were inescapable.

One such example of these seemingly trivial but necessary tasks centred on an Internal Revenue refund of fewer than five US dollars. Bertil Renborg, the former head of the Drug Control Service who transferred to the UN in the autumn of 1946, received a letter in early October 1947 informing him that he had been over-assessed for the taxation year of 1942, issuing him a cheque for the grand total of $4.53. As the League of Nations had reimbursed its US-based officials for taxes paid during their time in Princeton or Washington, DC, this money technically belonged to the League, and thus Watterson had to advise Renborg to cash the cheque, forward the amount onto him, before remitting the less-than-opulent windfall back to Geneva.[54] It was hardly a serious issue, but this was the kind of problem that had to be resolved in order to close an organization like the League in a compliant fashion. It did not matter if a question arose as a result of external forces or internal ineffectiveness, it could not be ignored.

Watterson was not the only former League Secretariat official trying to wrap up the organization's business in the United States. Ansgar Rosenborg, although employed by the UN since the summer of 1946, was still trying to oversee the release of the EFO's final publication: *Europe's Population in the Interwar Years* by Dudley Kirk. Rosenborg had agreed to oversee the publication in 1946 because, as a former EFO official – which Watterson was not – he had a greater understanding of the text and the review process. Unfortunately it had taken significantly longer than expected to finalize the contents due to various delays and absences, but it was finally published by Princeton University Press, the EFO's publication partner during its time at the Institute for Advanced Studies, on 22 September 1947.[55] Five thousand copies of the publication were shipped from New Jersey as planned and only one, outwardly straightforward, task remained: paying the Princeton University Press bill, using what was left of the Rockefeller Grant.[56]

Unfortunately for Rosenborg it was not as simple as it seemed. When the bill arrived, it was much higher than expected – only $5,184 remained of the Rockefeller Grant but the invoice was for over $10,000 – and Rosenborg was pressed into a war of words with his long-time contact at Princeton University Press, Norvell B. Samuels.[57] Over several weeks in October 1947 the debate went back and forth, Rosenborg worried because he now had to find an additional $5,000 from somewhere – hopefully the UN – while Samuels was obliged to justify the invoice by explaining that the Press had already lowered the bill as a favour and had foregone any profit in order to reduce the total.[58] Rosenborg endeavoured to convince his UN superiors to pay the additional sum needed to settle the bill – the invoice coming too late to be paid by the League before Stencek's departure – but by the end of January 1948 the amount was still unpaid. Samuels continued to send reminders – 'As I have told you, Princeton University Press did not make any profit at all on this book … we feel that it is somewhat unfair to expect us to continue to carry this account' – but Rosenborg, both frustrated that the UN had not yet agreed to the expenditure and that he was still trying to deal with League of Nations problems over eighteen months after he left the Secretariat, had to wait while the UN prevaricated.[59]

Nevertheless the major issue holding up the League's business was the much-derided income tax lawsuit brought against the US Internal Revenue. Before the case was heard by the Tax Court, Watterson had to spend the late part of August 1947 writing to former League officials who had been based in the United States during the Second World War, asking them to sign an agreement confirming that, should the lawsuit be successful, they would hand over the proceeds of any windfall to the League.[60] This meant that these monies could be gathered by Watterson, and then distributed among the organization's former members in accordance with the same distribution scheme established for the liquidation of the League's assets.[61] Nevertheless, despite all the work put in place to situate Watterson as trustee and liquidating agent, the case was dismissed by the Tax Court on 9 October 1947, as predicted by League legal advisor Émile Giraud one year earlier.[62] John F. Dailey Jr., working for law firm Edwards & Smith on behalf of former official John Chapman, made a number of different arguments to the Court but the judges presiding explained that it was not their place to evaluate the wisdom of taxing people, but instead to interpret the laws of Congress, and that the petitioner's 'elaborate arguments' were 'ineffective'.[63]

The negative, if unsurprising, result did not however mean that the League's responsibilities in this regard were complete; instead of distributing a windfall to members, Watterson's first task was to update the interested parties including

Chapman and other former US-based officials.[64] Watterson also wrote to Stencek at his home address in Geneva in early November, explaining that he would organize the final payment to Edwards & Smith and detailing his actions up to that point to halt the New York lawyers' desire to appeal the decision.[65] Despite receiving explicit instruction from Seán Lester before his departure that no further action should be taken in the case of a negative outcome, Edwards & Smith wrote to Watterson explaining that, as trustee and liquidating agent, he could authorize the pursuit of a Special Act of Congress designed to cover the payment of such taxes.[66] Watterson was forced to write to them on two separate occasions in early November, confirming that absolutely no action should be taken in further pursuance of the case and that their business was over.[67]

Stencek, meanwhile, was not surprised by the result – 'I felt all along that it was rather a weak [case]' – and in his now informal and unpaid role as the League's Genevan representative, he instructed Watterson to compile a report for members, and send his expenses to Brunskog so the final accounts might be audited.[68] These were Watterson's last official tasks as trustee and liquidating agent – his custodianship was over – and while he acknowledged in November 1947 that compiling the documents might take a little time to finish, by the end of January 1948 he was ready.[69] Copies of the Court Judgement were sent to all thirty-four League member states – and the nine Board of Liquidation members – alongside a covering letter from Watterson explaining the case outcome, and his decision to close the final administrative account as a result.[70]

The League's tangible institutions had been dead for several months but the continuation of business into 1948 challenges the notion that the end of the organization's physical framework was also the conclusion of its story. Watterson's letter to members were the League's last words; after January 1948 the organization was never heard from again in an official capacity. Watterson had fulfilled his obligations and could finally look forward to focusing his energies elsewhere. However, forces beyond the control of the League's last stalwarts meant they were not allowed to rest easy just yet.

The un-ending: Spring 1948 and beyond

Trying to wrap up the League of Nations was a difficult task; liquidation on this scale had not been attempted before and both the organization's leaders and its Secretariat consistently bumped up against unknowable problems as a result. Nonetheless, precedent or previous experience would not necessarily have prepared the League's last officials for obstacles conjured up by the actions and interests of external parties. The Board of Liquidation had dissolved itself, the secretary general had retired to Ireland, the Secretariat closed down and the last communication to members had been sent; those final devotees acting on the organization's behalf, specifically Ansgar Rosenborg, Valentin Stencek and Percy Watterson, had completed all the tasks asked of them, but outside forces had other plans.

Predictably, as it was the last piece of League business to be concluded before the end of January, the dismissal of the income tax lawsuit brought further fallout not long after Watterson dispatched his final report to members. In the spring of 1947, the League's leadership assumed that any negative consequences to come from pursuing the case would be confined to a cost in terms of both Watterson's time and the legal fees, and the Board believed this risk was worth the possible reward.[71] What neither the Board nor the League's lawyers in the United States anticipated, however, was an entirely different downside to the case's dismissal. Watterson wrote to Stencek at the end of January 1948 to explain that 'a grave problem has arisen' as a result of the US Court's ruling against the League in the Chapman case. The outcome of the lawsuit had since led the Tax Commissioner in the United States to reclassify the League officials based in the country during the war, for the purposes of income tax, as 'resident aliens' for the years 1944, 1945 and 1946; they had previously been assessed as 'non-resident aliens' for the entire time. He only discovered this change in their – and his own – status after a chance meeting with Rosenborg in New York which, as the latter explained, meant these officials could expect to be called before the Commissioner and asked to pay additional amounts, depending on salary, to cover the changes. Rosenborg, Folke Hilgerdt and John Chapman had all already received calls to do so, and the rest of the group – eighteen individuals in total – could expect the same in the near future.[72] As Watterson explained to Stencek: 'It does seem rather hard on the Princeton and Washington ex-officials still in this country that through no fault of their own may possibly be held liable for taxes to the extent of hundreds of dollars with, in my case at least, no recourse to another organisation.'[73]

League officials did not pay income taxes in Switzerland, and the organization had refunded those individuals expected to pay similar levies during their time in the United States. With the League's liquid assets transferred to members in October 1947, there was no money to compensate these officials for the additional taxes they now had to pay, leaving former League employees out of pocket. Both Watterson and Stencek were at a loss as to what could be done for these officials; there were no funds available to reimburse them and in all likelihood there was no way to help. Watterson tried to procure advice from Seymour Jacklin, then the South African Government's representative at the UN, while he was visiting New York, but the former League treasurer and Board of Liquidation member was unable to help, leaving Stencek to contact both Lester and Hambro for guidance.[74] He referred to the situation as 'hopeless' in his letter to Lester, and Stencek hoped the two men would agree with his assessment that unfortunately for those ex-officials affected, there was nothing to be done, but neither man was forthcoming with a response.[75] When Hambro finally answered the query it was two months later, and the Board of Liquidation chairman suggested nothing in the way of advice or solution, or even approval of the decision to leave officials to pay the income tax bills alone. Instead he offered only two sentences: 'Many thanks for your letter of February 14th 1948 which brought us the final document concerning the tax difficulties. I am glad that you sent the document to me and I have communicated it to Sir Cecil Kisch.'[76] The Board of Liquidation, so full of pride in the organization and its ethos just six months earlier, had always been distant from the Secretariat's officials but these events reiterated that it, and Lester, had moved on, both literally and figuratively, from the League of Nations.

The League's Archives do not reveal what happened to those former officials asked to pay increased income taxes in the United States; with no indication that the organization refunded them we can assume they were left to settle the bills by themselves. The same sources and Lester's personal papers also show the secretary general never responded to Stencek's query regarding Watterson's 'grave problem', and indeed there is no evidence he ever wrote to him after his departure in August 1947. Stencek was not a man to complain, but there are small hints that he felt frustrated by his former colleague's lack of contact, at least on a personal level. There were the updates sent in September and October 1947, and in his letter explaining the fallout of the lawsuit, he noted his disappointment at the lack of the 'long letter you promised to send me'.[77] It is not entirely clear at what point Stencek stopped coming to the Palais every day to check on the League's affairs; Watterson always wrote to Stencek at his home address after October 1947 but the latter still used official League stationery to respond to correspondence as late as February 1948.[78] However, as the files in the League Archives become thinner from the end of 1947 onwards, so too did Stencek fade from events, and there was a sense that he felt adrift after a long career as a civil servant both in the Secretariat and as part of the Austro-Hungarian Government. In a letter to Lester in February 1948 he noted that he was enjoying his 'freedom' but that while he was trying to fill his time as best he could, 'so far nothing has turned up that would be of any interest to me'.[79] Stencek's time with the League was coming to an end – the number of weeks between each unexpected request for assistance became greater and greater – and while he was not yet ready for retirement, he was struggling to find his place in the post-war system.

Percy Watterson meanwhile found that the end of his responsibilities as the organization's trustee and liquidating agent was not the end of his work for the League. Separate from the lawsuit, the US Internal Revenue Service sent a query in mid-February 1948 to John Chapman – coincidentally the former EFO official in whose name the tax case had been filed – regarding shortfalls in his income tax for 1942, 1943 and 1944.[80] These shortfalls were paid by the League in 1946, but the Revenue Service had misplaced the corresponding cheque information, and Watterson, once again fulfilling his role as the clearing house for all the League's business in the United States, spent the next two months following up with both Chapman and the Princeton Bank and Trust to track down the missing information.[81] On a number of occasions, Watterson offered to reimburse Lilian Stout, of the Princeton Bank and Trust, for the time she spent pursuing the query, suggesting she take money directly from his League account: 'As stated in my letter of February 28, any expenses incurred in this connection may be charged to my account as Trustee and Liquidating Agent of the League of Nations.' What makes Watterson's proposal particularly surprising in relation to the League's many endings is that he made these offers – the last of which was dated 13 April 1948 – after he had supposedly concluded the organization's financial affairs at the end of January. There is no other evidence in the League's Archives to either support or contradict this irregularity, making it difficult to state with any certainty, but Watterson's repeated offer strongly suggests that the League continued to hold financial assets into the spring of 1948.[82]

Despite their efforts to close the League as quickly and orderly as possible, the rearguard of officials found themselves struggling over a long period of time to terminate the last trifling bits of organizational business. In New York, Rosenborg was starting to despair of his continuing League errands. He finally convinced the UN Publication Board to pay the outstanding Princeton University Press bill in mid-February 1948, but he was not safe from the unexpected ignorance of others.[83] When Columbia University Press wrote to the 'League of Nations' at Princeton in March and April 1948, asking the organization to settle an outstanding $1 bill, the details were initially passed on to Rosenborg in New York.[84] Adamant that his responsibilities had been solely confined to the publication of *Europe's Population*, Rosenborg referred the matter to

Watterson and, in his letter to the latter, he seemed both resentful at the nature of the query and almost relieved to be absolved of any responsibility towards it. He mockingly noted that the demand was for 'the formidable amount of $1.00' and told Watterson, while noting there was nothing to be done about the situation: 'But that is your headache, not mine.'[85] Even the ever-composed Watterson struggled to contain his disbelief in his response to the Columbia University Press, replying, 'I am somewhat surprised to learn that the Press is not aware that the League ceased operations in Princeton some eighteen months ago.'[86] The Board of Liquidation publicly declared the end of closure work at the end of July 1947, and yet Watterson and Rosenborg, over nine months later, were learning that even the most carefully controlled dissolutions were not immune to the obliviousness of other parties.

Not that the persistent issues affected only those based in the United States. Otto Jenny (Treasury) and Peter Welps (Internal Control), both working at the ILO following their departures from the League, were roped in to help with an outstanding staff removals query received months after they left. Agnes Driscoll, a former official of the Permanent Court of International Justice, wrote to Welps in February 1948, requesting his help in chasing down D. J. Bruinsma (head of Internal Services at the International Court of Justice) in regard to an ongoing query from July 1947. Driscoll wanted to know why an amount of money had been deducted from her removals compensation, but Bruinsma had not responded to her questions. Her letter was passed onto Jenny who, perhaps misunderstanding the nature of Driscoll's query, instead instructed her to contact Bruinsma directly. Whether Driscoll was ever able to resolve the issue is unknown, but there was clearly frustration on Jenny's part at the prospect of resolving problems that should have been laid to rest the previous summer, suggesting to Driscoll that she was at fault for raising the query even though the former PCIJ official specifically apologized for having to chase the matter in the first place.[87]

These persistent leftover issues were littered throughout the late winter and spring of 1948, but the summer of that year seemed to bring an end to the outstanding questions. However, in the true spirit of the organization's already drawn-out dissolution, a query arrived at the UN in September 1949 from an unlikely source. The Columbia University Press demand for $1 less than a year after the League's demise seemed petty, if understandable, but that same understanding could not be extended to the chief accountant of UNESCO. Writing to 'The Secretary' of the Board of Liquidation, an R. Adams explained that a recent audit had highlighted an unpaid bill for Cecil Kisch's 1947 Board of Liquidation travelling expenses. Although an unpaid invoice was an obvious inconvenience for an organization's accounting, it seems implausible that UNESCO was unaware the League closed two years earlier or that it thought it likely the bill would be settled.[88] The UN at Geneva, in receipt of the letter at the Palais des Nations, decided to consult Otto Jenny once again in his capacity as a former League Treasury official, and replying to Adams, a UN finance officer explained that even if the claim was in order, there was no way the bill could be settled and reminded them: 'The United Nations has no responsibility for League affairs.'[89]

These men were dedicated to the League – how else to explain their continued willingness to get involved – but it was difficult to move forward when they kept being pulled back into something they physically left behind months or even years earlier. The problems were not always difficult to resolve – some of them were very small – but those planning the organization's ending did not appreciate the possibility of complications arising after the leadership disbanded. Therefore, when these unanticipated queries cropped up again and again, the resolution of the problems fell to the Secretariat's last officials by default. Nevertheless it was also true that even if every eventuality had been prepared for, every risk mitigated against in some fashion, it was unlikely that the organization's dissolution could be fully controlled. As the events of 1948 showed, officials like Rosenborg and Watterson, Stencek and Jenny were only able to manage proceedings as much as their positions and power allowed; there was no way of predicting the interests and expectations of outside parties.

Institutional memory

There is a nebulous nature to the League of Nations; when talking about the organization it can be difficult, without an agreed definition or specifics, to know exactly what we are referring to. The organization was a forum for state governments, a collection of physical and monetary assets, the technical functions and activities it provided; the League was all of these things and more. This final section looks at one of these components – the organization as an international civil service – and demonstrates how the accumulated experience of the League's officials was, and still is, used by the secretariats that followed. The UN Library at Geneva today has an Institutional Memory Section, committed to coordinating and preserving what it calls the 'heritage of invaluable historical collections', a key part of which are the League of Nations

Archives.⁹⁰ The knowledge contained within these Archives, and that held by the League's Secretariat officials became an equally central part of the UN and its agencies in the mid- to late 1940s, and consequently this section demonstrates how this element of the League – arguably the most enduring – survived well beyond the more tangible facets of the organization.

Even before the foundation of the UN, during the Second World War, a number of groups outside the League of Nations started to recognize the value of, and attempted to record, the Secretariat's knowledge and experience of international civil service. In London a group of former officials – including the first secretary general Eric Drummond, Adriaan Pelt and Frank Walters – worked quietly under the auspices of Chatham House to record their memories of establishing and maintaining the first major civil service designed to support an IGO. Benjamin Auberer has looked in greater depth at the group and its motivations, but its work culminated in a fifty-page document known as the London Report which, it was hoped, would be of use to those planning whatever came next in intergovernmental cooperation.⁹¹

In a similar vein, the Carnegie Endowment for International Peace's Division of International Law was working on its own International Administration project, which manifested itself in a number of small conferences, two of which were devoted to capturing the experiences and knowledge of League Secretariat officials, both current and former. The two conferences – the Exploratory Conference on the Experience of the League of Nations Secretariat, held in August 1942, and the Conference on Experience in International Administration, held in Washington, DC in January 1943 – featured attendees such as Alexander Loveday, Arthur Salter and Arthur Sweetser and, like the work in London, were aimed at documenting the experience of these officials so it might be used to inform UN planning.⁹² George A. Finch, director of the Division of International Law, liked to bring attention to a Winston Churchill speech from February 1945 to echo why he and the Endowment were drawing upon a defunct organization: 'All the work that was done in the past, all the experience that has been gathered by the working of the League of Nations, will not be cast away.'⁹³ Under Finch's leadership, the Division of International Law used its conferences as a springboard from which to publish ten works under the banner Studies in the Administration of International Law and Organization, covering topics such as international tribunals, drug control and a survey of the economic and financial organization of the League. The most significant work in this collection, however, was Egon Ranshofen-Wertheimer's review of the League Secretariat's structure and procedures, *The International Secretariat: A*

Great Experiment in International Administration, which Wertheimer specifically hoped would be of value to those building future administrations. In his preface and introduction, he wrote 'The value of this study is unique', that it 'should be a valuable handbook for experts and officials', and that 'much of the contents of the volume has already been made privately available to officials and official agencies working upon problems of post-war reconstruction'.[94] Although many tried to publicly distance themselves from the League name at the time, in private it became apparent early on that the Carnegie Endowment and Chatham House were not alone in wanting to take advantage of the knowledge and proficiency of Secretariat officials.

The recruitment of League of Nations officials by the UN and its agencies in 1946 was covered in greater detail in Chapter 2 – as well as some of the problems associated with it – but it bears repeating that the League's leadership was largely pleased with, and even encouraged, the transfer of the unique knowledge belonging to its officials. Ranshofen-Wertheimer was an early hire for the new UN Secretariat – he previously left the League after he was stranded in London in the spring of 1940 – and his experience of the peculiarities of international civil service were quickly put to use preparing memorandums for his new employer on subjects such as the hiring of individuals who were not citizens of UN member states, and the practicality of transferring certain League functions and activities to the new organization.[95] Branko Lukac and Martin Hill, of the Communications and Transit Section and the EFO respectively, were both released early from their Secretariat contracts at the request of the UN.[96] By the summer of 1946 the UN clamour for League officials was so high that Lester sent a request for respite to Adriaan Pelt – himself a former member of the Secretariat since recruited by the UN – noting that the demand had reached the point where 'in one case there were actually two requests for the same official'.[97]

Although a significant number of League staff left to apply their experience at the UN, ILO and other agencies, the opportunities for officials still with the organization started to diminish during 1947. The new UN Secretariats were mostly at capacity by that time with many of their internal structures in place, and the collective knowledge of the League's procedures was no longer in demand as before. However, not every member of the Secretariat's rearguard was left behind; many of these men and women still went on to use their years of experience in new roles, ensuring the continuation of the League's memory. Figures such as Émile Giraud, the League's legal advisor, and Tevfik Erim, a member of the Political Section, were directly head-hunted by the UN in the autumn of 1946 and both moved to New York for their new roles.[98] The Treasury's

Otto Jenny was first offered a new position with the ILO in July 1946, the latter organization hoping he could start work in January of the next year noting: 'We are most anxious to secure the services of [Jenny] of whose work we have heard most highly from Jacklin and others.'[99] Lester however was aghast at the thought of losing his most senior Treasury official during liquidation – having already lost Jacklin in July 1946 – and begged Edward Phelan to second Jenny back to the League until the work was complete.[100] Fortunately for Lester, the director general agreed, and while Jenny officially joined the ILO in January 1947, he remained with the League on secondment for another eight months.

Ansgar Rosenborg had been part of the League of Nations for twenty-five years when he was transferred to the UN in the summer of 1946 as part of the EFO, where he later became a significant figure in that organization's Secretariat. He headed UN missions to Haiti and Indonesia in the 1940s and 1950s, became the secretary general's representative to Guinea in the latter of those two decades, before retiring in 1959 at the age of sixty-five.[101] Rosenborg's fellow Princeton colleague, Percy Watterson, was snapped up by the FAO in 1946, but the accountant's skills were also noticed by another of the new UN agencies in the same year. The Interim Commission of the World Health Organization recruited Watterson to establish the new organization's budgetary and accounting procedures – a service he was happy to provide – meaning that, in the late summer and early autumn of 1946, Watterson's experience was so in demand he was working for three international organizations at once: the League, the FAO and the WHO.[102]

Some of the leaders of the new secretariats were more explicit than others in their desire to take advantage of the existing international civil servants available to them. In 1982, as part of its oral history programme, the WHO recorded two interviews with Milton P. Siegel, director and later assistant director general of the organization's Division of Administration and Finance, and previously part of the Interim Commission to establish the new body.[103] Siegel had also been involved in establishing the UN Secretariat in New York and came to Geneva in 1947 to complete a similar task for the WHO. In his interview, he explained that he was a great believer in learning from that which had gone before: 'I had the attitude that instead of trying to reinvent the wheel, as they often say, maybe we can learn something from the predecessor organization which was called the League of Nations.' He also took the position that the best way to gather that knowledge would be to obtain it from those who had lived the experience, which led him to both Valentin Stencek and Chester Purves. The former was tasked with creating the WHO staff rules and regulations, while the former Board of

Liquidation secretary became the acting chief of the Conference and General Services Division, managing the Second World Health Assembly in Rome in the summer of 1949.[104]

Siegel freely acknowledged the benefits of recruiting those with experience of international administration – 'Had I not had the assistance of people such as those two [Stencek and Purves], I am confident I would have made the same errors as have been made by many other people, such as myself, in other organizations' – and that this was frequently down to recognizing what not to do, as much as it was about what they should.[105] Working as part of the WHO Secretariat proved to be the challenge Stencek was looking for, adrift after his time at the League was over. Footnotes to the Siegel interview transcript note that Stencek was chief of personnel from September 1948 to April 1949, but he also served, intermittently, as an administrative consultant in the Division of Administrative Management and Personnel, part of Siegel's Department of Administration and Finance, between 1954 and 1966. Some of these contracts lasted for as little as a few weeks while his final tenure continued for eight years, taking him up to 1966 and his retirement at the age of eighty-two.[106] The arrangement was a win–win situation for both Siegel and Stencek; the former gained invaluable insight into the successful administration of an international civil service, while Stencek successfully delayed his retirement by another twenty years.

Seán Lester however was much more interested in the quiet life than his former colleague. In May 1946, in a letter to his brother-in-law, Lester made it clear his only plans for the future centred on retirement to the new family home in County Wicklow in Ireland, 'about forty miles from Dublin … a moderate sized house with about fifty acres of land, though I have not the faintest idea what do with land', and he continued to stress his lack of ambition both in the past and in the future.[107] He turned down offers of ambassadorial roles for the Irish Government in New York, Brussels, Stockholm and Pretoria, not wanting to serve in big cities and expressing a preference to stay in Ireland if at all possible.[108] In a conversation with Freddy Boland, secretary of the Irish Department of External Affairs, in July 1947, both men admitted that Lester's history as secretary general of an IGO made it difficult to find an appropriate role for him in the Irish Foreign Service. In a memo recalling the conversation, Lester said: 'I am something of an anomaly' – an assessment Boland agreed with. Short of taking a role as an advisor to Trygve Lie or becoming a very senior member of one of the new international civil service branches, there was no obvious position in the post-war system for a former secretary general.[109] The only possible future Lester saw for himself beyond permanent retirement at the age of fifty-eight was in either special mission or committee work, but less than a year later he reaffirmed his commitment to his retired existence when he declined an offer from Lie to lead the UN Security Council Commission established to 'deal with the India-Pakistan question'. The post was well-paid and prestigious but, as Lester explained in his response, while he was greatly flattered by Lie's confidence in him, 'difficult and urgent personal affairs' made it impossible for him to accept the role. He did not expand on the 'personal affairs' at the time, although one of his daughters – it is unknown which – decided to elaborate further some unknown years later, annotating Lester's papers by underlining the phrase in pencil and writing 'His fishing!' next to it.[110] Lester's experience made him an invaluable source of wisdom and knowledge about the management of an international civil service, but as he and Freddy Boland correctly identified in the summer of 1947, his seniority made it almost impossible to find an appropriate position for him after he left the League. Unlike many of his former colleagues, Lester's contribution to the organization's institutional memory ended in 1947, but the international civil service to which he had belonged lived on in the knowledge and experience of those League officials who moved into the new post-war institutions.

Not every member of the Secretariat found themselves in high demand either before or after their departure from the Palais, but the esteem in which many individuals were held by the UN, the ILO, the WHO and others shows the value attributed to their knowledge, experience and the international civil service framework they helped to cement. The work of scholars such as Karen Gram-Skjoldager, Haakon Ikonomou and Bob Reinalda has already made great inroads into the evolution of international civil servants and secretariats across the twentieth century, and there is still more to be written about the transplantation of the League blueprint onto the organizations that succeeded it, but in an intangible fashion the League of Nations Secretariat survived. The knowledge and memory belonging to the League lived on long after the more palpable elements of the organization drifted away in 1947 and 1948, and will likely continue to do so into the foreseeable future.[111]

Conclusions

The League was more than just an institutional framework in which representatives from governments gathered to discuss and debate the issues of the day, and this was especially true after April 1946, the last time these governments came together. The League was, instead, the sum of a number of different parts; some of these elements were physical – the Palais des Nations, the many Assembly meetings – while others were more incorporeal, such as the collective knowledge held by officials, or the idea that intergovernmental cooperation was possible on a truly global scale. To try and pinpoint an absolute ending for the League is, therefore, an almost Sisyphean task; it is all too easy to become trapped in a loop, trying to decide which of the endings mentioned in this chapter is the correct one, never reaching a satisfying conclusion.

In reality, all of the end points discussed in this chapter are legitimate. The end of August 1947 was the culmination of the Board of Liquidation's commitment to the institution and thus the end of the League's strategic decision-making. The organization's leadership was steadfast in its belief that the end of its work was the end of the League of Nations as a whole and, as the body was invested with the power of the Assembly, its authority on the subject cannot easily be dismissed. The League was legitimized and given life by its membership, and if the Board of Liquidation, acting on their behalf, announced the liquidation was over, this declaration carried weight. Nevertheless, examination of the evidence shows that the Board was wrong to assume that its existence was the lynchpin by which the League's survival should be judged; its high-level guidance and decision-making was only one part of what remained of the organization. And, of course, it is well established that the Board of Liquidation had a vested interest in portraying the League's dissolution work as complete earlier than it actually was. Chapter 4 demonstrated the body's focus on its own reputation, how its efforts would be perceived by members and the willingness of the group to obfuscate the reality of liquidation in an attempt to build a positive, long-lasting legacy for itself and the organization. August 1947 saw the end of the Board of Liquidation, and consequently the end of the League of Nations' formal leadership, but many other elements of the organization continued.

There is a more compelling argument to be made for 25 October 1947 as the most meaningful ending of the League of Nations. This date saw the last remaining structure of the organization dismantled – the Secretariat – as well as the completion of the majority of the League's outstanding work. After this point, the League of Nations had no physical home, no employees and no assets beyond a pot of just over $7,000 sitting in a bank account in New Jersey, United States. It was also the point at which Valentin Stencek, a more reliable narrator perhaps than figures within the League's leadership, announced the end of the organization that had been his home for over twenty-five years. Looking at the League of Nations as a purely bureaucratic administration as perhaps envisaged by Max Weber, the end of October 1947, with the closure of the last vestiges of the institutional structures and systems, was as close to a definitive end as might be possible.[112] Yet in spite of this it was not the end of all things; significant work was still to be completed, money remained in a bank account with the League's name attached to it and the organization's liquidating agent was only just starting to fulfil his obligations. If Percy Watterson was still in the midst of managing the League's last financial matters, the institution's narrative was not yet complete.

Moving into 1948 the League's responsibilities and work persisted even as its institutional structures evaporated. The end of January of that year marked the organization's last official contact with its membership, and the lawsuit against the US Internal Revenue service – the only reason Watterson was appointed liquidating agent – was seemingly settled, but as this chapter has shown, closure was not a process that could be fully controlled. Stencek continued to intermittently manage outstanding questions, Ansgar Rosenborg was trying to remove himself from the last vestiges of a publication originally scheduled for release at least a year earlier and the end of Watterson's official responsibilities did not mean he could ignore his unending collection of informal tasks. Despite these men's best efforts to draw a metaphorical line in the sand, there was no foolproof way to close the book on the League of Nations; while they might have been finished with the organization, that did not mean external forces felt the same way.

The closing months of the tangible League were haunted by a sense of death by a thousand cuts, slowly disappearing into the ether until only the incorporeal memory of the organization remained. The last tasks of liquidation took longer than anyone anticipated – brought on by both a lack of experience and the unforeseeable actions of others – and when the leadership moved on, both physically and mentally, the tedious but necessary winding-up fell on the shoulders of those left behind. The story of their commitment to the League is bittersweet in many ways; as the last remnants of a twenty-eight-year experiment, they watched the organization crumble into dust alone, with no one to commiserate with or to appreciate their work. It is unclear if these individuals believed their efforts were worth it, or if they even cared to that extent, but their experiences reveal a collection of endings that were, more often than not, both lonely and unspectacular. However, as has been established, the death of the League's more tangible components was not a mortal blow to every aspect of the organization; its knowledge and memory endured in its officials as they moved on to newer and greener pastures in the global institutions still at the centre of our world today.

Trying to reconcile the organization's diverse and many endings into one faultless and unassailable closure story, while accounting for the argument that one portion of the League of Nations never ended at all, may not be feasible. However, the inability to do so is not to the detriment, but to the benefit of our understanding of the organization and its end. It might be possible to force a definitive finale on the League of Nations but doing so would be a simplification of what we have learnt about the organization at the end of 1947 and into 1948. The process of coercing the narrative into a tidy denouement would compel us to apply our own definition of ending on an organization that struggled to do so itself; any conclusions drawn in the process could never be truly objective and would only exist to make us, as scholars, feel more satisfied with the endeavour. Perhaps the real error is to think of the League of Nations as a story, implying that the organization had a fiction-like beginning, middle and end – and satiate our human instinct to impose order on chaos – when the reality was much more complex.

The League of Nations' closure came about as a collection of endings: some small and some more significant. Accepting this, and resisting the urge to simplify the process, forces us to re-think our assumptions about the closure of international organizations. Combined with what has already been revealed about the League's relationship to the UN and its agencies, this only reinforces the idea that the League of Nations and likely other IGOs do not snap out of existence but instead blur and merge into what follows.

Conclusions

Since its closure in 1947–8, the final months and years of the League of Nations have often been relegated to the back page of the organization's history or ignored entirely. The result of this neglect is both a conscious and unconscious consensus that this time, a transformative period in the League's story, was without either note or scholarly merit. Through its analysis of the organization after its public funeral, this book has, step by step, dismantled this misconception, revealing a two-year period dominated by activity that was compelled by outside forces, changing power dynamics and an inability to appreciate the enormity of the task. This is alongside stories of extraordinary personal commitment, the previously unexplored obfuscation of the links between the League and the UN, and a behind-the-scenes willingness to recognize the organization's value as a trial run for the international system still in place today.

Many of the beliefs held about the League of Nations, and especially its closure, are either misguided or outright false. Publicly the organization was a maligned endeavour but privately there were many in the post-war world who not only appreciated what had come before but actively drew upon both its ideas and its assets. The League's commitment to structures and established propriety, ingrained in the organization from its inception, failed both staff and leadership in 1946 and 1947 as it became apparent the framework for closure was not fit for purpose. Instead, the closure period was full of contradictions and self-defeating undertakings. Time-wasting negotiations with the ILO, and the ill-conceived and costly entertainment of a tax lawsuit in the United States were both justified by the pursuit of the moral high ground, but at the cost of efficient liquidation. Strategic decisions were made on the basis of long-standing, but no longer relevant, priorities and ways of thinking, without pausing to consider the most appropriate means of addressing the issues at hand.

The leadership structure introduced to dismantle the League was both poorly defined and ill-equipped to manage a complex liquidation, leaving the

Secretariat frustrated by a lack of progress and without much-needed direction. The increasingly small number of officials left at the Palais des Nations also struggled with a lack of resources, a Board of Liquidation overly apprehensive about its reputation, as well as becoming tenants in the palatial complex built in their name. Scrutinizing the closure process has also highlighted the League's continued efforts to control and manipulate the ways in which the organization would be appraised and thought about in the future and, interestingly, how its endeavours to protect the institution's Archives have helped facilitate this and other research into the League.

These final thoughts are designed to break down these findings and elaborate on what they mean for our understanding of this one-of-a-kind experiment. Firstly, looking at the framework put in place to close the organization, these conclusions reveal how a timetable directed by UN and ILO deadlines forced the League into a reactive approach to its dissolution, and how this combined with the unknowable task of liquidation to extend the process far beyond the anticipated endpoint. Secondly it looks at the experience of closure from the perspective of those carrying it out, and how these relatable individuals demonstrated an entirely unconventional commitment to the organization and to each other. Finally, attention turns to the UN and the other IGOs that followed in the League's wake, reinserting the post-First World War institution back into the story of International Organization in the twentieth century, and revealing that the lines separating the League of Nations from its successor organizations are even more blurred than previously thought.

Planning, presentism and precedent

The closure of the League of Nations was a by-product of the Allies' decision, made in the course of the Second World War, to create a new institution for the post-war world. The League's fate was not a foregone conclusion before this – the organization and its functions could easily have been reinvigorated had governments chosen to do so – but the desire for a fresh start, free from any association with the circumstances that led to another global war just twenty years after the last, was a powerful incentive. The League's closure, however, took much longer than anyone originally anticipated – full dissolution was expected no later than the end of 1946 – and an examination of the process has not only detailed what happened in the two years following the final Assembly but also shown how and why an organization known for its bureaucratic efficiency could stumble when managing its own demise. Neither the League's leadership nor its Secretariat were well-prepared for closure, either before the process began or during. Key elements that might have made proceedings more manageable were not in place, or even necessarily discussed. There was no agreement of overall objectives or what liquidation 'looked like', the absence of which made it almost impossible to break the process down into manageable pieces and left the enormity of the undertaking to loom over proceedings. It was also unclear what level of autonomy the Secretariat had to make decisions independently of the Board of Liquidation, leaving officials frequently frustrated by a lack of momentum while they had to wait for correspondence from figures like Carl Hambro, or for the group to meet in person, the latter of which sometimes took months.

However a lack of preparation and inadequate planning does not mean that the League's officials were incompetent or idle; these individuals had proved themselves more than capable and their diligence was not in doubt. The vast majority of those still working for the Secretariat and as part of the Board of Liquidation had been part of the League's machinery during the Second World War, risking their safety and ensuring the organization's survival through its darkest days. What derailed the organization's liquidation was not ineptitude or an absence of motivation, instead it came about as a result of a lack of focus and direction caused by three things: the reactive approach the League took in order to meet the demands stemming from the rapid construction of the UN, the priorities of these new institutions and the unknowable problems that came with a truly unique challenge.

The months preceding the twenty-first Assembly in April 1946 were plagued by confusion while the League's leadership remained in the dark about the establishment of the UN and the new organization's plans for the League's assets, activities and people. This information was essential to understanding what work lay ahead for Lester and his officials, and while handover to the new bodies was not the only task that needed to be accomplished during closure, the organization's leadership rightly predicted that it would be the most pressing. While the new UN was busy establishing itself, as frustrating as it was, there was not much the League could practically do to remedy the situation. The organization simply did not have sufficient knowledge to plan for closure in a proactive way, and instead found itself stuck in a reactive cycle, waiting for information followed by a rush to keep up with events beyond its control.

The League's leadership originally considered holding two Assemblies before dissolving – one in the autumn of 1945 to agree a budget for 1946 and review wartime work, and another in the spring of 1946 after the UN General Assembly, to eulogize the organization and formally close its doors.[1] In an ideal world, this latter Assembly would have had a greater focus on closure and planning, but holding two Assemblies within a six-month period, straddling an even larger UN General Assembly, was simply not feasible. Consequently, with only one Assembly to cover a wide range of business, it is unsurprising that there was little time available to seriously consider a framework for closure or what might be involved in achieving it. The so-called Dissolution Resolution was drawn up by senior figures in the League, alongside input from the British Government, and while the text was obviously focused on closure, it was never meant to be a detailed guide to this unknown process. It provided high-level principles, including the creation of a Board of Liquidation and agreed quarterly reports to members, but its main purpose was to provide the Assembly with an official and legally binding means of announcing the organization's demise.[2] The speed at which the Resolution was composed – the final draft for discussion at the Assembly was still under review just two days before proceedings began – meant there was neither the time nor the inclination to expand the text.[3] If anything, Seán Lester was wary of placing constraints on what he rightly anticipated would be an administration-heavy process. Liaising with Hugh McKinnon-Wood in February 1946 he wrote:

> I am not sure if it necessary or desirable to have detailed directions given to the Administration on this and other administrative questions; there are enough complications and restrictions and pressure without adding to the stranglehold on the representative officers who must be counted upon to take all the necessary steps to carry out any decisions in the quickest and best way.[4]

He was, however, needlessly concerned that tying the Secretariat into a formalized structure for liquidation would only elongate the process. The note that 'liquidation should be effected as rapidly as possible' was the only specific guidance written into the Resolution and it was not enough.[5]

The presentism that left the League's leadership with minimal time in the early part of 1946 to focus on either what they wanted to achieve from liquidation or establishing how they would achieve it became a recurring problem throughout the closure period. The opportunity to think either strategically or long term about the dissolution process was a luxury the League of Nations could not afford in 1946–7. The immediate post-Assembly months were tumultuous as the UN hurriedly established its own Secretariat and the League rushed to meet its needs, and closure issues remained on hold during the autumn while the more pressing General Assembly in New York took precedence. The League plummeted down the list of priorities for the international community, and the UN now came first for both resources and attention. If the UN needed something, the League had no choice but to comply – its membership made that clear at the final Assembly – and this happened again and again while the new secretariats fell into place during 1946. International power dynamics irrevocably changed with the creation of the UN. As a result, it was not until 1947 that the League's leadership really had the opportunity to get to grips with the full scope of closure and its many complexities, resulting in thirty-two Board meetings in fewer than six months as it became clear that some issues, like the Pensions Funds or the removal of staff furniture, could not be resolved as quickly as imagined.

While the inability to be proactive about liquidation had a significant impact on the League's ability to deliver it, there was another element to blame for the problems with planning: no one had ever done this before. While the League had some experience of attempting the unknown, dismantling the various structures of the organization – including its international civil service – was a challenge unlike any other. There was no guidebook or precedent to draw from, meaning the League's leadership had little more than a blank page from which to start. The organization had, in its most recent past, proved both resilient and able to adjust to changing circumstances, surviving the war with most of its technical functions intact and ready for handover to the new organizations. However, the ability to adapt was not enough to anticipate the inherent issues with, or to prepare for, liquidation. There was a consistent underestimation of the complexity of closure throughout the process, whether it manifested itself in believing the absence of the Board of Liquidation in the latter half of 1946 would not be a problem, or failing to appreciate the League's diminished position in negotiations with the ILO. The decision-making framework put in place by the twenty-first Assembly was frequently insufficient to manage the challenges of liquidation, but it is important to remember that this approach – one overarching strategic group sitting in lieu of the Assembly – had worked relatively well during the war; the League's leadership simply did not appreciate that closure was an entirely different test that would require a new approach.

These two problems – the lack of precedent and being forced to act reactively rather than proactively – fed each other throughout dissolution, resulting in an inversely chaotic yet slow liquidation process. In many ways, facing these two problems combined meant the League was doomed in its efforts before it began and that it delivered liquidation as fully as it did was testament to the later determination of those involved to see the process through to its conclusion. The initially limited understanding of the challenge that lay ahead meant officials and decision-makers were less concerned about their inability to be proactive, yet the lack of time to sit back and think strategically about the closure process meant they never truly understood the scope of the challenge until much later. Understanding that there was a quandary at the heart of the organization's closure reveals why the dissolution unfolded in the way that it did, and emphasizes the League's position as a great experiment in not just intergovernmental cooperation but also liquidation.

People and experience

As important as structural elements were in the closure of the League, a key part of this research into the process has looked beyond the institutional aspects of the organization to also think about the individuals who worked there during the dissolution and their involvement in it. This increasingly small group of officials were pioneers in unknown territory, and their experiences bring a personal and distinctive viewpoint on what might otherwise seem a dispassionate or clinical set of events, especially considering the Secretariat and the Board of Liquidation were the only elements of the organization left by 1946.

A more actor-focused approach has revealed circumstances and individuals both ordinary and extraordinary in nature. In many ways their stories would seem deeply familiar to anyone who has shared a workplace with colleagues over a number of years. They shared rivalries and frustrations with one another – Włodzimierz Moderow and Seán Lester, for example – but at other times their affection and concern for their fellow officials shone through. They frequently inquired after each other's health and families, Lester wrote to the new international organizations trying to find roles for staff, while Valentin Stencek referred to Lester as a man 'to whom I could turn in all my troubles for advice and help'.[6] They worked in offices, took sick days when needed and complained about the Geneva weather in correspondence, yet their familiarity to us is countered by their extraordinary choices and accomplishments.[7] They chose to work for an organization unlike any other before it – usually leaving their home countries to do so – and the majority of those left in Geneva in 1946 and 1947 had made it their life's work. They chose to stay in Switzerland during a world war, and again chose to stay when the League was publicly criticized and effectively sentenced to death by the Allies' choice to create a new institution. Their long-term loyalty to the League of Nations and their first-hand experience of the closure process have been recurring themes in this research, and as a consequence their perspectives do not just shed light on the end of a political experiment, but also the social history of the institution.

One of the most glaring omissions from histories of both the League and of its closure has been the relegation of Seán Lester to a concluding paragraph or footnote. The secretary general's exclusion from the organization's story has preserved the scholarly inference that both he and the League's final years are not worthy of interest or of value to history, despite the fact he oversaw one of the League's most tumultuous periods and held the position for seven years, as long as his predecessor Joseph Avenol. He inarguably faced a challenging task in dissolving the League, especially with a lack of both real-world experience to draw upon and agreement as to what he was responsible for. The secretary general was critical in keeping the League together during the Second World War, and the close working relationships he forged in those years were just as important during liquidation. His links with Carl Hambro and Cecil Kisch meant lines of communication with the Board were always kept open, even if they were never clearly defined, and his established connection with Adriaan Pelt and burgeoning friendship with Trygve Lie meant UN–League relations remained gracious during the transfer turmoil of 1946. Even his difficult relationship with Moderow, which resulted in unnecessary hurdles in the early days of League and UN co-existence at the Palais, thawed with time.[8] Lester also nurtured close and productive working relationships with Secretariat officials like Valentin Stencek and Chester Purves, both of whom had major roles to play in liquidation, and he advocated on behalf of the whole Secretariat when he appealed to the UN and its agencies regarding future job opportunities.[9] Lester wrote of his moral duty to lead the League in the wake of the Avenol crisis in the summer of 1940, and he felt the same responsibility to see liquidation carried out to the best of his ability for the sake of members, staff and the future success of the UN.[10]

Lester was a relative newcomer to the organization in comparison to some of his colleagues, and his career was varied before becoming League High Commissioner to Danzig. He had a fruitful family life away from work, and throughout the liquidation there was a clear sense that he had a very real desire to move on from the League.[11] Lester made it continually clear that he had never aspired to the position of secretary general, and his seven-year tenure in the role was perpetually fraught with problems. If anything, the trials of closing an IGO weighed heavily on Lester – especially the unpredictable nature of an unstructured liquidation – and his enthusiasm for the organization waned towards the end. His eagerness to leave Geneva behind meant he readily jumped at the chance to travel to New York in the autumn of 1946, and while he continued to work on liquidation from the other side of the Atlantic, he also relished the opportunity to liaise with the UN Secretariat on its establishment. This was his chance to work on something both new and exciting that was a million miles away from the dreary day-to-day attempts to close a defamed IGO. His absence – alongside that of half of the Board of Liquidation – proved an obstacle to progress in later 1946, and while his decision to travel to the United States was made with the intention of maintaining close contact with Hambro, Kisch and others, he expressed no regret, either publicly or in his personal papers, for leaving Geneva behind. He also physically moved on in August 1947, leaving what was left of the Secretariat to fend for itself before liquidation had been fully realized and, once gone, he did not look back. The leadership and recourse to a higher authority that a secretary general might well have been expected to provide was missing from the Secretariat after the summer of 1947, leaving the League's final acts, entirely unofficially, in the hands of a few officials.

Valentin Stencek, one of these last stalwarts, had a very different experience of liquidation from his immediate superior. He was a bureaucrat rather than a diplomat, having worked as part of the Austro-Hungarian – and then Czechoslovakian – Civil Service, before joining the League in 1921, and took great pride in his formal and principled approach to work. He was a backstage player – like many others left in the Secretariat in 1946–7 he was accustomed to working behind-the-scenes – but this aspect of his nature did not mean he was anything less than dedicated to the organization. He had worked quietly but diligently throughout his League career and the closure period only highlighted the value of his steadfast reliability. When other members of the League's leadership were absent, both during the latter half of 1946 and from the summer of 1947, he could be trusted to take the reins and ensure the organization's interests were looked after, even after he left the Secretariat's employ. In truth, unlike Lester, his personal circumstances left him little to focus on besides the League and his commitment to international civil service by the mid-1940s. He was almost five years older than the secretary general, his children were by then in their twenties and established in their adulthood, his much-loved wife Emily passed away in 1944 and he had no intention of returning to a Silesia that bore little resemblance to the place he left before the First World War.[12] He also had no interest in retiring, despite turning sixty-three in 1947, continuing to look for work following his departure from the League, and eventually finding it at the World Health Organization where he worked intermittently in a consultancy role until he finally retired at the age of eighty-two.

Percy Watterson, despite officially leaving the League's employ in the autumn of 1946, held a similarly trusted place in the Secretariat. Like Stencek he did not have a showy role – he was chief accountant within the Treasury – but he was one of the longest-serving officials, having joined in July 1919 at the age of thirty-one, and demonstrated a similar dedication to the League as his colleague. He crossed Vichy France in the summer of 1940 to travel to Princeton and become the Secretariat's Treasury agent in the United States and, following the transfer of the EFO to the UN in July 1946, Watterson became, by default, the League's primary – and sole – representative in North America. It was not a position he sought out – it was not even an official position until the middle of 1947 when he became the organization's trustee and liquidating agent – and Watterson was not well-compensated for his time, but he felt a responsibility to take on the role regardless and, with the assistance of Stencek, oversaw the last nine months of League activity.[13] When former officials faced an unexpected tax bill in the United States in the spring of 1948, the League's leaders were nowhere to be found; instead it was figures like Stencek and Watterson who tried to find an acceptable solution. However, unlike both Stencek and Lester, who both struggled to immediately find appropriate post-League roles, Watterson found himself in demand from the new international organizations both before and after his departure from the Secretariat. He was recruited to draw up the Draft Financial Regulations for the WHO in the summer of 1946, joined the Food and Agriculture Organization a few weeks later, all while continuing to work for the League in a part-time, and then a side-role, capacity.

He was not the only one looking to continue their work supporting the League's brand of internationalism. Most of the organization's last officials – Lester being one of the exceptions – chose to stay in the international civil services, either moving to the UN (Ansgar Rosenborg, Cosette Nonin and Émile Giraud), the ILO (Otto Jenny and Peter Welps), the FAO (Henri Vilatte and Watterson), or the WHO (Raymond Gautier and Chester Purves). Even those who were not initially able to find work in the new organizations, like Stencek, chose to stay in Geneva because the city, and its international community, had become their home. Connie Harris, having lived in the city for over twenty-five years by the mid-1940s, also stayed in Switzerland despite not being able to find a position in one of the new secretariats that was commensurate with her rise through the ranks at the League, not returning to England until the 1970s when she retired.[14] Those individuals who stayed with the organization until the bitter end were exceptionally dedicated to the League and the internationalism on which it was founded. They were not always rewarded for this loyalty – either in terms of financial recompense or in being unable to find adequate positions following their departure – but their commitment to the League and to one another explains how the liquidation of the organization, despite taking longer than expected, was completed as fully as it was. While the Board of Liquidation and Lester took their leave of the process in the summer of 1947, it was figures like Stencek, Watterson, Peter Welps and Otto Jenny – the last of the Secretariat's rear guard – who ensured the organization's final tasks were completed.

What came next

While the League quietly died in 1946–8, much of what it created lived on – and continues to do so – in the international system that followed. Scrutinizing the end of the League of Nations rightly reinserts those transformative months back into the narratives of twentieth-century history, international relations and of those IGOs we take for granted today. This reinsertion is not about picking a side in the interminable success or failure debate that often envelopes studies of the League, but rather pointing out that it did not disappear without a trace into the ether, and instead demonstrating that many remnants of the organization – and lessons learnt from its experience – found their way into the UN and its agencies. The League of Nations was a great experiment in the field of international organization, and whether or not one believes that experiment was a success, the results of that trial run were taken onboard by what followed in its wake.[15]

The decision to build a new IGO in the aftermath of the Second World War was predicated on the idea that it would be nothing like the 'failed' League of Nations. The founders of the UN wanted to distance the new organization from what had come before – an understandable endeavour necessitated by a fragile new world order. If the UN was to succeed, it needed the faith and trust of its members; the League's efforts to manage the antagonistic political environment of the 1930s were proof of how crucial member support was for an IGO's survival. Any authority they had was imbued in them by their membership and without the backing of governments, both financially and politically, these organizations offered only empty platitudes. The efforts in the mid-1940s to distance the UN from the League were perhaps therefore warranted, but more recent scholarship continues to perpetuate this myth, in part because the extent of the entwining of the League and the UN in 1946–7 has, until now, been unappreciated.

The outward attempts to distance the new international system from the League of Nations were often quite different behind the scenes, as a number of those in charge of establishing the new secretariats were much more willing to draw upon the lessons learnt during the organization's quarter of a century of experience. While the UN and its associated institutions needed to be seen to create something new to take advantage of post-war reconstruction enthusiasm and to inspire confidence, away from the spotlight they were free, and eager, to take advantage of the League of Nations' many assets. The long-term impact of the League on international governance has yet to be comprehensively explored but, even in the short term, the UN and other IGOs were privately willing to take note of its lessons. As Milton Siegel explained when describing his work establishing the WHO Secretariat, the League experiment provided invaluable guidance as to both the right and wrong way to build an international civil service:

> I tried to obtain, tried to identify people who had had previous experience in the League of Nations so that we would be able to benefit from their experience in the League, and maybe we would learn more about what not to do and would help us identify what we should do.[16]

Far from every element of the UN and its associated agencies began life in the League – the UN is significantly broader in remit, membership and budget – but examining how much of the League was handed over to the UN yields surprising results. Almost every element that remained of the League in the mid-1940s ultimately became part of the UN. The organization's physical assets, from major structures such as the Palais des Nations, the rest of the Ariana Estate and the League Archives, to paintings, office equipment and vacuum cleaners, were all transferred wholesale to the new organization. As highlighted in the last chapter, many of the League officials still with the organization in 1946-7 were headhunted by the UN, WHO, ILO and others for their unique skills and experience in an effort to establish and strengthen the new institutions. Technical activities and services provided to governments around the world, including the various drug control bodies, the EFO, and the Weekly Epidemiological Record – as well as the people supporting them – were transferred over to new management but otherwise stayed intact. Numerous financial assets covering pensions, renovations and publications all became part of the UN bubble, including the troublesome Staff Pensions Funds. Even the League's final liquid assets – money sat in bank accounts in various countries and officially owned by the League's members – were indirectly transferred to the new organization in the form of credits for those also part of the UN. The only financial assets remitted directly, in cash, to League members were those belonging to Finland, Ireland, Switzerland and Portugal, who were not yet part of the new organization. Only a handful of funds and some destitute functions, such as the Forstall Fund and the Nansen Office, were genuinely liquidated or transferred to non-UN institutions.[17]

Not only are the lines separating the League and the UN blurred by the transfer of a significant portion of the former into the latter, but the two organizations lived, quite literally, side-by-side for over a year. Traditionally the institutions are portrayed as siloed bodies, with the UN rising out of the League's ashes, suggesting the post-First World War organization was long dead by the time the new IGO arrived. This is another fallacy, especially in the halls of the Palais des Nations in 1946 and 1947, where both organizations shared expertise and resources. This does not just change the way scholars might think about both the liquidation of the League and the creation of the UN, but also more widely about the lifecycles of IGOs and how they are written about in the academic field of international organization. The League's example not only counters the misconception that international organizations do not die, contrary to the position of some international relations scholars, but it also checks the impulse to portray these institutions as neatly delineated from one another.[18] The League and the UN both had an impact on the other's dissolution and foundation respectively, whether through the delays to League planning and the handover of physical and liquid assets to the new organizations, or via the UN headhunting of Secretariat officials. The League bled into the UN and its agencies and vice versa, demonstrating that organizations like this are not always the fully independent bodies they are consistently portrayed as. This blurring of one institution's end and another's beginning challenges the assumptions we hold about these transformative periods in the histories of the League and the UN and asks us to reconsider the nature of the relationships between IGOs.

The institutions created in the wake of the Second World War were not the only bodies thinking long term in 1946 and 1947; the Board of Liquidation, charged with dissolving the organization as quickly as possible, spent a significant portion of its time creating a foundation on which a positive and long-lasting legacy for the League might be built. The organization's emphasis on public relations and the power of narrative was ingrained in the League Secretariat and leadership from its earliest days, and this way of thinking remained a part of the institution even after its fate was sealed. The League of Nations Museum, still managed by the UN as part of the Palais des Nations, began its life as a means of presenting a curated image of the organization and was designed as a rebuttal to a world that had refocused on post-war opportunities. The preservation of the League's Archives and the guarantee of access to them were prioritized by the Board of Liquidation in the hope that, in the future, research like this would lead to a reassessment of the organization's achievements and the restoration of its reputation. Some of the Board's endeavours were more cynical than others – the crafting of its Final Report to members was an exercise in presenting a very particular version of events – but much of the League's memory did not materialize naturally but was instead meticulously planned.

As a final note, it should be pointed out that one major lesson of the League's experience has been ignored by both the organizations that sprang up in the wake of the Second World War and those that have followed since: the problems of closing an IGO. This has stemmed, in part, from the lack of awareness surrounding the League's closure, but it is also the result of these new institutions being compelled to work reactively, the same issue that plagued the Secretariat in 1946. This need or choice to focus only on the most pressing issues remains as much of a problem today as it was when the League was undergoing liquidation, and the perils of closing an IGO without adequate thought or preparation have not been given their due. Major organizations including the UN and agencies such as the World Health Organization and the ILO, as well as newer bodies like the European Union and NATO, have all chosen to omit closure provisions from their institutional charters or treaties. Perhaps the founders and current leaders of these organizations believe they have found the magic formula for an immortal IGO that, unlike the League, will never have to think about its own demise, but it is more likely that the modus operandi of reactive thinking has left closure as a question for another day. Long-term thinking is often the first casualty of pressurized schedules, and it is understandable that IGOs – or any organization – are typically focused on the most vital questions. Designing a liquidation process does not qualify as a critical issue; there is little obvious incentive to take time away from urgent problems in order to plan for a theoretical closure that may never take place. Nevertheless, the League's dissolution ought to be a warning to any international organization convinced of its own immortality: not only is it possible for these institutions to die, but preparing for an unlikely demise may save much time and effort should it come to pass. The League of Nations was not fortunate enough to have a forerunner's experience to look to for guidance during its liquidation, but its own struggles with the process have left a precedent from which others might draw in future.

Final conclusions

The League of Nations was an organization of firsts, and its end was no different. It was the first multi-member, multi-remit international organization to live, and it was the first to die. Considering the scope of the institution, its assets, its membership and its connections, it is not at all surprising that the prospect of dismantling it was a daunting one, and the reality of the situation in 1945–8 only made the job even harder. The end of the League was in many ways a victim of both presentism and precedent. Its leaders did not know what the closure of the organization meant in practical terms; they had a broad outline in their minds but no time to expand on it or determine how to make it happen. As a consequence, the Secretariat's usual flair for all things efficient and bureaucratic had to be put aside for an approach that was more instinctual and freewheeling, that ultimately dragged on for much longer than imagined.

The foundation of a new international system, agreed in 1945, not only cemented the end of the League but also dictated what could happen and when, as fresh deadlines took precedence over the old organization's liquidation. For twenty-five years the League of Nations had effectively been at the top of the pecking order when it came to the priorities and power in international cooperation; the creation of the UN quickly reversed that, catapulting the League to the bottommost position. Languishing in its new situation, the organization – having publicly pronounced its death at the final Assembly in April 1946 – found it difficult to raise much in the way of interest or concern from anyone outside its immediate sphere of influence. Reports of the League's demise in the press passed without significant comment from the public, and not even members had much to say beyond perfunctory acknowledgements upon receipt of the Board of Liquidation's Final Report. The new UN bodies cared about the transfer of assets, activities and knowledge, but their interest did not extend to the closure as a process or to elements of the organization beyond their remit. These new institutions neither had, nor have, the figurative time or space to think about less-than-urgent concerns, and as the new 'top dogs' in international affairs, they had the power to control what happened and when. The change in power dynamics was not always accepted or handled with ease by the Board of Liquidation, whose insecurity about its performance manifested itself in pointless quarrelling with the ILO and financing increasingly extravagant additions to the League Museum. The group understood the world had changed but found it difficult to relinquish either its relative prestige or their pride in the organization.

Meanwhile the UN was a spectre haunting the League as it closed, looming over events both physically and psychologically. Even once most of the transfer was completed in 1946, the League Secretariat still had to go to work every day in the same building as their replacements, ask them nicely for the use of resources they created and watch quietly while the League was publicly forsaken for the greater good. These officials were just as proud of the League of Nations as the Board of Liquidation, but much less able to do anything about it. Surrounded by their successors they nevertheless carried on with the same determination as in the past, and this was especially prevalent in those who stayed with the League until the bitter end. They were not particularly prominent or public figures; they were a small collection of European bureaucrats and administrators, doing the best they could to efficiently close the organization to which they had pledged their professional lives.

Fortunately for many of these individuals, while the League of Nations was buried, the basis on which it was founded – providing a centre for multilateral cooperation and discussion – lived on. The unique knowledge and experience of the Secretariat meant many former League officials were able to find new homes in the UN, and the direct transfer of assets, functions and funds demonstrates a previously unappreciated strength to the links between the old and the new. The two organizations were bedfellows for over eighteen months in 1946 and 1947, sharing both offices and people; the supposed temporal and institutional distance between the League and the UN was not as great as thought, both at the time and in the present day. The creation of the UN is a crucial element in the end of the League, but the same is also true vice versa; telling one story without the other is injudicious.

The League of Nations suffered a quiet death, overseen by a small group of international civil servants in a discreet corner of the Palais des Nations. Following the twenty-first Assembly in April 1946, there were no grand celebrations or parties, nor were there any public disputes or death throes. Quiet does not, however, mean boring or without value to scholars; the eighteen months or more constituting the League's liquidation period were disordered and surprising. This time challenges our assumptions about the organization's story, its relationship with the post-war institutions that replaced it and the dangers of embarking on closure without a strategy. There were spectacular highs (the final Assembly), a plethora of bittersweet moments (the handover of the Palais to the UN) and more than a few low points (sending a bill for broken crockery to UNRRA following its conference in the summer of 1946). The League's last chapter was full of unexpected developments but it was finally over, leaving those embroiled in its demise to turn, like the rest of the world had several years earlier, to the future and the UN. Writing to Seán Lester on hearing of the Board of

Liquidation's dissolution, Arthur Sweetser summed up the feelings of many of those involved in the League's final years:

> If there is any satisfaction in this world of ours, it comes, I think, from doing well and thoroughly the thing you have to do, and you certainly have done that up to the last second of the last hour. You can look the world in the face with the clearest of consciences, knowing that you have fulfilled the mandate entrusted to you ... and that, God knows, with too little appreciation or recognition.[19]

Notes

Introduction

1 League of Nations, *Official Journal Special Supplement No. 194: Records of the Twentieth (Conclusion) and Twenty-First Ordinary Sessions of the Assembly* (Geneva: League of Nations, 1946), 30.
2 LN, *Records of the 21st Assembly*, 1–17; an official newsreel briefly featuring the twenty-first Assembly and the Palais des Nations shows the event in 'full swing': https://www.britishpathe.com/video/VLVA72PEE0JN6QAYCJBACTUKP2CKG-NO-INFORMATION/query/%22league+of+nations%22.
3 LN, *Records of the 21st Assembly*, 68.
4 The Board of Liquidation's final report has a publication date of 31 July 1947 but was not distributed to members until 2 September, while Valentin Stencek – the last Secretariat official remaining – left his post on 25 October 1947. League of Nations, *Board of Liquidation Final Report, Presented to States Members of the League of Nations in Accordance with the Requirement of the Final Article of the Resolution for the Dissolution of the League of Nations Adopted by the Assembly on April 18th, 1946, at Its Twenty-First Ordinary Session* (Geneva: League of Nations, 1947); League of Nations Archive, 2 September 1947, letter from Valentin Stencek to Trygve Lie, informing him that the Final Report was circulated to members that day, R5816.4 50/44023/43844. Stencek's leaving date can be found in his personnel file: LNA, Personnel File, Stencek, Valentin Joseph. As for continuation of the League into 1948, a number of issues remained outstanding and required action past the October 1947 shutdown. For an example, see a February 1948 letter from Valentin Stencek to Percy Watterson, written on official League of Nations headed paper: LNA, 9 February 1948, letter from Stencek to Percy Watterson regarding the US Treasury decision on income taxes, C1784–4.
5 Dijkstra and Debre defined 'major international organisations' as those that fulfilled at least one of the following criteria: 50 per cent of existing state membership, high levels of institutionalization and substantial administrative support. The specific details were further elaborated on in Hylke Dijkstra and Maria J. Debre, 'The Death of Major International Organizations: When Institutional Stickiness Is Not Enough', *Global Studies Quarterly* 2 (2022), 1–13.

6 Zara Steiner, *The Lights That Failed: European International History 1919–1933* (Oxford: Oxford University Press, 2005), 349–54; F. P. Walters, *A History of the League of Nations* (Oxford: Oxford University Press, 1952), 43.
7 At the end of 1920, there were 182 Secretariat officials in post. By late 1932, this number had increased to 700. Egon R. Ranshofen-Wertheimer, *The International Secretariat: A Great Experiment in International Administration* (Washington, DC: Carnegie Endowment for International Peace, 1945), 241–2. Membership of the League also increased during this period, from forty-seven members in 1920 to fifty-seven by the end of 1932. Walters, *History of the League*, 64–5.
8 Eric Hobsbawm, *The Age of Extremes: The Short Twentieth Century, 1914–1991* (London: Abacus, 1994), 37; F. S. Northedge, *The League of Nations: Its Life and Times, 1920–1946* (Leicester: Holmes & Meier, 1986), 256–70.
9 Figures taken from Ranshofen-Wertheimer, *The International Secretariat*, 224; and from Annex 4, submitted to the Second (Finance) Committee at the Twenty-First Assembly: LN, *Records of the Twenty-First Assembly*, 159.
10 Steiner, *The Lights That Failed*, 368–71; Ranshofen-Wertheimer, *The International Secretariat*, 160–1.
11 Cordell Hull wrote to Joseph Avenol in early February 1939 stating that the US Government 'looked forward to the development and expansion of the League's machinery for dealing with these problems, would continue to collaborate therein, and would willingly consider the means of making its collaboration more effective'. Quoted in Walters, *History of the League*, 760–1.
12 For a more detailed look at the combined efforts of Avenol and Bruce, see: Martin D. Dubin, 'Toward the Bruce Report: The Economic and Social Programs of the League of Nations in the Avenol Era', in United Nations Library, *The League of Nations in Retrospect: Proceedings of the Symposium Organized by the United Nations Library and the Graduate Institute of International Studies Geneva, 6–9 November 1980* (Berlin: de Gruyter, 1983), 42–65; James Barros, *Betrayal from Within: Joseph Avenol, Secretary-General of the League of Nations, 1933–1940* (New Haven, CT: Yale University Press, 1969), 195–7.
13 From *Official Journal*, Special Supplement No. 183, pages 97 and 140, referenced in the Second (Finance) Committee at the Twenty-First Assembly: LN, *Records of the Twenty-First Assembly*, 109.
14 Ranshofen-Wertheimer, *The International Secretariat*. For other, earlier, works written by League officials, see: Arthur Sweetser, *The League of Nations at Work* (New York: Macmillan, 1920); Philip Noel-Baker, *The League of Nations at Work* (London: Nisbet, 1926); Robert Cecil, *A Great Experiment: An Autobiography* (London: Jonathan Cape, 1941).
15 There were ten works published by the Carnegie Endowment under this banner: Nicholas Murray Butler, *The International Law of the Future: Postulates,*

Principles, Proposals (Washington, DC: Carnegie Endowment for International Peace, 1944); Manley O. Hudson, *International Tribunals: Past and Future* (Washington, DC: Carnegie Endowment for International Peace, 1944); Ranshofen-Wertheimer, *The International Secretariat*; Vladimir D. Pastuhov, *A Guide to the Practice of International Conferences* (Washington, DC: Carnegie Endowment for International Peace, 1945); P. de Azcárate, *League of Nations and National Minorities: An Experiment* (Washington, DC: Carnegie Endowment for International Peace, 1945); Martin Hill, *The Economic and Financial Organization of the League of Nations: A Survey of Twenty-five Years' Experience* (Washington, DC: Carnegie Endowment for International Peace, 1946); Bertil A. Renborg, *International Drug Control: A Study of International Administration by and through the League of Nations* (Washington, DC: Carnegie Endowment for International Peace, 1947). Martin Hill, *Immunities and Privileges of International Officials: The Experience of the League of Nations* (Washington, DC: Carnegie Endowment for International Peace, 1947); H. Duncan Hall, *Mandates, Dependencies and Trusteeship* (Washington, DC: Carnegie Endowment for International Peace, 1948); Jacob Viner, *The Customs Union Issue* (Washington, DC: Carnegie Endowment for International Peace, 1950).

16 Fosdick wrote several books about his relationship with the League and its existence in more general terms, including: Fosdick Raymond, *The League and the United Nations after Fifty Years: The Six Secretaries-General* (Newtown: Raymond B. Fosdick, 1972); and Raymond Fosdick, *Letters on the League of Nations* (Princeton, NJ: Princeton University Press, 1966).

17 Lester wrote to Frederic Hapgood – formerly of the League Registry service and transferred to the UN at the end of August 1946 – confirming that he and Włodzimierz Moderow had agreed to grant Walters access to the Archives. LNA, 11 December 1946, memo from Lester to Frederic Hapgood, S568.

18 Walters, *History of the League*.

19 Hobsbawm, *Age of Extremes*, 34; Mark Mazower, 'An International Civilization? Empire, Internationalism and the Crisis of the Mid-Twentieth Century', *International Affairs* 82, no. 3 (2006), 564; Stephen C. Schlesinger, *Act of Creation: The Founding of the United Nations. A Story of Superpowers, Secret Agents, Wartime Allies and Enemies and Their Quest for a Peaceful World* (Boulder, CO: Westview, 2003), 9, 125.

20 Alexandru Grigorescu, 'Mapping the UN-League of Nations Analogy: Are There Still Lessons to Be Learned from the League?', *Global Governance* 11, no. 1 (2005), 25–6.

21 Ibid., 39.

22 E. H. Carr, *The Twenty Years' Crisis, 1919–1939* (London: Palgrave Macmillan, 2016), 29–35. In his preface to the reissued edition of *The Twenty Years' Crisis* in 2016, Michael Cox explained that Carr was not necessarily the conservative

antagonist of all international organizations that he has been portrayed as by the academy.

23 J. Martin Rochester, 'The Rise and Fall of International Organization as a Field of Study', *International Organization* 40, no. 4 (1986), 790.

24 For more information on the increasing interest in the League of Nations, see Susan Pedersen, 'Back to the League of Nations: Review Essay', *American Historical Review* 112, no. 4 (2007), 1091–117.

25 Iris Borowy, *Coming to Terms with World Health: The League of Nations Health Organisation 1921-1946* (Frankfurt: Peter Lang, 2009), 462–3.

26 Northedge, *The League of Nations*, 276; George Scott, *The Rise and Fall of the League of Nations* (London: Hutchinson, 1973), 401.

27 See Susan Pedersen, *The Guardians: The League of Nations and the Crisis of Empire* (Oxford: Oxford University Press, 2015), 402; Patricia Clavin, *Securing the World Economy: The Reinvention of the League of Nations 1920-1946* (Oxford: Oxford University Press, 2013), 358; Mazower, *Governing the World*, 211.

28 Douglas Gageby, *The Last Secretary-General: Sean Lester and the League of Nations* (Dublin: Townhouse, 1999), 256. Torsten Kahlert, '"The League Is Dead, Long Live the United Nations": The Liquidation of the League and the Transfer of Assets to the UN', in Haakon A. Ikonomou and Karen Gram-Skjoldager (eds), *The League of Nations: Perspectives from the Present* (Aarhus: Aarhus University Press, 2019), 256–64.

29 Emma Mary Edwards, *The Wartime Experience of the League of Nations, 1940-1947*. Unpublished doctoral thesis, National University of Ireland, Maynooth, 2013, 296–310.

30 Carolyn N. Biltoft, *A Violent Peace: Media, Truth, and Power at the League of Nations* (Chicago: University of Chicago Press, 2021); C. N. Biltoft, 'Decoding the Balance Sheet: Gifts, Goodwill, and the Liquidation of the League of Nations', *Capitalism: A Journal of History and Economics* 1, no. 2 (2020), 379–404.

31 See the section titled 'La SDN et l'OIT à l'épreuve de l'après-guerre' in: Victor-Yves, *Organisation Internationale et Guerre Mondiale. Le Cas de la Société des Nations et de l'Organisation Internationale du Travail Pendant la Second Guerre Mondiale. Édité par Robert Kolb* (Bruxelles: Bruylant, 2013).

32 Bob Reinalda, *Routledge History of International Organizations: From 1815 to the Present Day* (Abingdon: Routledge, 2009), 756–8; David Armstrong, Lorna Lloyd and John Redmond, *International Organisation in World Politics*, 3rd edn (Basingstoke: Macmillan, 2004), 10.

33 Susan Strange, 'Why Do International Organizations Never Die?' in Bob Reinalda and Bertjan Verbeek (eds), *Autonomous Policy Making by International Organizations* (London: Routledge, 1998), 213–20; Reinalda, *History of International Organizations*, 756–8.

34 Mette Eilstrup-Sangiovanni, 'Death of International Organizations. The Organizational Ecology of Intergovernmental Organizations, 1815–2015', *Review of International Organizations* 15 (2020), 339–70; Dijkstra and Debre, 'The Death of Major International Organizations', 1–13.

35 Ilaria Scaglia, *The Emotions of Internationalism: Feeling International Cooperation in the Alps in the Interwar Period* (Oxford: Oxford University Press, 2020), 51–9.

36 Karen Gram-Skjoldager and Haakon A. Ikonomou, 'Making Sense of the League of Nations Secretariat – Historiographical and Conceptual Reflections on Early International Public Administration', *European History Quarterly* 49, no. 3 (2019), 420–44; Karen Gram-Skjoldager and Haakon A. Ikonomou, 'The Making of the International Civil Servant c. 1920–60: Establishing the Professions', in Karen Gram-Skjoldager, Haakon A. Ikonomou and Torsten Kahlert (eds), *Organizing the 20th-Century World: International Organizations and the Emergence of International Public Administrations, 1920–1960s* (London: Bloomsbury, 2020).

37 Bob Reinalda, *International Secretariats: Two Centuries of International Civil Servants and Secretariats* (Abingdon: Routledge, 2020).

38 Ranshofen-Wertheimer, *The International Secretariat*, 351–69.

39 Klaas Dykmann, 'How International Was the League of Nations Secretariat', *International History Review* 37, no. 4 (2015), 721–44.

40 Kahlert, Torsten, 'Prosopography: Unlocking the Social World of International Organizations', in Gram-Skjoldager, Ikonomou and Kahlert (eds), *Organizing the 20th-Century World*, 49–69; Myriam Piguet, 'Gender Distribution in the League of Nations: The Start of a Revolution?', in Haakon A. Ikonomou and Karen Gram-Skjoldager (eds), *The League of Nations: Perspectives from the Present* (Aarhus: Aarhus University Press, 2019), 62–73.

41 See: Patricia Clavin, 'Europe and the League of Nations', in Gerwarth, Robert (ed.), *Twisted Paths: Europe 1914–1945* (Oxford: Oxford University Press, 2007), 344–9; Clavin, *Securing the World Economy*, 308–19; Borowy, *Coming to Terms with World Health*, 427–44.

42 Fosdick's review and that of Rovine were published only two years apart, and the similarities between the structure of the two can be attributed to their previous working relationship: Rovine worked as Fosdick's research assistant on the latter's volume. Fosdick, *The League and the United Nations after Fifty Years*; Rovine, *The First Fifty Years*.

43 Gerard Keown, 'Seán Lester: Journalist, Revolutionary, Diplomat, Statesman', *Irish Studies in International Affairs* 23 (2012), 143–54; Stephen Barcroft, *The International Civil Servant: The League of Nations Career of Sean Lester, 1929-1947*. Unpublished doctoral thesis, Trinity College Dublin, 1973; Gageby, *The Last Secretary-General*, 250–8. The only other published work on Lester, written by Marit Fosse and John Fox in 2016, is similarly based on Lester's papers although,

in using only these papers – and no other primary sources – Fosse and Fox's work is significantly more simplistic than Gageby's. Marit Fosse and John Fox, *Sean Lester: The Guardian of a Small Flickering Light* (Lanham: Hamilton Books, 2016).

44 Paul Kennedy refers to some of the League's actions as 'pathetic' in the opening chapter of *Parliament of Man*, while Hinsley dismissed the League as doomed to failure from its inception. See Paul Kennedy, *Parliament of Man: The United Nations and the Quest for World Government* (New York: Random House, 2006), 21; F. H. Hinsley, *Power and the Pursuit of Peace: Theory and Practice in the History of Relations Between States* (Cambridge: Cambridge University Press, 1963), 311–21.

45 Meisler, Stanley, *United Nations: The First Fifty Years* (New York: Atlantic Monthly Press, 1995), 26.

46 The UN Secretariat figures are taken from the United Nations Library website: http://ask.un.org/faq/14626. The League figures for 1931 come from Ranshofen-Wertheimer, *The International Secretariat*, 242.

47 David Macfadyen, Michael D. V. Davies, Marilyn Norah Carr and John Burley, *Eric Drummond and His Legacies: The League of Nations and the Beginnings of Global Governance* (Basingstoke: Palgrave, 2019); Reinalda, *History of International Organizations*, 286; Hinsley, *Power and the Pursuit of Peace*, 338–41.

48 Evan Luard, *The United Nations: How It Works*, 2nd edn (Basingstoke: Macmillan, 1994), 128.

49 One recent exception to this trend can be found in the work of Gram-Skjoldager, Ikonomou and Kahlert: Gram-Skjoldager, Ikonomou and Kahlert (eds), *Organizing the 20th-Century World*.

50 There are any number of examples: Glenda Sluga and Patricia Clavin (eds), *Internationalisms: A Twentieth-Century History* (Cambridge: Cambridge University Press, 2017); Simon Jackson and Alanna O'Malley (eds), *The Institution of International Order: From the League of Nations to the United Nations* (Abingdon: Routledge, 2018); David Brydan and Jessica Reinisch (eds), *Internationalists in European History: Rethinking the Twentieth Century* (London: Bloomsbury, 2021); William B. McAllister, *Drug Diplomacy in the Twentieth Century* (London: Routledge, 2000); Elisabetta Tollardo, *Fascist Italy and the League of Nations, 1922–1935* (London: Palgrave Macmillan, 2016).

51 As an example, Langrod discussed the continuation of the Secretariat during the Second World War, but he failed to mention Lester by name, instead referring to him only as 'Avenol's successor': Georges Langrod, *The International Civil Service: Its Origins, Its Nature, Its Evolution* (Leyden: Oceana Publications, 1963), 141; Fosdick, *The League and the United Nations after Fifty Years*, 72.

52 Ken W. Parry and Alan Bryman, 'Leadership in Organizations', in Stewart R. Clegg, Cynthia Hardy, Thomas B. Lawrence and Walter R. Nord (eds), *The Sage Handbook of Organization Studies*, 2nd edn (London: Sage, 2006), 447–57.

53 Even Emma Edwards's study of the League during the Second World War only mentions Stencek in passing: Edwards, *The Wartime Experience of the League of Nations*, 299, 307.
54 Keith Hopkins suggested that social history's supposed 'trivialities' can be used to infer broader conclusions than critics once thought, and Raphael Samuel noted the value of the discipline's concern with 'real life rather than abstractions': Keith Hopkins, 'What Is Social History?', *History Today* 35, no. 3 (1985), 38–9; Raphael Samuel, 'What Is Social History?', *History Today* 35, no. 3 (1985), 34–8.
55 Moderow was director of the UN Office at Geneva from 1946 and consequently worked closely with those League staff remaining at the Palais des Nation. Pelt, a former League official, was undersecretary general for conferences and general services under Trygve Lie and spent considerable amounts of time liaising with the League Secretariat in 1945–7.

1 The beginning of the end, 1940–April 1946

1 F. P. Walters, *A History of the League of Nations* (Oxford: Oxford University Press, 1952), 806–7.
2 Egon F. Ranshofen-Wertheimer, *The International Secretariat: A Great Experiment in International Administration* (Washington DC: Carnegie Endowment for International Peace, 1945), 371–3.
3 This included the Health Committee for example: Iris Borowy, *Coming to Terms with World Health: The League of Nations Health Organisation 1921–1946* (Frankfurt: Peter Lang, 2009), 426.
4 Patricia Clavin, *Securing the World Economy: The Reinvention of the League of Nations, 1920–1946* (Oxford: Oxford University Press, 2013), 252–5.
5 League of Nations Archives, 21 March 1940, letter from Skylstad to S. W. Harris, R4659, 11A/40032/40032; LNA, 24 April 1940, League of Nations Advisory Committee on Social Questions, *Social aspects of the Problems Arising out of Movements of Civil Populations, prepared for the special meeting of the Emergency Sub-Committee of the Advisory committee on social questions, taking place in Geneva, 15 May 1940*, R4659, 11A/40294/40032.
6 Alexander Loveday recounted his difficulty in travelling to Portugal via France and Spain in a letter to Lester: Seán Lester's Diary, 25 August 1940, letter from Alexander Loveday to Lester.
7 As explained by Supervisory Commission President C. J. Hambro at the Second (Finance) Committee of the Twenty-First Assembly: League of Nations, *Official Journal Special Supplement No. 194: Records of the Twentieth (Conclusion) and Twenty-First Ordinary Sessions of the Assembly* (Geneva: League of Nations, 1946),

149; League of Nations, *Report on the Work of the League during the War: Submitted to the Assembly by the Acting Secretary-General* (Geneva: League of Nations, 1945), 139–40.

8   LNA, 15 May 1940, J. Avenol, Internal circular 43.1940, R5398, 18A/39002/39002.
9   Celinski's continued presence can be found in documentation sent to the Swiss authorities: LNA, July 1945, [unknown author], Listes des membres du secretariat de la societe des nations, p. 1, R5357, 18A/604/534.
10 LNA, 15 May 1940, J. Avenol, Internal Circular 43.1940, R5398, 18A/39002/39002.
11 Staff numbers are taken from Ranshofen-Wertheimer, *The International Secretariat*, 242.
12 For more information about Avenol's time as secretary general see Barros, James, *Betrayal from Within: Joseph Avenol, Secretary-General of the League of Nations, 1933–1940* (New Haven, CT: Yale University Press, 1969); Rovine, Arthur, *The First Fifty Years: The Secretary-General in World Politics 1920–1970* (Leyden: A. W. Sijthoff, 1970); Walters, *History of the League*; Elmer Bendiner, *A Time for Angels: The Tragicomic History of the League of Nations* (New York: Book World Promotions, 1975).
13 James Barros's 1969 account of his tenure as secretary general remains the most in-depth study of the Frenchman: Barros, *Betrayal from Within*.
14 Rovine, *The First Fifty Years*, 162–3.
15 Ranshofen-Wertheimer, *The International Secretariat*, 381.
16 Kopecky, speaking at the Fourth plenary meeting of the Twenty-First Assembly on 11 April 1946: LN, *Records of the Twenty-First Assembly*, 42.
17 For an example of their concern, see this entry from Lester's diary in 1940: Lester's Diary, 22 July 1940, personal diary entry.
18 Lester's Diary, 17 July 1940, personal diary entry.
19 Barros, *Betrayal from Within*, 241–8.
20 Lester's Diary, 2 August 1940, personal diary entry.
21 Rovine, *The First Fifty Years*, 173–4.
22 Lester's Diary, 10 April 1997, lecture delivered by Douglas Gageby to the Military History Society, titled 'Seán Lester: A lecture for the Military History Society'.
23 From the minutes of the Second (Finance) Committee at the Twenty-First Assembly: LN, *Records of the Twenty-First Assembly*, 111.
24 Douglas Gageby, *The Last Secretary-General: Sean Lester and the League of Nations* (Dublin: Townhouse, 1999), 209–12.
25 LN, *Report on the work of the League during the war*, 10–11.
26 Taken from LNA, 6 April 1946, Press Service release [unknown author], titled Session of the Assembly, April 1946: Work of the League of Nations during the war, 5, R5704, 50/40142/3535.
27 Ibid., 6.

28 LNA, January 1943, [unknown author], Listes des members du secretariat de la société des nations, R537, 18A/604/534; LNA, 12 January 1944, letter from Renborg to Vigier, R5006, 12/42303/31213.
29 Seán Lester to the Second (Finance) Committee at the Twenty-First Assembly in LN, *Records of the Twenty-First Assembly*, 108.
30 See the list of publications detailed in LN, *Report on the work of the League during the war*, 151–67.
31 LNA, Personnel files: Maria de Steller. LNA, 15 May 1940, J. Avenol, internal circular 43.1940, R5398, 18A/39002/39002; LNA, 29 May 1940, letter from Wertheimer to Skylstad, R4710, 11B/33121/33121; LNA, 3 May 1940, note from Wertheimer to Miss Ray, of the Social Questions Section, regarding the translation of a document pertaining to the Prevention of Prostitution into French, R4710, 11B/33121/33121; LNA, Personnel files: Egon Ranshofen-Wertheimer.
32 LNA, 2 October 1941, letter from Aghnides to Lester, R4659, 11A/41266/41266. Following consultation with Vigier, as well as Raymond Gautier from the Health Section, Aghnides reported to Lester that 'There was general agreement that the work formerly entrusted to her should be carried on to the fullest possible extent.' LNA, memo from Lester to Aghnides, 24 September 1941, asking the latter to investigate how the Secretariat will continue the work of the Social Questions Section, R4659, 11A/41266/41266; LNA, 2 October 1941, memo from Aghnides to Lester, R4659, 11A/41266/41266; LNA, 7 October 1941, memo from Stencek to Aghnides, R4659, 11A/41266/41266. LNA, Personnel files: Constance Harris.
33 There are several letters back and forth on Lenroot's proposal. These include: LNA, 20 May 1941, letter from Katharine F. Lenroot, to Arthur Sweetser, R4659, 11A/41292/41292; LNA, 13 June 1941, handwritten note from Biraud to Lester, warning the latter of ensuring the work does not cross over into the remit of the ILO, R4659, 11A/41292/41292; LNA, 18 July 1941, letter from Sweetser to Lester, covering Lenroot's desire to make a temporary League appointment to look into this research, R4659, 11A/41292/41292; LNA, 5 September 1941, letter from Sweetser to Lester, regarding the ever-solidifying plans and the possibility of a $10,000 grant, R4659, 11A/41292/41292.
34 LNA, 10 December 1941, letter from Lester to Sweetser, R4659, 11A/41292/41292.
35 LNA, August 1942, memo by Renborg, titled Concerning Preparation for the Post-War Period, R5037, 12/43096/43096. LNA, March 1944, memo by Renborg, titled 'Note on the post-war organisation of international drug control', R5037, 12/43096/43096; McAllister, *Drug Diplomacy*, 134.
36 LNA, 10 February 1943, letter from Renborg to Jacklin, R5037, 12/43096/43096.
37 See both: Jessica Reinisch, 'Introduction: Relief in the Aftermath of War', *Journal of Contemporary History* 43, no. 3 (2008), 371–404; Jessica Reinisch, 'Internationalism

in Relief: The Birth (and Death) of UNRRA', *Past & Present* 210, Issue Supplement 6 (2011), 258–89.
38 Lester's Diary, [exact date unknown – catalogued as March 1944], personal diary entry in which Lester notes the lack of faith in the League's future.
39 Clark Eichelberger, *Organizing for Peace: A Personal History of the Founding of the United Nations* (London: Harper and Row, 1977), 204.
40 Mark Mazower, *Governing the World: The History of an Idea* (London: Penguin, 2012), 194–205; Inis L. Jr. Claude, *Swords into Plowshares: The Problems and Progress of International Organizations*, Fourth Edition (New York: McGraw-Hill, 1984), 57–65.
41 Lester's Diary, 25 November 1944, letter from Loveday to Lester.
42 Lester's Diary, exact date unknown – listed as September 1944, handwritten notes by Lester.
43 Stephen C. Schlesinger, *Act of Creation: The Founding of the United Nations. A Story of Superpowers, Secret Agents, Wartime Allies and Enemies and Their Quest for a Peaceful World* (Boulder, CO: Westview, 2003), 113–18; Lester's Diary, 8 February 1945, letter from Lester to J. P. Walshe, secretary of the Irish Government's Department of External Affairs.
44 Lester's Diary, 8 February 1945, letter from Lester to Walshe; Lester's Diary, 12 April 1945, letter from Lester to Walshe.
45 Lester's Diary, 12 April 1945, letter from John Winant (US Ambassador in London) to Lester.
46 Lester's Diary, 12 April 1945, Lester personal diary entry.
47 Lester's Diary, 30 April 1945, Lester personal diary entry.
48 Lester's Diary, 15 May 1945, Lester personal diary entry.
49 Plesch, Dan, *America, Hitler, and the UN: How the Allies Won World War II and Forged a Peace* (London: I. B. Tauris, 2011), 168.
50 Lester's Diary, 30 April 1945, personal diary entry relaying the treatment received by the League delegation in San Francisco, including Soviet opposition to Lester's presence.
51 Lester's Diary, 15 May 1945, personal diary entry describing Jacklin as 'very sore' following his treatment at a committee meeting, and Lester's personal desire to move on from San Francisco as soon as possible.
52 LNA, 25 June 1945, official press communication from the US Office of War Information detailing the establishment of the United Nations Preparatory Commission, S565.
53 Denys Myers, 'Liquidation of League of Nations Functions', *American Journal of International Law* 42, no. 2 (1948), 323.
54 LNA, 25 June 1946, official press communication from the US Office of War Information, S565.

55 Myers, 'Liquidation of League of Nations Functions', 322.
56 For a list of the Executive Committee delegates, see Lord Gladwyn, *The Memoirs of Lord Gladwyn* (London: Weidenfeld and Nichols, 1972), 173.
57 See Lester's Diary, 23 July 1945, letter from Lester to Alexander Loveday; Mazower, Governing the World, 199; E. J. Hughes, 'Winston Churchill and the Formation of the United Nations Organization', *Journal of Contemporary History* 9 (October 1974), 181.
58 LNA, 11 September 1945, Lester notes on a meeting between Gladwyn Jebb, David Owen and Lester, S565.
59 LNA, 1 September 1945, letter from Jebb to Lester requesting assistance, S565.
60 LNA, 26 November 1945, letter from Lester to Jebb, S565.
61 See both: LNA, 11 September 1945, Lester notes on a meeting between Jebb, Owen and Lester, S565; LNA, 24 September 1945, letter from Jebb to Lester, S565.
62 LNA, 28 September 1945, Lester memo on meeting with Jonkheer Beelaerts van Blokland, S565.
63 UK National Archives (TNA), 28 November 1945, Committee 7: League of Nations, Second Meeting, FO 371/57248.
64 TNA, 14 March 1946, from 'Report of the Committee set up by the United Nations Preparatory Commission', sent to League members by Lester, originally published 28 January 1946, FO 371/57321.
65 LNA, 7 January 1946, letter from Gladwyn Jebb to Lester, S565.
66 LNA, 5 January 1946, telephone message from Seymour Jacklin regarding a conversation with Moderow, S565.
67 Lester's Diary, 10 January 1946, letter from Lester to Jacklin.
68 LNA, 14 March 1946, 'Report on Discussion with the Representatives of the United Nations on Questions of the Transfer of League of Nations Assets', pp. 1–3, S567.
69 LNA, 20 February 1946, draft report on Discussions with UN Representatives on Asset Transfer, S565.
70 TNA, 1 February 1946, proceedings of the UN General Assembly League of Nations Committee, second meeting – Moderow presenting, FO 371/57248. In the same meeting, when discussing a section of the Common Plan related to arrangements allowing the ILO to use the Geneva Assembly Hall, Moderow noted that the downgrade from 'entitled to use' to 'may use' had finally been accepted by the ILO.
71 TNA, 28 January 1946, 'Report of the Committee set up by the Preparatory Commission', p. 4, FO 371/57248.
72 LNA, 14 March 1946, Report on Discussions with the Representatives of the United Nations on Questions of the Transfer of League of Nations Assets, pp. 1–10, S567.
73 Bertil Renborg, Head of the League's Drug Control Service through the war, compiled a comprehensive overview of its work – funded by the Carnegie Endowment – following his departure from the organization: Bertil A. Renborg,

International Drug Control: A Study of International Administration by and through the League of Nations (Washington, DC: Carnegie Endowment for International Peace, 1947), 38–43.

74 United Nations, *Report of the Preparatory Commission of the United Nations* (London: United Nations, 1946), 116–18.

75 Thomas Campbell and George Herring, *The Diaries of Edward Stettinius Jr., 1943–46* (New York: Littlehampton, 1974), 132. For more on the development of the Bruce Report, see: Martin D. Dubin, 'Towards the Bruce Report: the Economic and Social Programs of the League of Nations in the Avenol Era', in United Nations Library (ed.), *The League of Nations in Retrospect: Proceedings of the Symposium 6–9 November 1980* (Berlin: de Gruyter, 1983); Lester's Diary, 13 August 1945, personal diary entry on confidential information from a member of the US delegation to the Preparatory Commission.

76 See both: TNA, 28 November 1945, Committee 7: League of Nations, Second Meeting, FO 371/57248; and TNA, 5 December 1945, Committee 7: League of Nations, Fifth Meeting, FO 371/57248.

77 LNA, 3 December 1945, letter from Lester to Hambro reporting the results of a telephone conversation with Jebb, S565. See also: Porter, Louis H., *Cold War Internationalisms: The USSR in UNESCO, 1945–1967*. Unpublished doctoral thesis, University of North Carolina at Chapel Hill, 2018.

78 TNA, 12 October 1945, records from Executive Committee meeting review of Committee 9 report, T236/431; Lester's Diary, 11 October 1945, letter from Loveday to Lester; TNA, 20 March 1946, UN General Assembly Resolutions affecting the League of Nations, FO 371/57321.

79 LNA, 20 February 1946, letter from Lester to Hambro recounting a recent meeting with Owen, S565.

80 LNA, January 1943, [unknown author], *Listes des membres du secretariat de la societe des nations*, R5357; LNA, July 1945, [unknown author], *Listes des membres du secretariat de la societe des nations*, R5357.

81 For example, Major Gerald Abraham joined the Secretariat in January 1920 before leaving in April 1939. He was re-engaged in June 1945, working for Division I in London. See LNA, 6 July 1945, letter from Valentin Stencek to Lester regarding Abraham's reengagement date of 19 June 1945, S565; also LNA, Personnel File: Gerald Huguerty Furtado Abraham.

82 LNA, 7 May 1945, letter from Stencek to Janet Smith, S565.

83 LNA, 1 January 1946, [unknown author], list of League Secretariat staff, S698.

84 Lester's Diary, 4 December 1944, letter from Lester to Loveday.

85 LNA, 25 July 1945, Lester personnel memo on staff questions, S565.

86 TNA, 12 November 1945, report by the Executive Committee, 108, FO 372/4382.

87 Lester's Diary, 18 December 1945, letter from Lester to Loveday regarding the expected outcomes from the Preparatory Commission report and the impact on staff.
88 TNA, 1 February 1946, records from the second meeting of the UN General Assembly's League of Nations Committee, FO 371/57248.
89 LNA, 16 January 1946, Lester's personal notes on a Supervisory Commission meeting, S565.
90 LNA, 25 February 1946, Lester's personal notes on a Supervisory Commission meeting from the previous day, S565.
91 Ibid.
92 LNA, 16 February 1946, Lester's personal notes on a Supervisory Commission meeting, S565.
93 LNA, 26 February 1946, letter from Lester to Hambro, S565.
94 United Nations Archives Geneva, 22 January 1946, report by Hugh McKinnon-Wood titled 'The extent to which the liquidation of the League depends on the assumption by the United Nations of activities hitherto exercised by the League', A/LA/W/13., G.I. 4/1.
95 LNA, 3 August 1945, Lester personal memorandum, S565.
96 LNA, 4 August 1945, proposed timetable of UN/League of Nations meetings and negotiations 1945–6, S565.
97 The original message to members suggesting the single Assembly approach was sent in August 1945: LNA, 23 August 1945, draft telegram to League members, S565. The final confirmatory communiqué was sent in October: LNA, 17 October 1945, communiqué to League members, S565. For a breakdown of Hambro and Lester's reasoning for this approach: LNA, 7 September 1946, letter from Lester to Francisco Castillo Najera, Mexican Supervisory Commission member, S565.
98 LNA, 24 January 1946, letter from Lester informing Jebb that he has been directed to convoke an Assembly for 8 April, S565.
99 Lester's Diary, [exact date unknown – listed as February 1946], letter from Sweetser to Hambro regarding plans for the 21st Assembly.
100 The Supervisory Commission agreed that a member of the League should propose the resolution at the Assembly, and Britain – the most prominent remaining member of the League – was heavily involved in the organization's affairs until its closure. See LNA, 21 February 1946, letter from Lester to Hambro, S565; Lester's Diary, 25 April 1946, Lester personal diary note on the proceedings of the Assembly and the British Government's help in its planning; LNA, 6 April 1946, letter from Lester to Jacklin querying some of the wording in the latest British draft of the dissolution resolution, S565.
101 LN, *Report on the work of the League during the war*. Also see: LNA, 18 February 1946, letter from Lester to Stencek explaining that Hambro has some queries

regarding the earphone interpreter system, S565; LNA, 2 March 1946, [unknown author], Annotated Provisional Agenda of the Assembly, R5704 15/40199/40199; LNA, 29 March 1946, memo from Lester to Hambro, forwarding the latter a script for his opening speech to the Assembly, S565.

102 See LNA, 12 February 1946, letter from Owen to Lester agreeing to pass on the former's request for additional support from United Nations' officials during the upcoming Assembly, S565.

103 Numbers taken from: LNA, 1 April 1946, [unknown author], list of Secretariat staff, including temporary and UN officials, present for the 21st Assembly, broken down by department and availability, S913.

104 LN, *Records of the Twenty-First Assembly*, 11–17.

105 The first Assembly attracted representation from forty of forty-two total members, and even the tenth Assembly in 1929 – arguably taking place at the height of the League's power – could not manage a full house of attendance. League of Nations, *Official Journal Special Supplement: Records of the First Session of the Assembly* (Geneva: League of Nations, 1920), 10–19; League of Nations, *Official Journal Special Supplement: Records of the Tenth Session of the Assembly* (Geneva: League of Nations, 1929), 11–22.

106 The Assembly Room at the Palais des Nations had a capacity of just over 1,500 when first built: TNA, 28 January 1946, Appendix to the Common Plan for the Transfer of League of Nations Assets established by the UN Committee and the Supervisory Commission of the League of Nations, pp. 3–7, FO 371/57248.

107 The two major committees were the First and Second Committees. The First Committee was also known as the General Committee as it dealt with general questions, while the Second Committee, aka the Finance Committee, considered financial and administrative issues. LN, *Records of the Twenty-First Assembly*, 26.

108 The discussions take up a significant portion of the official records of the Assembly – twenty-two different member representatives spoke – and many examples of the delegates' lamentations can be found therein. Ibid., 27–54. Sweetser's speech was published a few months later: Arthur Sweetser, 'From the League to the United Nations', *Annals of the American Academy of Political and Social Science* 246 (1946), 1.

109 LNA, 17 April 1946, Report and Resolution of the First Committee on the Dissolution of the Permanent Court of International Justice, from the Twenty-first Ordinary Session of the League of Nations Assembly, R3820 3C/43816/42549.

110 LN, *Records of the Twenty-First Session of the Assembly*, 277–8.

111 Ibid., 280. The thanks to the Soviet Union were added to avoid the government demanding a portion of the League's assets – as an expelled member it was not, in theory, subject to the same exclusion rules that a resigned member was. The League's leadership, however, did not want to include the Soviet Union in any

distribution of assets, and thus the Assembly resolution was positioned as an effort to placate any demands.
112 Ibid., 278.
113 'Resolution for the Dissolution of the League of Nations' in ibid., 281–4.
114 Taken from the Report of the First Committee to the Assembly, led by rapporteur Professor K. H. Bailey, delegate of Australia: ibid., 250.
115 Ibid., 281–4.
116 The Belfast Telegraph's report was heavily influenced by Reuters correspondent Boris Kidel: *Belfast Telegraph*, 19 April 1946, [unknown author], 'Packed Public Galleries Watch League End', 5. For examples of the coverage from the *Manchester Guardian* and *The Times of London*, see the former's article on the end of the mandates system, and the latter's editorial on the failure of states to live up to the League's promise: *Manchester Guardian*, 10 April 1946, [unknown author], 'Carrying on the League's Work on Mandates', p. 5; *The Times of London*, 12 April 1946, [unknown author], 'The End of the League', 5.

2 Transfer troubles, April–July 1946

1 Mette Eilstrup-Sangiovanni, 'Death of International Organizations. The Organizational Ecology of Intergovernmental Organizations, 1815–2015', *Review of International Organizations* 15 (2020), 339–70.
2 League of Nations, *Official Journal Special Supplement No. 194: Records of the Twentieth (Conclusion) and Twenty-First Ordinary Sessions of the Assembly* (Geneva: League of Nations, 1946), 82.
3 A sub-committee of representatives from the Assembly's First and Second Committees proposed the candidates. This included delegates from China, France, Canada, Poland, Turkey, Uruguay and the UK – as well as the chairmen of the First and Second Committees, Maurice Bourquin and Atul Chatterjee respectively. Ibid., 139–40.
4 Ibid., 281. The dissent focused on the Board's remuneration package was given voice by Louis Atzenwiler – a member of the PCOB Secretariat from 1931 through 1946 – in his interview on 5 July 1970 with Barcroft: Barcroft, *The International Civil Servant*, 298. See Chapter 4 for more details on the 'voluntary' salary contribution scheme, which details how related Secretariat disquiet came to a head in 1947.
5 League of Nations Archives, 1 May 1946, [unknown author], Board of Liquidation document titled Rules of Procedure for the Board of Liquidation, B.L.3(1), S570; LNA, 23 April 1946, Board of Liquidation: Minutes of First Meeting, B.L./First Session/P.V.1., S569.

6 The first official set of meeting dates for the Board were 23 and 30 April, and 1 May 1946. The second group took place on 15, 16, 17, 18, 19, 24 and 27 July 1946. The secret meetings were on 1 May, 16 July, 23 July and 29 July 1946. Minutes for the official meetings can all be found in LNA, Various dates, B.L./P.V.1-10, S569. The first set of secret meeting minutes are held in LNA, 1 May 1946, Board of Liquidation: Minutes of secret meeting, R5816.2 50/43856/43844. Records of the three other secret meetings are held in LNA, Various dates, Board of Liquidation: minutes of secret sessions, R5816.2 50/43856/43844.
7 LNA, 2 May 1946, note from Lester to Chester Purves requesting the latter take on responsibility for the fortnightly update reports to the Board of Liquidation, R5816.3 50/43877/43844. The first report produced can be found at LNA, 15 May 1946, First Fortnightly Progress Report to the Board of Liquidation, B.L./F.P.R.1, S923.
8 LNA, 26 April 1946, Board of Liquidation Document titled Claim of the Italian Government to share in League assets, B.L.1., R5812 50/43851/43262.
9 LNA, 2 May 1946, note from Lester to Purves in which Lester stresses that only liquidation issues should be addressed to the Board, R5816.3 50/43877/43844.
10 LNA, 1 May 1946, Board of Liquidation: Minutes of Third Meeting, B.L./P.V.3., S569.
11 For example, see: LNA, 31 May 1946, letter from Lester to Kisch in which he provides an update on officials' furniture, staff numbers and secondments to the UN, R5816.3 50/43877/43844; LNA, 11 June 1946, letter from Hambro to Purves regarding member contributions in arrears, R5816.3 50/43877/43844.
12 LNA, 24 July 1946, Board of Liquidation: Minutes of Tenth Meeting, B.L./P.V.10., S569.
13 Detail about the League estates comes from LNA, 31 October 1945, document prepared by Stencek for the Supervisory Commission titled 'League Estates', C.C.1453, S565. Information concerning Ariana Park: LNA, 31 October 1945, document prepared by Stencek for the Supervisory Commission titled 'The League Buildings: Ariana Park', C.C.1450, S565. Details of the fixtures and fittings: UK National Archives (TNA), 28 January 1946, Appendix to the Common Plan for the Transfer of League of Nations Assets established by the UN Committee and the Supervisory Commission of the League of Nations, pp. 3-7, FO 371/57248.
14 LNA, 14 March 1946, Report on Discussions with the Representatives of the United Nations on Questions of the Transfer of League of Nations Assets, A.8.1946.X., pp. 1-10, S567.
15 LNA, 16 February 1946, Lester personal memo regarding the creation of a UN Negotiating Committee, S565.
16 LNA, 14 March 1946, letter from Lie to Lester explaining that the Negotiating Committee will arrive in Geneva on 6 April, S565 50/43684/43262; LNA, 6 April

1946, [unknown author], memo detailing the hotel arrangements for each member of the Negotiating Committee party, S565.
17 LNA, 3 April 1946, letter from Lester to Włodzimierz Moderow, welcoming the latter to Switzerland and expressing his hopes for useful negotiations, R5812 50/43684/43262; LNA, 5 April 1946, letter from Moderow to Lester, thanking the latter in advance for his assistance with the Negotiating Committee, S565.
18 LNA, 10 April 1946, letter from Lester to Moderow, S565. Also: Seán Lester's Diary, 11 April 1946, letter from Moderow to Lester in which the former apologized for the inconvenience; Lester's Diary, 26 April 1946, Lester personal diary entry recalling the events of a post-Assembly dinner hosted by Moderow, and his impressions of the host.
19 Lester's Diary, 5 August 1946, Lester personal note covering the handover celebrations taking place in Geneva, in which he described Lie as 'a man of personality and character' and Moderow as 'a bloody fool'. Also see LNA, 8 August 1946, letter from Lester to Lie thanking him for his work in establishing good relations between the two organizations, R5813 50/43874/43262.
20 For example: LNA, 24 June 1946, memo from Stencek to Moderow relaying Lester's proposed minor amendments to the asset transfer agreement, R5813 50/43874/43262.
21 LNA, 17 April 1946, memo from Émile Giraud to Lester regarding his legal opinion on what will be required for a transfer of assets to take place, R5813 50/43874/43262.
22 LNA, 30 April 1946, letter from Adriaan Pelt to Lie, listing the main problems involved in transfer of League assets and activities, R5812 50/43298/43262.
23 A draft version of the agreement can be found at: LNA, 1 May 1946, [unknown author], Draft agreement concerning the transfer of certain League assets to the UN, R5813 50/43874/43262. Also see: LNA, 17 June 1946, letter from Stencek to Moderow outlining some final minor changes, R5813 50/43874/43262.
24 LNA, 7 May 1946, letter from Stencek to Pelt suggesting Lester have the continued use of La Pelouse, R5813 50/43874/43262; LNA, 26 June 1946, memo from Moderow to Lester suggesting a simplified version of the agreement could be used, R5813 50/43874/43262; LNA, 28 June 1946, memo from Stencek to Moderow, agreeing to the latter's final changes, R5813 50/43874/43262.
25 The agreements with the Geneva Canton can be found in: LNA, 22 July 1946, 'Projet d'acte de transfert S.D.N. - O.N.U. - Ariana - Palais', R5813 50/43874/43262; LNA, 22 July 1946, 'Projet d'acte de transfert S.D.N. - O.N.U. - Terraine et villas privés, R5813 50/43874/43262. See also: LNA, 28 June 1946, memo from Stencek to Moderow confirming that the agreement can be finalized and signed on 1 August as planned, R5813 50/43874/43262.

26 Carolyn Biltoft, 'Decoding the Balance Sheet: Gifts, Goodwill, and the Liquidation of the League of Nations', *Capitalism: A Journal of History and Economics* 1, no. 2 (2020), 379–404.
27 LNA, 22 July 1946, 'Agreement Concerning the Execution of the Transfer to the United Nations of Certain Assets of the League of Nations', R5813 50/43874/43262.
28 LNA, 30 July 1946, letter from Stencek to J. Lachavanne – of the Genevan government – inviting the latter to the Palais to sign the legal agreement transferring the League assets to the United Nations, R5813 50/43874/43262.
29 Thomas Campbell, and George Herring, *The Diaries of Edward Stettinius Jr., 1943–46* (New York: Littlehampton, 1974), 132; Louis H. Porter, *Cold War Internationalisms: The USSR in UNESCO, 1945–1967*. Unpublished doctoral thesis, University of North Carolina at Chapel Hill, 2018, 6.
30 See both: TNA, 28 November 1945, Committee 7: League of Nations, Second Meeting, FO 371/57248; TNA, 5 December 1945, Committee 7: League of Nations, Fifth Meeting, FO 371/57248.
31 UNOG Archives, 29 April 1946, report prepared by Egon Ranshofen-Wertheimer for the UN entitled 'Notes on some Problems Raised by the Continuation of certain League Activities', G.I. 4/11 1260. Also see: United Nations, *Report of the Preparatory Commission of the United Nations* (London: United Nations, 1946), 116–17. The PCOB was created by the International Convention relating to Dangerous Drugs 1925, and the DSB by the Convention for limiting the Manufacture and Regulating the Distribution of Narcotic Drugs 1931. For more on the role of the League in drug control, see Bertil A. Renborg, *International Drug Control: A Study of International Administration by and through the League of Nations* (Washington, DC: Carnegie Endowment for International Peace, 1947).
32 TNA, 20 March 1946, UN General Assembly Resolutions affecting the League of Nations, FO 371/57321.
33 Iris Borowy, *Coming to Terms with World Health: The League of Nations Health Organisation 1921–1946* (Frankfurt: Peter Lang, 2009), 421–44.
34 LNA, 26 February 1946, letter from Jebb to Lester requesting the presence of a League representative at the Technical Preparatory Committee of the ECOSOC, in order to consult on plans for an international health conference in June 1946, S565; LNA, 4 April 1946, first meeting minutes of the Sub-Committee to Study Relations between the Future Organizations and Other Bodies, part of the Technical Preparatory Committee for the International Health Conference, held 29 March 1946, R6150 8A/43889/41755.
35 See: Lester's Diary, 28 February 1945, letter from Lester to Walshe. Other areas of the League's Administration also stressed continuity in function: LNA, 7 May 1946, 'Memorandum on the relations of the Supervisory Body to the United Nations', produced by the Drug Supervisory Body, R5146 12B/43890/8707.

36 UNOG Archives, 29 April 1946, report by Ranshofen-Wertheimer titled 'Notes on some Problems Raised by the Continuation of certain League Activities', G.I. 4/11 1260; UNOG Archives, 19 May 1946, report by Ranshofen-Wertheimer titled 'Transferrable Activities and Functions', G.I. 4/11 1260.
37 LNA, 31 July 1946, League Internal Circular 21, Note by the secretary general regarding the transfer of certain services to the UN, R5812 50/43625/43262.
38 Egon F. Ranshofen-Wertheimer, *The International Secretariat: A Great Experiment in International Administration* (Washington, DC: Carnegie Endowment for International Peace, 1945) remains the most comprehensive review of the League's Secretariat, covering all imaginable areas including its structure, functions, external relations, personnel ranks, benefits and pay scales.
39 UNOG Archives, 29 April 1946, report prepared by Ranshofen-Wertheimer titled 'Notes on some Problems Raised by the Continuation of Certain League Activities', G.I. 4/11 1260.
40 Id. For more on the transfer of the League's Archives, see Chapter 4.
41 LNA, 29 July 1946, letter from Moderow to Lester requesting continued use of the League's Distribution and Publications Service for the foreseeable future, R5813 50/44053/43262.
42 LNA, 31 July 1946, Internal Circular 21, written by Lester, confirming how usage of central Palais functions will work from 1 August 1946, R5812 50/43625/43262.
43 TNA, 12 October 1945, records from Executive Committee meeting review of Committee 9 report, T 236/432; UNOG Archives, 29 April 1946, report by Ranshofen-Wertheimer titled 'Notes on some Problems Raised by the Continuation of certain League activities', G.I. 4/11 1260.
44 See both LNA, 14 May 1946, letter from Lester to Lie regarding the transfer of the Publications Department, R5610 19/43868/43868; LNA, 16 May 1946, letter from Lester to Lie regarding the transfer of the drug control bodies, R5505 12A/43883/2131.
45 LNA, 7 June 1946, letter from Alexander Elkin to Lester advising the latter that the UN intended to transfer Princeton functions and staff from 1 August 1946, R5813 50/43945/43262.
46 LNA, 9 April 1946, letter from Lie to Lester, thanking the latter for releasing Branko Lukac from his contract, S568.
47 See LNA, 21 May 1946, memo from Gregoire Frumkin to Lester, expressing his frustration about the continued division of the EFO, S568; LNA, 17 June 1946, letter from Lester to Pelt, noting his concern that the UN is only proposing one-year contracts for the Princeton EFO officials, S568; LNA, 17 June 1946, letter from Lester to Pelt, expressing his disappointment that the UN will not be transferring the Geneva elements of the EFO alongside those at Princeton, S927 50/43945/43262.

48 LNA, 25 July 1946, handwritten note from Stencek to Lester, noting that two of the Geneva-based EFO officials have already accepted their temporary contracts, S922.
49 LNA, 29 July 1946, letter from Moderow to Lester explaining that the UN will now be transferring all Geneva elements of the EFO alongside those from Princeton, from 1 August 1946, R5813 50/44053/43262; LNA, 29 July 1946, memo from Lester to Stencek, expressing his hopes that the new UN contracts for Geneva EFO staff will arrive before 1 August, R5813 50/44053/43262.
50 UNOG Archives, 24 July 1946, letter from Owen to Moderow, G.I. 4/9 251.
51 LNA, 31 July 1946, letter from Lester to Moderow, in which the former expresses his hope that the Geneva EFO officials now have their UN contract offers, R5813 50/44053/43262.
52 LNA, 1 April 1946, [unknown author], report entitled 'The Present Organisation of the Secretariat of the League of Nations' detailing the different sections of the Secretariat, the different functions performed by these and the officials working therein, S922.
53 LNA, 29 April 1946, telegram from Lester to Lie explaining that the former is happy to second Yves Biraud to the United Nations in preparation for the World Health Conference, R5813 50/43905/43262.
54 LNA, 10 July 1946, letter from Lester to Moderow in which the former forwards a note by Henri Vigier on the work of the Social Questions Section, R4659 11A/43999/41292.
55 LNA, 26 July 1946, cable from Pelt to Moderow, informing the latter that the UN intends to transfer the remaining Department III activities from 1 August 1946, S568.
56 LNA, 31 July 1946, letter from Lester to Moderow, R5813 50/44054/43262; LNA, 29 July 1946, letter from Lester to Moderow, noting that he will not bear responsibility for any repercussions from the last-minute request to transfer Department III, R5813 50/44054/43262.
57 LNA, 29 July 1946, cable from Moderow to Pelt, urgently requesting a one-month delay in the transfer of Department III activities, R5813 50/44054/43262.
58 LNA, 6 August 1946, letter from Lie to Lester regarding the possible transfer of the P.C.O.B. secretariat in September, R5813 50/44054/43262.
59 Lester's Diary, 25 August 1940, letter from Loveday to Lester regarding his journey from Geneva to the United States.
60 LNA, 25 February 1946, Lester's personal notes on a Supervisory Commission meeting from the previous day, S565.
61 LNA, 21 March 1946, letter from Lester to Hambro confirming that he will be giving notice to a large number of officials that day, S565. Also see: Lester's Diary, 3 April 1946, personal memo on decision to issue notice to all staff with a termination date of 31 July 1946.

62 Lester's Diary, 18 December 1945, letter from Lester to Loveday regarding the expected outcomes from the Preparatory Commission report and the impact on staff.
63 LNA, 23 July 1946, letter from Pelt to Lester apologizing for delays in appointing League officials to the United Nations, S927.
64 See both: LNA, 29 April 1946, list of League officials interviewed by the two UN interview boards between 24 and 29 April 1946, S927; LNA, 2 May 1946, letter from Pelt to Lester thanking the latter and his colleagues for their help with the interview board process, S927; Ellen J. Ravndal, *In the Beginning: Secretary-General Trygve Lie and the Establishment of the United Nations* (Bristol: Bristol University Press, 2023), 126–9.
65 This was a concern Lester himself expressed to Pelt: LNA, 17 June 1946, letter from Lester to Pelt concerning League staff staying with the organization after the end of July, S922.
66 LNA, 17 June 1946, letter from Phyllis van Ittersum to Ansgar Rosenborg, C1626.
67 Two figures with long service who would later take on important roles in the liquidation of the League were Constance (Connie) Harris and Percy Watterson. Harris joined the organization on 12 August 1919, while Watterson joined one month earlier on 14 July 1919. LNA, Personnel File: Harris, Constance Myra; LNA, Personnel File: Watterson, Percy Gill.
68 LNA, 14 June 1946, letter from Stencek to Lester with an update on staffing, including Martin Hill's departure, S922; LNA, 15 May, telegram from Lester to Lie agreeing to second Léon Steinig to the UN from 1 June 1946, R5813 50/43905/43262.
69 LNA, 1 June 1946, [unknown author], table showing allowances and pensions contributions for seconded staff, including Branko Lukac and Yves Biraud, R5813 50/43905/43262.
70 UNOG Archives, 9 April 1946, letter from Lie to Lester, P188 Papers of Włodzimierz Moderow 1921–60.
71 LNA, 8 June 1946, letter from Stencek to Lester suggesting Pelt take over as the point of contact on secondment requests, S568.
72 LNA, 17 June 1946, letter from Lester to Pelt expressing concerns about the high volume of secondment requests and the possible disadvantages seconded officials may face when pursuing permanent positions at the UN, S568.
73 Lester's Diary, 3 April 1946, Lester personal note on a Supervisory Commission meeting during which Jacklin confirmed his wish to leave the Secretariat in July 1946. Privately Lester found Jacklin paranoid and in possession of a 'deep-seated inferiority complex': Lester's Diary, 1 March 1946, personal diary entry.
74 LNA, 31 May 1946, letter from Lester to Kisch explaining that staff numbers would likely go up in coming weeks due to an increase in workload, R5816.3

50/43877/43844; LNA, 13 June 1946, memo from E. A. Lloyd – head of the Publications Department – to Stencek urgently requesting additional staff for the department, S937 19/43868/43868.
75 LNA, 24 July 1946, memo from Henri Vilatte to Elkin explaining how he plans to manage the League's Personnel Office from 1 August onwards, S922.
76 LNA, 24 April 1946, letter from Stencek to Julian Huxley – at UNESCO – requesting details of all available UNESCO posts so they can be forwarded to League officials, S942.
77 Elmer Bendiner, *A Time for Angels: The Tragicomic History of the League of Nations* (New York: Book World Promotions, 1975), 402.
78 Ranshofen-Wertheimer, *The International Secretariat*, 259–62; Reinalda, Bob, *International Secretariats: Two Centuries of International Civil Servants and Secretariats* (Abingdon: Routledge, 2020), 122–3.
79 Extract from the sixth meeting of the Second (Finance) Committee of the 21st Assembly: LN, *Records of the Twenty-First Assembly*, 130–3. LNA, 9 April 1946, report by Lester on the Administrative Tribunal ruling of 26 February 1946, S942.
80 LNA, 3 July 1946, letter from Gordon Graham – representing the Staff Committee – to Lester, relaying the committee's views and suggestions regarding the termination of contracts taking effect from 31 July, S918. For an outline of the officials' furniture problem, see LNA, 3 June 1946, memo from Stencek to Moderow, R5385 18A/39144/3471.
81 LN, *Records of the Twenty-First Assembly*, 118.
82 LNA, 3 July 1946, letter from Graham – representing the Staff Committee – to Lester, relaying the committee's views and suggestions regarding the termination of contracts taking effect from 31 July, S918.
83 LNA, 30 July 1946, letter from Stencek to Graham regarding the Staff Committee queries of 3 July, S918.
84 LNA, 28 July 1946, document prepared by Stencek – for Lester – looking at the Staff Sickness Insurance Association and the proposed options for its future, S913.
85 LNA, 31 July 1946, [unknown author], report on the anticipated contractual positions of staff on 31 July 1946, S922; LNA, 31 July 1946, report by Stencek providing a breakdown of all staff in League employ from 1 August 1946, and any anticipated transfers that remain outstanding, S927.
86 The best source of information on the rise and dominance of the EFO is Patricia Clavin's 2013 work *Securing the World Economy* which covers the League's work in economics and financial management from its beginnings: Patricia Clavin, *Securing the World Economy: The Reinvention of the League of Nations, 1920–1946* (Oxford: Oxford University Press, 2013).

Notes 201

87 Clavin goes into significantly more detail on the work of the Princeton group during the war in Chapter 8 of *Securing the World Economy*, titled 'Made in the USA, 1940–1943': ibid., 267–304.
88 LNA, 1 April 1946, [unknown author], report entitled 'The Present Organisation of the Secretariat of the League of Nations' detailing the different sections of the Secretariat, the different functions performed by these and the officials working therein, S922.
89 TNA, 20 March 1946, UN General Assembly Resolutions affecting the League of Nations, FO 371/57321.
90 LNA, 8 April 1946, letter from Lester to Rosenborg regarding issues arising as a result of terminating the contracts of those officials still working at Princeton, S922.
91 Ibid.
92 LNA, 24 April 1946, letter from Folke Hilgerdt to Rosenborg expressing concerns regarding the guidelines from the League's leadership relating to leave journeys, C1784-4.
93 See LNA, 20 June 1946, memo from Stencek to Lester explaining that Rosenborg had granted a leave journey for Paul Deperon's wife and daughter, S942; LNA, 25 June 1946, letter from Stencek to Rosenborg regarding Deperon's request for an additional leave journey for himself, S942.
94 LNA, 4 May 1946, letter from Martin Hill to Rosenborg, suggesting the latter refrain from proposing procedure for transfer of functions, S568.
95 LNA, 29 May 1946, report by Stencek covering all current officials and possible offer of temporary contracts from 1 August, S922.
96 LNA, 17 June 1946, letter from Lester to Pelt regarding the UN decision to assume the EFO functions based in Princeton from 31 July, R5813 50/43945/43262.
97 LNA, 29 June 1946, cable from Lester to Pelt regarding offers of employment for League officials currently based at Princeton, R5813 50/43945/43262.
98 LNA, 18 July 1946, letter from Rosenborg to Lester in which the former explains that he has been holding the EFO together as best he can in the face of uncertainty, R5813 50/43945/43262.
99 LNA, 17 July 1946, memo from Vilatte to Lester noting that UN contract offers have now come through for four of the Princeton-based officials, R5813 50/43945/43262.
100 LNA, 16 July 1946, cable from Pelt to Lester confirming that UN contracts for League officials at Princeton are being finalized, and that he hopes to resolve the local staff 'issue' within the next two weeks, R5813 50/43945/43262; LNA, 20 July 1946, cable from Lester to Rosenborg apologizing that the League cannot extend the contracts of locally recruited staff, R5813 50/43945/43262.
101 LNA, 18 July 1946, letter from L. Malania – executive officer at the UN Department of Economic Affairs – to Una M. Russell – a local staff member of

the EFO at Princeton – inviting her to attend an interview in New York on 22 July 1946, R5813 50/43945/43262.

102 LNA, 26 July 1946, cable from Lester to Rosenborg in which the former notes that he now understands David Owen has stepped in to resolve the issue, R5813 50/43945/43262.

103 LNA, 17 June 1946, letter from Lester to Stencek asking the latter to forward Pelt's telegram of 8 June – regarding the UN takeover of the Princeton EFO functions – to Rosenborg, S922.

104 See: LNA, 18 June 1946, memo from Stencek to Lester on the Princeton transfer and the expected effect on publications, R5813 50/43945/43262; LNA, 26 July 1946, letter from Lester to Moderow explaining that the Princeton situation has been settled but that he would prefer more notice in future, R5813 50/43945/43262; LNA, 17 June 1946, letter from Lester to Pelt regarding the new UN contracts for Princeton-based staff, S927 50/43945/43262.

105 LNA, 20 July 1946, letter from Watterson to Lester, outlining a list of what he believed were the principal issues in relation to the liquidation of the Princeton office, R5813 50/43945/43262.

106 LNA, 3 August 1946, letter from Lester to Watterson, issuing instructions on the liquidation of the Princeton Office, and the agreements already in place with the UN, R5813 50/43945/43262.

107 LNA, 1 September 1946, League of Nations Board of Liquidation: First Interim Report presented in accordance with Paragraph 9 of the Assembly Resolution of April 18, 1946, C.83.M.83.1946., S570.

108 LNA, 18 July 1946, letter from Rosenborg to Lester, updating the latter on the current situation regarding the Princeton group, R5813 50/43945/43262.

109 LNA, 31 July 1946, letter from Rosenborg to Lester, in which the former explains that the work and experience of the EFO group at Princeton is expected to stay much the same for at least the next three to four weeks, R5813 50/43945/43262.

110 For an example of Lester's writings to Kisch, see: LNA, 31 May 1946, letter from Lester to Cecil Kisch, R5816.3 50/43877/43844. Lester's predecessor, Joseph Avenol, had previously refused to set a budget for 1941, without which the Secretariat would have been unable to function. James Barros's account of Avenol's tumultuous tenure remains the most comprehensive, over forty years since it was first published: Barros, James, *Betrayal from Within: Joseph Avenol, Secretary-General of the League of Nations, 1933–1940* (New Haven, CT: Yale University Press, 1969).

111 LNA, 17 August 1945, letter from Owen to Lester, asking the latter if they can have dinner together when he is next in London, S565.

112 LNA, 29 July 1946, letter from Lester to Moderow, noting that he could not bear any responsibility for the last-minute transfer should it go ahead, R5813 50/44054/43262.

3 Geneva and New York, August–December 1946

1 The Secretariat was made up of fifty-six officials on 1 August, but by 1 January 1947 this number had dropped to just twenty. See: League of Nations Archives, 1er Août 1946, Listes des Membres du Secrétariat de la Société des Nations, S698; LNA, 1er Janvier 1947, Listes des Membres du Secrétariat de la Société des Nations, S698.
2 Chester Purves, secretary to the Board of Liquidation, kept a list of outstanding issues requiring Board intervention at any point in time. For example, see LNA, 26 September 1946, report by Purves entitled 'Board of Liquidation: items carried over from the July meetings', R5816.4 50/44081/43844; LNA, 11 October 1946, report by Purves entitled 'Board of Liquidation: summary list of outstanding items (revised)', R5816.4 50/44081/43844.
3 The first point of the Common Plan stated 'The League of Nations agrees to transfer to the United Nations, and the United Nations agrees to receive on or about August 1st, 1946': LNA, 14 March 1946, Report by the League Supervisory Commission: Report on Discussions with the Representatives of the United Nations on Questions of the Transfer of League of Nations Assets, A.8.1946.X., S567.
4 For more on the rapid construction of the UN Secretariat in 1946, see: Ellen J. Ravndal, *In the Beginning: Secretary-General Trygve Lie and the Establishment of the UN* (Bristol: Bristol University Press, 2023), 128–9.
5 For examples of their correspondence in early August, see: LNA, 7 August 1946, letter from Trygve Lie to Seán Lester, R5813 50/43874/43262; LNA, 8 August 1946, letter from Lester to Lie, R5813 50/43874/43262.
6 Seán Lester's Diary, 5 August 1946, personal diary entry.
7 LNA, 7 August 1946, letter from Lie to Lester, R5813 50/43874/43262; LNA, 8 August 1946, letter from Lester to Lie, R5813 50/43874/43262.
8 In a personal memo, Lester noted that at a UN General Committee meeting of the night before, it was agreed by all participants to treat Lester (and others invited to the General Assembly) as 'distinguished visitors': Lester's Diary, 29 October 1946, personal diary entry.
9 Lester confirmed the 1 September 'moving' day in a letter to Hambro: Lester's Diary, 6 August 1946, letter from Lester to Carl Hambro.
10 For example, the official communique to governments regarding the transfer of the PCOB and the DSB was issued on 26 August 1946: LNA, 26 August 1946, Transfer

to the United Nations of the Activities of the League of Nations relating to the Control of Narcotic Drugs, C.L.15.1946.XI., R5813 50/44054/43262, 127–31.

11 LNA, 1 December 1946, League of Nations, *Board of Liquidation Second Interim Report*, C.89.M.89.1946, S923.

12 See Chapter 2 for more on the EFO transfer and liquidation.

13 Details of the different elements of the Princeton Office's liquidation can be found in Percy Watterson's first liquidation report: LNA, 3 September 1946, Board of Liquidation: League's Missions in the USA, Report No. 1, R5813 50/43945/43262.

14 Frank Aydelotte and the Princeton IAS continued to show much of the same generosity and warmth towards the League at this time as they had during the war. Watterson continued to use, with their permission, the Institute's Courier Service, throughout his efforts to close the League's office there: Shelby White and Leon Levy Archives Center, 23 August 1946, letter from Jane Richardson – Secretary to Aydelotte – to Percy Watterson confirming the latter can continue to use the courier service as needed, Director's Office: General Files: Box 38: League of Nations Correspondence Since August 1940, 70675 Princeton I.A.S. files: Aydelotte and the League.

15 Watterson's continued work with the League is a feature throughout this book.

16 Valentin Stencek and Alexander Elkin agreed the protocols for how these services would be transferred and used along the same lines as those drawn up for the Palais handover: LNA, 26 August 1946, memo from Elkin to Stencek, R5813 50/43874/43262. The transfer dates for the Documentation, Printing, and Publications Services Details can be found in: LNA, 1 December 1946, League of Nations, Board of Liquidation Second Interim Report, C.89.M.89.1946, S923.

17 Carolyn Biltoft, 'Decoding the Balance Sheet: Gifts, Goodwill, and the Liquidation of the League of Nations', *Capitalism: A Journal of History and Economics* 1, no. 2 (2020), 379–404.

18 UNOG Archives, [exact date unknown], memo from Elkin to Moderow, G.I. 4/4 (26).

19 For the reasoning behind the original low value of 50,000 Swiss francs and the debates between Moderow and Lester, see: LNA, 2 September 1946, personal memo written by Lester regarding his conversations with Moderow, S567; LNA, 6 September 1946, letter from Lester to Hambro regarding the original 50,000 Swiss francs value assigned to publications, S567.

20 Delays to these transfers were significant enough to cause Elkin to apologize to Stencek in October: LNA, 12 October 1946, memo from Elkin to Stencek, R5502 18B/43967/38729.

21 Just some of the Funds earmarked for transfer to the UN but not moved until 1947 were the Léon Bernard Fund, the Darling Foundation and the proceeds of the Wateler Peace Prize: LNA, 18 December 1946, cable from Lester to Adriaan Pelt

regarding the long-awaited UN decision on the Darling Foundation and the Léon Bernard Fund, R6115 8A/13512/13060.
22 Board members expressed some concerns about the inability to reach quorum during the UN General Assembly, suggesting the possibility of either liaising by correspondence or flying a Europe-based Board member to New York, but no decisions were made: LNA, 24 July 1946, Board of Liquidation: Provisional Minutes of Tenth Meeting, B.L./P.V.10, S569.
23 Carl Hambro, Cecil Kisch, Seymour Jacklin and Adolfo Costa du Rels were all in New York for the UN General Assembly, although Kisch did leave proceedings earlier than the others at the start of November. This left Atul Chatterjee, Daniel Secrétan, Émile Charvériat, F. T. Cheng and Jaromír Kopecky in Europe; an almost even split of members between the North American and European continents. For details of Kisch's earlier departure, see: LNA, [No date], letter from Kisch to Hambro confirming the latter's imminent departure, S567.
24 Lester recounted Lie's invitation to New York in a letter to Hambro: Lester's Diary, 6 August, letter from Lester to Hambro. He later confirmed his decision to attend in another letter to Hambro two weeks later: LNA, 22 August 1946, letter from Lester to Hambro, S567.
25 LNA, 30 August 1946, letter from Martin Hill to Lester requesting details of the latter's stay in New York in order to book accommodation for him, S567.
26 There are numerous examples of Watterson's logistics work preparing for Lester's trip: LNA, 9 September 1946, letter from Cosette Nonin to Watterson requesting the latter's assistance with documents, S567; LNA, 3 October 1946, letter from G.S. Stephenson, assistant treasurer at the Bankers Trust Company in New York, to Watterson, confirming establishment of a new account in Lester's name, S567; LNA, 23 December 1946, letter from Watterson to Nonin regarding outstanding issues on Lester's US bank account, S567.
27 We do not have an exact date for Hambro's departure from Oslo, although a telegram to Chester Purves, dated 14 September 1946, confirmed he had just left Europe: LNA, 14 September 1946, [unknown author], cable to Purves, R5816.3 50/43953/43844. Hambro departed New York on 21 December 1946: LNA, 20 December 1946, telegram from Hambro to Lester, R5816.4 50/44101/43844.
28 LNA, 24 October 1946, telegram from Purves to Lester, requesting Hambro's New York address, R5816.3 50/43953/43844.
29 LNA, 24 July 1946, Board of Liquidation: Provisional Minutes of Tenth Meeting B.L./P.V.10, S569.
30 Atlantic crossing time data comes from: Peter J. Hugill, *World Trade Since 1431: Geography, Technology, and Capitalism* (Baltimore: Johns Hopkins University Press, 1995), 128; Martin Stopford, *Maritime Economics*, Third Edition (London: Routledge, 2008).

31 Lester left on 14 October before sending confirmation of his arrival to Stencek on 24 October. His return passage left on 29 November, and he was back in Geneva by 10 December: LNA, 11 October 1946, letter from Lester to Lloyds and National Provincial Bank London, confirming the former's absence from 14 October, R5299 17/3934/3933; LNA, 24 October 1946, letter from Lester to Stencek confirming the former's arrival in the US, S567; LNA, 21 November 1946, letter from F.J. Saunders of the UN Transportation Services to Lester, confirming details of the latter's tickets for the Queen Elizabeth departing on 29 November, S567; LNA, 10 December 1946, letter from Lester (in Geneva) to Terence Maxwell regarding the Staff Pensions Fund, S568.
32 LNA, 22 August 1946, letter from Lester to Hambro confirming the former's 'ten days leave', S567.
33 One example of a lengthy update to Stencek is a letter he sent on 1 November, covering a number of different topics across three pages: LNA, 1 November 1946, letter from Lester to Stencek, S567.
34 The meeting minutes were eventually issued as a Board of Liquidation document on 6 December: LNA, 6 December 1946, Board of Liquidation document titled Notes on an Informal Meeting held in New York on 29 October 1946, B.L.68, S568.
35 United Nations Archive, 21 September 1946, memo from Moderow to Pelt and Egon Ranshofen-Wertheimer, G.V 4/1/114.
36 LNA, 1 May 1946, Board of Liquidation Rules of Procedure, B.L.3.(1), S570.
37 In a document prepared by Ernest Haury, the costs of holding a 6-day Board meeting in New York – including travel expenses and subsistence allowance for both Board members and Secretariat officials – came to a total of 66,624 Swiss francs: LNA, 19 September 1946, report prepared by E.H. Haury entitled 'Board of Liquidation: Meeting in New York (November 1946: 6 days), Estimated Cost', R5816.4 50/44081/43844. Lester later confirmed the impossibility of a meeting in letters to both Jaromír Kopecky and Kisch: LNA, 1 November 1946, letter from Lester to Jaromír Kopecky, S567; LNA, 5 November 1946, letter from Lester to Kisch, S567.
38 LNA, 1 November 1946, letter from Lester to Stencek updating the latter on the unofficial Board meeting, S567.
39 For example: LNA, 18 November 1946, letter from Kopecky to Purves regarding the next Board of Liquidation meeting, R5816.4 50/44101/43844.
40 League of Nations, *Official Journal Special Supplement No. 194: Records of the Twentieth (Conclusion) and Twenty-First Ordinary Sessions of the Assembly* (Geneva: League of Nations, 1946), 282.
41 LNA, 1 December 1946, League of Nations, Board of Liquidation Second Interim Report, C.89.M.89.1946 S923; LNA, 14 November 1946, letter from Purves to Daniel Secrétan in which the former explains the second report 'will contain

only a bare recital of events that have taken place since the last Report', R5816.3 50/44023/43844.
42 Chapter 4 examines this in greater detail. See also: Emil Eiby Seidenfaden, 'Legitimizing International Bureaucracy: Press and Information Work from the League of Nations to the UN', in Karen Gram-Skjoldager, Haakon A. Ikonomou and Torsten Kahlert (eds), *Organizing the 20th-Century World: International Organizations and the Emergence of International Public Administration, 1920–1960s* (London: Bloomsbury, 2020); Carolyn N. Biltoft, *A Violent Peace: Media, Truth, and Power at the League of Nations* (Chicago: University of Chicago Press, 2021).
43 LNA, 18 November 1946, letter from Lester to Sweetser, S567. Also see: Lester's Diary, 6 August 1946, letter from Lester to Hambro.
44 LNA, 22 August 1946, letter from Lester to Hambro, S567.
45 LNA, 5 November 1946, letter from Lester to Stencek, S567. LNA, 18 November 1946, letter from Lester to Sweetser in which he recalls a trip to see Hudson, S567; LNA, 22 November 1946, telegram from Lester to Sweetser confirming dinner plans, S567.
46 Martin Hill wrote to Lester in early October as he was concerned Lie had not gained USSR approval for Lester's visit to the General Assembly and, while he was not convinced of it, he was worried there might be a repeat of the events of San Francisco: Lester's Diary, 7 October 1946, letter from Hill to Lester.
47 LNA, 1 November 1946, letter from Lester to Kopecky confirming the General Assembly delegate status of Hambro, Kisch and Jacklin, S567.
48 See Chapter 2 for more details of the Jacklin-Lester relationship.
49 Lester complained most often – in regard to Jacklin – to Cecil Kisch: LNA, 5 November 1946, letter from Lester to Kisch, S567.
50 Lester expressed his concerns about the unwieldy size of the Board in a letter to Hambro: LNA, 10 September 1946, letter from Lester to Hambro, S567.
51 LNA, 18 November 1946, letter from Lester to Sweetser, S567.
52 See: LNA, 17 July 1946, Board of Liquidation: Provisional Minutes of Sixth Meeting B.L./P.V.6, S569; LNA, 26 July 1946, Board of Liquidation document titled Claim of Manley Hudson to relief from US income tax on arrears of salary B.L.45(c), S569; LNA, 3 December 1946, letter from Hambro to Lester regarding Hudson's income tax claims, S567.
53 LNA, 27 December 1946, letter from Stencek to Loveday, R5276 17/40603/1371.
54 Over twenty Board of Liquidation documents were produced across this period, plus a further seven Secretariat progress reports. For two examples, see: LNA, 15 October 1946, Board of Liquidation: Eighth Fortnightly Progress Report, B.L./F.P.R.8, S923; LNA, 21 November 1946, Board of Liquidation document titled Disposal of the Surplus in respect of the Financial Year 1945, B.L.66, S569.
55 Biltoft, 'Decoding the Balance Sheet', 379–404.

56 LNA, 14 March 1946, Supervisory Commissions document titled Report on Discussions with the Representatives of the United Nations on Questions of the Transfer of League of Nations Assets A.8.1946.X, S567.
57 Stencek provided a detailed breakdown of the negotiations in a letter to Lester in early November: LNA, 7 November 1946, letter from Stencek to Lester, R5813 50/43874/43262.
58 The transfer of the Staff Pensions Fund is covered in Chapter 5.
59 LNA, 14 December 1946, letter from Lester to Hambro regarding the ILO/Pensions Fund situation, S567.
60 Giraud prefaced a larger memo on the matter with a note to Lester, in which he wrote 'The claim, to my mind, has no legal ground and the suit will be lost.' LNA, 22 October 1946, note from Émile Giraud to Lester, S567; LNA, 22 October 1946, memo by Giraud titled 'Is there a legal basis for the claim that the salaries of the League of Nations officials who have exercised their functions in the USA. should be exempted from taxation?', S567.
61 The background, progression and outcomes of this lawsuit are covered in more detail in both Chapters 4 and 5. See also: LNA, 19 November 1946, Lester personal note on conversation between himself and Jacklin, R3748 3A/41136/705.
62 LNA, 18 November 1946, letter from Kopecky to Purves regarding the next Board of Liquidation meeting, R5816.4 50/44101/43844; LNA, 10 December 1946, handwritten letter from Atul Chatterjee to Lester regarding the next Board of Liquidation meeting, S567.
63 The outcomes of the twenty-first Assembly were not clear on the relationship between the Board and the Secretariat: LN, *Records of the Twenty-First Assembly*, 269–72.
64 See Chapter 2 for more details on the rush to build the UN Secretariat.
65 For an example of the back-and-forth regarding the report into January, see Purves's cable to Hambro in January: LNA, 3 January 1947, cable from Purves to Hambro regarding edits to the Second Interim Report, R5816.3 50/44023/43844. See also LNA, 1 December 1946, League of Nations, Board of Liquidation Second Interim Report, C.89.M.89.1946, S923.
66 Lester outlined some of his concerns with the 1947 budget in a letter to Kisch in November: LNA, 19 November 1946, letter from Lester to Kisch, R5353 17/44093/44093.
67 LNA, 11 October 1946, Summary List of Outstanding Items for the Board of Liquidation, produced by Chester Purves, R5816.4 50/44081/43844.
68 LNA, 11 October 1946, letter from Lester to the manager of the Lloyds and National Provincial Bank in London, R5299 17/3934/3933.

69 For details of Stencek's work in this area, see his update for Lester in mid-October: LNA, 11 October 1946, letter from Stencek to Lester on the staff furniture situation, S567.
70 LNA, 4 October 1946, letter from Stencek to Kamal Kumar, head of the New Delhi Office, regarding the reimbursement of the purchase of a length of garden hose, R5353 17/43613/43553.
71 LNA, 26 February 1945, letter from Evelyn Curry to Loveday, S750; LNA, 22 March 1945, letter from Bertil Renborg to Lester, S750. Stencek later wrote to Renborg, head of the Drug Control Service, in early August 1946, suggesting Curry's move to the Treasury to 'prop up' that department, as well as preventing her from having to work alongside Steinig again: LNA, 9 August 1946, letter from Stencek to Renborg, S750.
72 LNA, 11 November 1946, letter from Stencek to Lester, S567.
73 See: LNA, 11 November 1946, letter from Purves to Lester, R5816.3 50/44023/43844; LNA, 11 November 1946, letter from Purves to Kisch, R5816.3 50/44023/43844.
74 On 1 August 1946 there were fifty-six Secretariat officials in post, nineteen of whom were women. By 1 January 1947 the total number of officials was down to twenty, twelve of whom were women. See: LNA, 1er Août 1946, Listes des Membres du Secrétariat de la Société des Nations, S698; LNA, 1er Janvier 1947, Listes des Membres du Secrétariat de la Société des Nations, S698.
75 See Harris's personnel file for the full details of her various roles: LNA, [unknown date and author], C.M. Harris curriculum vitae, S789.
76 LNA, 27 August 1947, letter from Lester to Constance Harris, S789.
77 LNA, 18 September 1946, letter from Stencek to Curry, S750.
78 LNA, 29 July 1946, letter from Cecily Babington to Stencek, S707.
79 LNA, 2 August 1946, letter from Babington to Stencek, S707.
80 For examples, see contract renewals for Marie Boiteux in July and December 1946: LNA, 11 July 1946, letter from Stencek to Marie Boiteux, S723; LNA, 13 December 1946, memo from Stencek to Boiteux, S723.
81 For details on the agreement to hold the Council meeting at the League see: LNA, 12 July 1946, letter from Ranshofen-Wertheimer to Moderow regarding the use of the Palais des Nations for the UNRRA Council Session, R5810 50/43985/42168. Also see: LNA, 11 September 1946, [unknown author], Protocol Signed by Representatives of the United Nations, the League of Nations, and the United Nations Relief and Rehabilitation Administration, in Geneva, R5810 50/43985/42168.
82 Ilaria Scaglia, *The Emotions of Internationalism: Feeling International Cooperation in the Interwar Period* (Oxford: Oxford University Press, 2020), 76–9.

83 Giraud officially left on 31 December 1946, Vilatte on 5 November 1946 and Watterson departed on 31 October 1946. See LNA, Personnel file: Émile Giraud; LNA, Personnel file: Henri Vilatte; LNA, Personnel file: Percy Gill Watterson.
84 LNA, 1er Janvier 1947, Listes des Membres du Secrétariat de la Société des Nations, S698.
85 LNA, 29 October 1946, letter from Valentin Stencek to Seán Lester, S567.

4 (Un)Avoidable delays, January–July 1947

1 Ilaria Scaglia, *Emotions of Internationalism: Feeling International Cooperation in the Alps in the Interwar Period* (Oxford: Oxford University Press, 2020), 3–17.
2 Ranshofen-Wertheimer, *The International Secretariat*, 201; Emil Eiby Seidenfaden, 'Legitimizing International Bureaucracy: Press and Information Work from the League of Nations to the UN', in Karen Gram-Skjoldager, Haakon A. Ikonomou, and Torsten Kahlert (eds), *Organizing the 20th-Century World: International Organizations and the Emergence of International Public Administration, 1920–1960s* (London: Bloomsbury, 2020), 131.
3 Seán Lester's Diary, February 1946 [exact date unknown], letter from Sweetser to Hambro.
4 See Chapter 3 for more on the backdating of the Board's Interim Reports.
5 League of Nations Archives, 12 June 1947, Board of Liquidation: Minutes of Twenty-Eighth Meeting B.L./P.V.28, S569.
6 In its sixteenth meeting, the Board spent time considering how its decisions regarding contributions might be interpreted by members, and how the presentation of these decisions could be manipulated to avoid criticism. LNA, 14 February 1947, Board of Liquidation: Provisional Minutes of Sixteenth (Private) Meeting B.L./P.V.16, S569.
7 The Final Report was discussed at nine out of the ten last Board meetings. For examples see: LNA, 9 July 1947, Board of Liquidation: Provisional Minutes of Thirty-Fourth Meeting B.L./P.V.34, S569; LNA, 23 July 1947, Board of Liquidation: Provisional Minutes of Forty-Second Meeting B.L./P.V.42, R5816.2 50/43856/43844.
8 LNA, 26 April 1947, letter from Purves to F. T. Cheng regarding the Final Report publication date, R5816.3 50/44023/43844; LNA, 1 May 1947, Board of Liquidation: Fourth Interim Report, covering the period March 1st–30th April, 1947, C.4.M.4.1947, S923.
9 LNA, 27 June 1947, Board of Liquidation document, prepared by Purves, titled Preliminary Draft of Final Report to States Members B.L.164, R5816.4 50/44023/43844.

10 LNA, 23 July 1947, Board of Liquidation: Provisional Minutes of Forty-Second Meeting B.L/P.V.42, R5816.2 50/43856/43844.
11 See LNA, 22 July 1947, Board of Liquidation: Provisional Minutes of Forty-First Meeting B.L./P.V.41, R5816.2 50/43856/43844; LNA, 23 July 1947, Board of Liquidation: Minutes of Forty-Second Meeting B.L./P.V.42, R5816.2 50/43856/43844.
12 League of Nations, *Board of Liquidation Final Report, Presented to States Members of the League of Nations in accordance with the Requirement of the Final Article of the Resolution for the Dissolution of the League of Nations Adopted by the Assembly on April 18th, 1946, at Its Twenty-first Ordinary Session* (Geneva: League of Nations, 1947), 51.
13 The ILO Governing Body was in session from 13 June to 10 July 1947, but the negotiations regarding the transfer of the Pensions' Funds did not feature in that time, nor did the Governing Body officially approve the decision of its sub-committee led by Myrddin-Evans: International Labour Office, *Minutes of the 102nd Session of the Governing Body. Geneva – 13 June -10 July 1947* (Geneva: International Labour Organization, 1947).
14 Very few governments acknowledged the issuance of the Final Report; two examples are: LNA, 12 September 1947, letter from La Secretaría de Estado de Relaciones Exteriores de la República Dominicana to the Secretary-General League of Nations, R5816.4 50/44023/43844; LNA, 14 October 1947, letter from La Secretaría de Relaciones Exteriores de los Estados Unidos Mexicanos to the Secretary-General of the League of Nations, R5816.4 50/44023/43844.
15 The official transfer of the Archives to UN ownership in August 1946 was laid out in a letter to Hambro: LNA, 6 September 1946, letter from Lester to Hambro, S567.
16 At an early May 1946 Board meeting, Kisch suggested 'vandalism' might follow the UN takeover of the Palais: LNA, 1 May 1946, Board of Liquidation: Minutes of Third Meeting B.L./P.V.3, S569. And in a message to Moderow at the end of July 1946, Pelt suggested the Archives would be transferred to New York: LNA, 26 July 1946, cable from Pelt to Moderow, R5813 50/44054/43262.
17 LNA, 3 June 1947, memo from Stencek to Lester regarding the Board's archives, R5816.4 50/44126/43844.
18 Registry file box R5294 of the League's Archives contains files on gifts and legacies to the League, dated 1933–47, alongside the Board's work on contributions.
19 LNA, 12 June 1947, Board of Liquidation: Provisional Minutes of Twenty-Eighth Meeting B.L./P.V.28, S569; LNA, 5 June 1947, Board of Liquidation memorandum, prepared by Lester, titled Disposal of the Board's Archives, R5816.4 50/44126/43844.
20 Moderow, confirming the establishment of the new procedures, wrote to Lester in mid-April and, at the wish of Pelt, conveyed the UN's commitment to the

League's Archives: LNA, 15 April 1947, letter from Moderow to Lester, R5813 50/44104/43844.
21 UNA, 12 November 1946, letter from Moderow to Pelt, G.V. 2/2/5 (346).
22 The future management of the League's Archives was outlined in: LNA, 24 February 1947, memo by Renborg entitled Note Concerning Transfer to United Nations, Lake Success, of League of Nations Registry Files, R5813 50/44104/43262.
23 Lester's Diary, February 1946 [exact date unknown], letter from Sweetser to Hambro.
24 LNA, 27 February 1947, letter from Lester to Moderow, R5813 50/44104/43262.
25 LNA, 5 June 1947, Board of Liquidation memorandum, prepared by Lester, titled Disposal of the Board's Archives, R5816.4 50/44126/43844.
26 LNA, 12 June 1947, Board of Liquidation: Provisional Minutes of the Twenty-Eighth Meeting B.L./P.V.28, S569.
27 Ilaria Habermann-Box, 'From the League of Nations to the United Nations: The Continuing Preservation and Development of the Geneva Archives', in Madeleine Herren, (ed.), *Networking the International System: Global Histories of International Organizations* (Heidelberg: Springer, 2014), p. 28. For more on the UNESCO Memory of the World Programme, see: https://en.unesco.org/partnerships/partnering/memory-world (retrieved 3 December 2021).
28 Lester wrote to Frederic Hapgood – formerly of the League Registry service and transferred to the UN at the end of August 1946 – confirming that he and Moderow had agreed to grant Walters access to the Archives, and that Hapgood should provide all necessary services to him. LNA, 11 December 1946, memo from Lester to Hapgood, S568.
29 Lester's Diary, 5 August 1947, letter from Sweetser to Lester.
30 LNA, 1 May 1947, letter from Lester to Kisch, S567; LNA, 14 May 1947, letter from Lester to Hambro, S567.
31 Two separate plans for the museum, from 1933 and 1937, were enclosed in a letter from the secretary of the Building Committee to Stencek: LNA, 15 May 1937, letter from F.I. Lloyd to Stencek, R5265 16/33081/33080.
32 LNA, 30 April 1946, Board of Liquidation: Minutes of the Second Meeting B.L./P.V.2, R5816.2 50/43856/43844; LNA, 16 May 1946, memo from Lester to an unknown recipient regarding the decision to continue with the planned 'portrait gallery', R5265 16/33082/33080.
33 LNA, 10 July 1946, memo from Tevfik Erim and Willem van Asch van Wijck to Lester, R5265 16/33082/33080.
34 Stencek made his note on the lack of women, alongside some suggestions, in a personal memo: LNA, 11 July 1946, Stencek personal memo, R5265 16/33082/33080. The Board of Liquidation asked for example photo sizes so it could decide the best dimensions for portraits at a secret meeting in July 1946: LNA,

23 July 1946, Board of Liquidation: Minutes of the Secret Meeting, R5816.2 50/43856/43844. LNA, 10 July 1946, report by Erim and van Asch van Wijck on figures to be included in the exhibit, R5265 16/33082/33080; LNA, 26 November 1946, letter from Hambro to Lester agreeing the purchase of glass cabinets, S567.
35 LNA, 9 August 1946, letter from Secrétan to Lester, R5265 16/33080/33080; LNA, 16 January 1947, letter from John D. Rockefeller Jr. to Sweetser, R5265 16/33080/33080.
36 Biltoft, 'Decoding the Balance Sheet', 379–404.
37 LNA, 23 May 1946, memo from Arthur Breycha-Vauthier to Stencek, R5265 16/33082/33080.
38 In a letter to Alexander Loveday at the start of 1945, Lester described Breycha-Vauthier as 'extremely energetic and resourceful'. Lester's Diary, 3 January 1945, letter from Lester to Loveday.
39 For example, see: LNA, 11 July 1947, letter from G. Kaeckenbeeck – of the Belgian Foreign Affairs and Commerce Ministry – to Breycha-Vauthier regarding a portrait of Hymans, R5265 16/33080/33080.
40 LNA, 15 April 1947, Board of Liquidation: Provisional Minutes of Twenty-Second Meeting B.L./P.V.22, S569; LNA, 16 July 1947, memo from van Asch van Wijck to Stencek regarding new suggestions for the museum from Breycha-Vauthier, R5265 16/33082/33080.
41 LNA, 12 September 1946, letter from Stencek to Hambro suggesting the inclusion of the tapestries, S567; LNA, 5 November 1946, letter from Stencek to Watterson, S567; LNA, 4 June 1947, list of the tapestries and their themes prepared by Breycha-Vauthier, R5265 16/33080/33080.
42 LNA, 12 March 1947, letter from van Asch van Wijck to A. Ganem – of the French Foreign Ministry – regarding a portrait of Briand, R5265 16/33080/33080.
43 LNA, 14 June 1946, letter from Stencek to Watterson, asking the latter if he can procure a duplicate medal to replace the one that had been lost, R5265 16/33080/33080.
44 LNA, 15 April 1947, Board of Liquidation: Provisional Minutes of Twenty-Second Meeting B.L./P.V.22, S569.
45 LNA, 8 July 1947, Board of Liquidation: Provisional Minutes of Thirty-Third Meeting B.L./P.V.33, S569.
46 Adolfo Costa du Rels made the initial suggestion of film footage at the Board's 22nd meeting: LNA, 15 April 1947, Board of Liquidation: Provisional Minutes of Twenty-Second Meeting B.L./P.V.22, S569. Meanwhile, Jaromír Kopecky mentioned gramophone recordings of speeches from the League's Final Assembly to Lester in July: LNA, 16 July 1947, memo from Lester to van Asch van Wijck, S567. Ranshofen-Wertheimer explained the expansion of the Information's Section in the 1930s to include the production of films and audio recordings demonstrating the League's work: Egon F. Ranshofen-Wertheimer, *The International Secretariat: A*

Great Experiment in International Administration (Washington, DC: Carnegie Endowment for International Peace, 1945), 206–7.

47 LNA, 8 July 1947, Board of Liquidation: Provisional Minutes of Thirty-Third Meeting B.L./P.V.33, S569.

48 Stencek suggested that Secretariat directors and heads of departments and sections should be allowed to review, and provide commentary on, the proposals of the Erim, van Asch van Wijck, and Breycha-Vauthier sub-committee: LNA, 11 July 1946, personal memo by Stencek, R5265 16/33082/33080.

49 LNA, 16 July 1947, [unknown author], internal circular titled Board of Liquidation, Historical Gallery, providing details of attendees and timings, R5265 16/33082/33080.

50 LNA, 9 May 1947, Lester to van Asch van Wijck regarding the possibility of an opening ceremony in July, S567.

51 UNOG Archives, 18 July 1947, memo from Moderow to Pelt providing an overview of the handover ceremony and Moderow's speech, G.I. 4/15 (1978).

52 The organization's aim was 'Lasting Peace Through Social Justice'. David A. Morse, *The Origin and Evolution of the ILO and Its Role in the World Community* (Ithaca: W. F. Humphrey Press, 1969), 9.

53 Ibid., 15.

54 The book in which O'Connor's essay appears was a compilation of Phelan's unfinished memoirs and was published as part of the ILO Century Project in 2009: Emmet O'Connor, 'Edward Phelan: A Biographical Essay', in International Labour Organization (ed.), *Edward Phelan and the ILO: The Life and Views of an International Social Actor* (Geneva: International Labour Organization, 2009), 33.

55 The Philadelphia Declaration is widely considered a key moment in the ILO's history. Daniel Maul called it 'a turning point', David Morse described it as 'the rebirth of steadfast confidence in the mission of the ILO', while Antony Alcock suggested it set a precedent for the UN Charter and the Universal Declaration of Human Rights. Daniel Maul, *The International Labour Organization: 100 Years of Global Social Policy* (Berlin: De Gruyter Oldenbourg, 2019), 111; Morse, *Origin and Evolution of the ILO*, 28–30; Antony Alcock, *History of the International Labour Organisation* (London: Palgrave Macmillan, 1971), 182–3.

56 Maul, *The International Labour Organization*, 137–8.

57 From O'Connor, 'Edward Phelan', 32.

58 Ibid., 24–7.

59 As outlined in: LNA, 12 April 1947, Board of Liquidation document, prepared by Lester, titled Removal and repatriation expenses of former and present League officials B.L.118, S569; LNA, 14 April 1947, Board of Liquidation: Provisional Minutes of Twenty-First Meeting B.L./P.V.21, S569.

60 The transfer was outlined in a letter to Phelan on 2 April 1947, and by 15th of that same month, it had been carried out: LNA, 2 April 1947, letter from Lester to Edward Phelan regarding the transfer of the Working Capital Fund, R5306 17/43861/8461; LNA, 15 April 1947, letter from Phelan to Lester thanking the latter for the transfer, R5306 17/43861/8461.
61 Ranshofen-Wertheimer, *The International Secretariat*, 312–13.
62 LNA, 28 January 1947, Board of Liquidation document, written by Lester, titled Staff Pensions Fund B.L.83, S569.
63 Lester's 28 January 1947 telegram to Phelan was distributed to Board members as part of a Board of Liquidation document: LNA, 8 February 1947, Board of Liquidation document, prepared by Lester, titled Staff Pensions Fund B.L.94, S569.
64 LNA, 5 February 1947, telegram, dictated over the telephone, from Phelan to Lester, S568.
65 The 2.5m Swiss francs figure was confirmed following a face-to-face conversation between Lester and Myrddin-Evans at the end of February: LNA, 27 February 1947, letter from Lester to Guildhaume Myrddin-Evans, S568.
66 Myrddin-Evans explained in a letter to Lester: 'it is most unlikely that the Governing body would agree to accept a calculation based on any higher figure': LNA, 19 March 1947, letter from Myrddin-Evans to Lester, S568.
67 Lester wrote of 'shock' and 'great disappointment' following the Governing Body session: LNA, 14 March 1947, letter from Lester to Cecil Kisch, S568.
68 LNA, 18 February 1947, Board of Liquidation: Provisional Minutes of Seventeenth (Private) Meeting B.L./P.V.17, S569. Lester made his proposal to Myrddin-Evans in later February: LNA, 27 February 1947, letter from Lester to Myrddin-Evans, S568.
69 In 1947 the Governing Body was made up of sixteen government representatives, eight from the employment group and eight from the worker's groups, reflecting the wider organization's tripartite structure. For details of the 1947 members see: ILO, *Minutes of the 102nd Session of the Governing Body*.
70 LNA, 14 March 1947, letter from Lester to Kisch outlining the results of the ILO Governing Body session, S568. Lester would also write to Hambro five days later, noting he was 'still suffering from the shock and disappointment': LNA, 19 March 1947, letter from Lester to Carl Hambro, S568.
71 A letter, dated 19 March 1947, from Myrddin-Evans to Lester, was read out during the Board's twenty-third meeting on 16 April 1947: LNA, 16 April 1947, Board of Liquidation: Provisional Minutes of Twenty-Third Meeting B.L./P.V.23, S569.
72 LNA, 27 May 1947, cable from Lester to Kisch detailing planned dates for negotiation with the Governing Body delegation, R5816.4 50/44117/43844.
73 LNA, 28 January 1947, Board of Liquidation document, written by Lester, titled Judges' Pensions Fund B.L.84, S569.

74 Details of the technical opinion obtained from Nationale Levensverzekering-Bank N.V. were sent to Board members in April 1947: LNA, 10 April 1947, Board of Liquidation document, written by Lester, titled Judges' Pensions Fund B.L.115, S569.
75 LNA, 7 May 1947, letter from Lester to Hambro regarding the conversations he had over a dinner in Geneva with Phelan, Myrddin-Evans, G.A. Johnston and Wilfred Jenks, S568.
76 Phelan outlined the ILO position in a letter to Lester in mid-April: LNA, 14 April 1947, letter from Phelan to Lester, R5306 17/43861/8461.
77 LNA, 7 May 1947, letter from Lester to Hambro regarding the conversations he had over a dinner in Geneva with Phelan, Myrddin-Evans, G. A. Johnston and Wilfred Jenks, S568.
78 Ibid.
79 Phelan wrote: 'I therefore venture to suggest that the decision concerning the allocation of certain arrears to the Reserve Fund should not be considered as final until the consultation … has taken place.' Phelan's 2 June 1947 letter was distributed to Board members via a Board of Liquidation document: LNA, 5 June 1947, Board of Liquidation document, prepared by Lester, titled Application of Article 33(b) of the Financial Regulations: Further correspondence with the director general of the International Labour Office B.L.137(a), S569.
80 LNA, 7 May 1947, letter from Lester to Hambro regarding the conversations he had over a dinner in Geneva with Phelan, Myrddin-Evans, G. A. Johnston and Wilfred Jenks, S568.
81 In his memoirs, collected in a volume by the ILO, Phelan wrote that the financial system between the two organizations was 'far too complicated' and that 'its successful operation depended entirely on the existence of a large measure of goodwill and understanding between them'. ILO (ed.), *Edward Phelan and the ILO*, 242.
82 See LNA, 13 June 1947, Board of Liquidation: Provisional Minutes of Thirtieth Meeting B.L./P.V.30, S569.
83 LNA, 14 June 1947, Board of Liquidation: Provisional Minutes of Thirty-First Meeting B.L./P.V.31, S569.
84 C. N. Biltoft, 'Decoding the Balance Sheet: Gifts, Goodwill, and the Liquidation of the League of Nations', *Capitalism: A Journal of History and Economics* 1, no. 2 (2020), 391–3; LNA, 11 February 1947, Board of Liquidation: Provisional Minutes of Twelfth Meeting B.L./P.V.12, S569.
85 LNA, 10 April 1946, statement of the proportion of the total contributions of each state member paid to the League up to 31 March 1946, R5294 17/43857/3223.
86 The precise outstanding debt was 6,267,468.09 Swiss francs. This figure did not include those member debts which were forgiven, that is, wiped clean, during the liquidation process. A detailed breakdown of the contributions' calculations is in

the Final Report issued by the Board of Liquidation. It should be noted that while this publication has a listed publication date of 31 July 1947, it was not completed and distributed until the start of September 1947: LN, *Board of Liquidation: Final Report to Members*, 28–45.
87 Documents prepared for the Board outlined the position of publication sales debts in January and July of 1947: LNA, 29 January 1947, Board of Liquidation document, prepared by Lester, titled League Publications Accounts B.L.85, S569; LNA, 23 July 1947, [unknown author], Board of Liquidation document titled Publications Service: Outstanding Accounts B.L.176, S569.
88 LNA, 14 June 1947, Board of Liquidation: Provisional Minutes of Thirty-First Meeting B.L./P.V.31, S569; LNA, 27 May 1947, letter from Stencek to Watterson asking the latter to pursue the debt with the Alien Property Custodian in Washington D.C., C1784-4 18A/11022/1919.
89 LNA, 14 April 1947, Board of Liquidation: Provisional Minutes of Twenty-First Meeting B.L.P/V.21, S569.
90 LNA, 2 April 1947, Board of Liquidation document, prepared by Lester, titled Renovation Fund and containing correspondence between Lester and Phelan in regard to the League Renovation Fund B.L.113, S570.
91 LNA, 5 May 1947, letter from Kisch to Lester, S568.
92 LNA, 21 April 1947, Board of Liquidation: Provisional Minutes of Twenty-Sixth Meeting B.L./P.V.26, S569.
93 LNA, 17 June 1947, letter from Hambro to Myrddin-Evans officially accepting the terms of the agreement, R5306 17/43861/8461; LNA, 27 June 1947, letter from Lester to Terence Maxwell explaining the agreement reached between the League and the ILO and the dates of transfer, S568 18A/27605/3411; LNA, 28 June 1947, letter from Lester and Stencek to the Manager of the Lloyds & National Provincial Foreign Bank Ltd. confirming the bolstering of the Staff Pensions Fund by 2.2m Swiss francs, R5299 17/3934/3933.
94 LNA, 1er Janvier 1947, Listes des Membres du Secrétariat de la Société des Nations, S698; LNA, 23 August 1947, letter from Lester to Stencek confirming the staffing arrangements for September 1947 onwards, S723.
95 LNA, [no date], Curriculum Vitae of C.M. Harris prepared by League of Nations Secretariat, S789.
96 The other four officials who had more than one appointment all had two in total. Cecily Babington and Alma Schibli both worked for the Secretariat in the 1920s before returning after the Second World War, while Chester Purves and Roger Fuss both left the service in mid-1940 before being recruited again in 1946 and 1942 respectively.
97 LNA, 10 August 1934, letter from unknown author to N. Williams regarding Winifred Oberdorff's request to return to the Secretariat, S844; LNA, 2 April 1947,

memo written by Stencek explaining that he had convinced Oberdorff to stay with the League following her resignation earlier that day, S844.
98. LNA, 19 January 1945, letter from Alma Raisin to Stencek asking the latter to keep her in mind for any English secretarial roles, S876.
99. Purves left the Secretariat, for the first time, in 1940 following Avenol's call for resignations: LNA, 19 July 1940, letter from Stencek to Purves acknowledging the latter's resignation, S860.
100. Purves did not want to leave his niece in London when he returned to Geneva, and thus directly asked if he could bring her with him and have her work for the League. LNA, 30 January 1946, letter from Jacklin to Lester outlining the reappointment (and appointment) of Purves and his niece, S860.
101. LNA, 12 September 1946, letter from Stencek to Watterson suggesting he remain on the League payroll on a part-time basis, S904.
102. League of Nations Archives, 4 June 1947, letter from Watterson to Stencek, C1784-4.
103. LNA, 17 July 1946, cable from Lester to Ansgar Rosenborg regarding the agreement with the FAO in regard to Watterson, S904.
104. Rosenborg, now working at the UN, took on the responsibility for the publication of the final EFO publication, titled *Europe's Population in the Interwar Years*, in late November 1946. As Watterson had not been part of the EFO and Geneva was keen to close the Princeton accounts as soon as possible, it was felt that Rosenborg would be a better figure to oversee the process: LNA, 26 November 1946, letter from Stencek to Ansgar Rosenborg asking if the latter would accept responsibility for the publication, C1741 19/43868/43868.
105. Watterson discovered in February 1947 that fire insurance covering League publications held in Trenton, New Jersey, was still active, over six months after it should have been cancelled: LNA, 14 February 1947, letter from A. W. Volz of Walter F. Smith and Company to Watterson, C1784-4. For examples of Watterson pursuing debts see: LNA, 7 May 1947, letter from Watterson to Stencek regarding League monies held with the Banque de l'Indochine in Hanoi, C1784-4, or LNA, 5 June 1947, letter from Watterson to David L. Bazelon regarding outstanding publications debts, C1784-4. LNA, 3 February 1947, letter from Benjamin Gerig to Dean Lockwood of Haverford College, Pennsylvania, regarding the removal of League tapestries from the College to Geneva, C1784-4.
106. Watterson explained the situation regarding the publication of *Europe's Population in the Interwar Years* in a letter to Stencek: LNA, 20 May 1947, letter from Watterson to Stencek, C1784-4.
107. In a letter to Rosenborg in early January 1947, Watterson wrote: 'Despite the few people that still remain in League service in Geneva, it seems that they have little to do with one another.' LNA, 9 January 1947, letter from Watterson to Rosenborg,

C1741. He wrote to Chester Purves about the above incident, reminding him that he left Princeton some months earlier: LNA, 9 January 1947, letter from Watterson to Purves, C1784-4 10A/43320/41207.
108 LNA, 4 July 1946, [unknown author], Board of Liquidation document titled Income Tax on Salaries of League Officials in USA. B.L.17, S570.
109 See Edwards' letter to Hambro: LNA, 12 March 1947, letter from Harold Edwards – of Edwards & Smith in New York – to Carl Hambro, R3748 3A/41136/705.
110 In a letter to Lester, Hambro wrote: 'Under the circumstances, I can do nothing but ask them [Edwards & Smith] to keep on': LNA, 3 December 1946, letter from Hambro to Lester, S567.
111 Hambro wrote 'I do not like the whole situation and we shall have to discuss whether it would not be the best course to cut our losses and get out of this whole disgusting law suit.' LNA, 18 March 1947, letter from Hambro to Lester, R3748 3A/41136/705.
112 LNA, 12 April 1947, League of Nations: Board of Liquidation, Provisional Minutes of Twentieth Meeting B.L./P.V.20, S569.
113 LNA, 24 April 1947, letter from Hambro to Edwards, R3748 3A/41136/705.
114 Cecil Kisch told his fellow Board members: 'A Government faced with a similar situation would certainly decide in favour of a continuance.' LNA, 12 April 1947, Board of Liquidation: Provisional Minutes of Twentieth Meeting B.L./P.V.20, S569.
115 Watterson wrote to Stencek in May 1947 to check if the case was still happening as he had not received any information on the subject: LNA, 2 May 1947, letter from Watterson to Stencek, R3748 3A/41136/705.
116 LNA, 4 June 1947, letter from Watterson to Stencek, C1784-4.
117 LNA, 20 June 1947, letter from Stencek to Watterson outlining the position of trustee, C1784-4 3A/41136/705(2).
118 LNA, 25 June 1947, telegram from Watterson to Stencek, R3748 3A/41136/705.
119 This meant 984,761 Swiss francs of the voluntary contributions had been 'used for ordinary Secretariat expenditure': LNA, 14 June 1947, letter from Stencek to Lester, S922.
120 LNA, 12 June 1947, letter from Yves Biraud to Hambro, S922. A full list of signées can be found at: LNA, 26 juin 1947, Liste des signataires de la pétition concernant le remboursement de la contribution volontaire et auxquels ont a envoyé copie de la lettre adressée en réponse, au Dr. Biraud, S922.
121 LNA, 16 June 1947, Board of Liquidation document, prepared by Lester, titled Voluntary Contributions B.L.160, S922.
122 LNA, 12 June 1947, letter from Biraud addressed to 'Monsieur le Président du Comité de Liquidation de la Société des Nations', S922. When forwarding Biraud's letter to Lester, Stencek noted that several current officials had also been approached to co-sign but, while feeling sympathy for the request, had thought it best to abstain. LNA, 14 June 1947, letter from Stencek to Lester, S922.

123 Lester wrote: 'I am asked to inform you that the Board does not see its way to grant the request.' LNA, 23 June 1947, letter from Lester to Biraud, S922; LNA, 16 June 1947, Board of Liquidation: Provisional Minutes of Thirty-Second Meeting B.L./P.V.32, S569.

124 The original request from Watterson is detailed in a Board of Liquidation document: LNA, 14 January 1947, [unknown author], Board of Liquidation document, written by Lester, titled Claim of Mr. P.G. Watterson for Loss sustained on his Motor Car B.L.77, R5501 18B/40436/37845. Watterson acknowledged his 1,000 Swiss francs indemnity roughly six weeks later in a letter to Lester: LNA, 25 February 1947, letter from Watterson to Lester, C1784-4.

125 The claims are laid out in a Board of Liquidation document: LNA, 30 January 1947, [unknown author], Board of Liquidation document titled Claims for Indemnity made by Dr. C. L. Park and Dr. S. Dakshinamurthi, ex-officials of the League's former Epidemiological Bureau at Singapore B.L.86, S569.

126 Lester noted in the Board's thirteenth meeting, where the claims were discussed, that the League had been particularly strict about claims for war damage for fear of setting precedent, but 'that danger was now over and these two cases only remained.' LNA, 12 February 1947, Board of Liquidation: Provisional Minutes of Thirteenth Meeting B.L./P.V.13, S569.

127 LNA, 12 June 1947, [unknown author], Board of Liquidation document titled Staff Pensions Fund, Contribution of 15,000 francs to relieve cases of hardship B.L.155, S569.

128 LNA, 21 April 1947, Board of Liquidation: Annex to Twenty-Seventh meeting, prepared by Lester and titled Claim of E. Henneberger, S569.

129 LNA, 16 April 1947, Board of Liquidation document, prepared by Lester, titled Demande d'indemnité de Mlle de Peganow B.L.125, S569.

130 LNA, 5 March 1947, letter from Léon Steinig to Stencek asking the League to refund the additional $957 he has been charged by the US Government, C1784-4.

131 For just two examples see the salary increases granted to Constance Harris and Cecily Babington, which were backdated to January and March respectively: LNA, 27 May 1947, letter from Lester to Harris, S789; LNA, 21 March 1947, letter from Stencek to Babington, S707.

132 LNA, 7 January 1947, letter from Lester to Moderow, R5385 18A/44108/3471.

133 LNA, 13 June 1947, letter from Lester to Phelan, S916; LNA, 13 June 1947, letter from Lester to the executive secretary of the Preparatory Commission for the Refugee Organisation, S927; LNA, 13 June 1947, letter from Lester to Moderow, S927; LNA, 13 June 1947, letter from Lester to Trygve Lie, S927; LNA, 13 June 1947, letter from Lester to the director general of UNESCO, S942.

134 LNA, 4 February 1947, letter from Lester to Nonin, S568.

135 Lester continued: 'Your invariable kindness to the staff and readiness to consider their point of view won you their highest regard and esteem. I would ask you to accept my renewed thanks for your cooperation and my best wishes for the future.' LNA, 7 August 1947, letter from Lester to Stencek, S887.
136 LNA, 19 July 1947, letter from Boiteux to Stencek, S723.
137 A case that came to the Board on a couple of occasions during the liquidation period involved two former officials of the PCIJ. Both men were obliged to resign in 1940 but continued to work through 1945, without pay, to ensure the Court remained functional. The claim was first put to the Board for financial compensation in June 1946, and discussed at the fourth meeting in July of the same year, but the group refused to consider the issue as it had already been heard at the Supervisory Commission: LNA, 27 June 1946, Board of Liquidation document, written by W. J. M. van Eysinga, titled Situation of two former officials of the Permanent Court B.L.12, S569; LNA, 15 July 1946, Board of Liquidation: Provisional Minutes of Fourth Meeting B.L./P.V.4, S569.
138 Scaglia, *Emotions of Internationalism*, 17.

5 Many endings, August 1947 and beyond

1 Lester's Diary, 5 August 1947, letter from Sweetser to Lester.
2 League of Nations Archives, 23 July 1947, Board of Liquidation: Provisional Minutes of Forty-Second Meeting B.L./P.V.42, R5816.2 50/43856/43844.
3 League of Nations, *Official Journal Special Supplement No. 194: Records of the Twentieth (Conclusion) and Twenty-First Ordinary Sessions of the Assembly* (Geneva: League of Nations, 1946), 284.
4 LNA, 14 August 1947, letter from Purves to Secrétan asking for comments on the French version of the Final Report to Members, R5816.4 50/44023/43844; LNA, 19 August 1947, letter from Émile Charvériat to Purves passing on his modifications to the French text of the Final Report, R5816.4 50/44023/43844.
5 LNA, 12 August 1947, Hambro to Purves, R5816.4 50/44023/43844.
6 LNA, 16 August 1947, Purves to Kisch, R5816.4 50/44117/43844.
7 Purves could not understand the reason for Hambro's tardy response and the Chairman's insistence on continuing to make changes: LNA, 27 August 1947, letter from Purves to Lester R5816.4 50/44023/43844.
8 Purves explained in a letter to Kisch that his 'private affairs have been much neglected during the last year, and I must now go home and try to tidy them up.' LNA, 16 August 1947, Purves to Kisch, R5816.4 50/44117/43844. See also: LNA, 29 August 1947, letter from Purves to Hambro, R5816.4 50/44023/43844.

9 LNA, 6 August 1947, telegram from Ranshofen-Wertheimer to Purves requesting 1,500 copies of the Board's Final Report to Members, R5816.4 50/44023/43844.

10 LNA, 30 August 1947, communique issued to members of the League 'Final Report to States Members of the League' C.L.2.1947, R5816.4 50/44023/43844. Meanwhile, the press communique, in its final paragraph, stated that 'all valid claims had been met and the affairs of the League of Nations had terminated in good order'. LNA, 30 August 1947, Press Communique titled 'Work by the Board of Liquidation', R5816.4 50/44023/43844.

11 The unnamed author of the article went on to suggest that the League would soon be no more than a historic memory: 'la Société des Nations ne sera plus qu'un souvenir historique'. LNA, 5 August 1947, [unknown author], 'La liquidation de la S.D.N.', Tribune de Genève, R5813 50/43874/43262.

12 *The Times of London*, 4 August 1947, [unknown author], 'Winding Up League of Nations: Disposal of Assets'. Meanwhile *The New York Times* article began 'Liquidation of the League of Nations has been completed, Sean Lester, secretary of the liquidation commission, announced today.' *The New York Times*, 5 August 1947, [unknown author], 'League of Nations Assets Are Finally Liquidated', 12.

13 One example of Sweetser's many letters to *The New York Times* came in November 1941: *The New York Times*, 23 November 1941, letter to the editor from Arthur Sweetser titled 'Correcting a False Impression About the League', Section 4, 7.

14 The Secretariat received few official acknowledgements of the League's closure from governments. For two examples, see: LNA, 12 September 1947, letter from La Secretaría de Estado de Relaciones Exteriores de la República Dominicana to the Secretary-General League of Nations, R5816.4 50/44023/43844; LNA, 14 October 1947, letter from La Secretaría de Relaciones Exteriores de los Estados Unidos Mexicanos to the Secretary-General of the League of Nations, R5816.4 50/44023/43844.

15 Lester informed Trygve Lie of the credit shares in a letter sent at the beginning of August. The USD equivalent of the 46m Swiss francs total was reached using a conversion rate of $23.40 USD to 100 Swiss francs – this was the rate effective at the date of transfer and that used in Lester's calculations: LNA, 4 August 1947, letter from Lester to Lie, R5812 50/43672/43262.

16 Lester's Diary, 27 August 1947, letter from Lie to Lester.

17 Lester's Diary, 5 August 1947, letter from Sweetser to Lester.

18 LNA, 29 August 1947, letter from Stencek to Hambro, S816.

19 LNA, 5 September 1947, letter from Stencek to Welps confirming the prolongation of Lester's contract, S816.

20 Jenny (Treasury), Curry (Drug Control Service and Internal Administration), van Asch van Wijck (Department I) and Harris (Department I and Personnel Office) served as officials for almost one hundred years between them – just over

ninety-five years in total. Other officials leaving in July and August, beyond those already mentioned, were Cecily Babington (Board of Liquidation Secretariat), Aline Buffle (Stenographic Service, Internal Administration, and Secretary-General's Office), Dagny Gran (Board of Liquidation Secretariat), Kathleen Harrison (Treasury), Winifred Oberdorff (Treasury), Chester Purves (Board of Liquidation Secretariat) and Alma Schibli (Treasury).

21 See Chapter 2 for more details on staff contracts from 1946 onwards.
22 For examples, see: LNA, 29 August 1947, letter from Stencek to Babington, S707; LNA, 17 August 1947, letter from Lester to Harris, S789.
23 LNA, 18 August 1947, letter from Stencek to Curry, S750.
24 LNA, 20 August 1947, letter from Stencek to Uno Brunskog, R5353 17/44134/44093.
25 LNA, 30 July 1947, van Asch van Wijck to The Secretary of the High Commissioner for the Union of South Africa in London, R5265 16/33080/33080; LNA, 28 August 1947, letter from Stencek to G. Kaeckenbeeck, Belgian Foreign Ministry, R5265 16/33080/33080. In addition, Hambro explained in a letter to Stencek that he had been told that 'the [portrait] frame should be in light gold to create a Halo round the representative of the North'. LNA, 7 August 1947, letter from Hambro to Stencek, R5265 16/33082/33080.
26 LNA, 4 August 1947, letter from Stencek to 'The Manager, Lloyds Bank Ltd, London' checking confirmation of a transfer to the League from the Indian Office, R5353 17/43613/43553; LNA, 29 July 1947, letter from Stencek to Byron Price, assistant secretary general for Administrative & Financial Services, United Nations, New York, regarding League officials seconded to the UN in New York, R5813 50/43905/43262.
27 LNA, 20 August 1947, letter from Stencek to Hambro, R5385 18A/44108/347; LNA, 30 August 1947, letter from Stencek to Phelan, R5385 18A/35884/3471.
28 Just one example of bank accounts closed at this time was the League's 'General Account' at the Lloyds & National Provincial Foreign Bank in London: LNA, 13 August 1947, letter from Stencek to 'The Manager, Lloyds & National Provincial Foreign Bank Limited, London', R5299 17/3934/3933. See also: LNA, 23 September 1947, letter from Stencek to Breycha-Vauthier regarding the transfer of the Library Building Fund to the United Nations, R5265 16/33082/33080.
29 LNA, 23 August 1947, letter from Lester (writing from Avoca in Ireland) to Stencek, S723.
30 In a letter to Stencek, Brunskog explained that he would be coming to Geneva in October regardless as he would be examining the ILO accounts at that time and did not think he could justify the expense of two separate trips to Switzerland: LNA, 29 August 1947, letter from Brunskog to Stencek, R5353 17/44134/44093.

31 LNA, 5 September 1947, letter from Stencek to The Manager of Hugh Rees, Ltd. regarding the payment of a subscription to *The Times*, R5299 17/3934/3933; LNA, 10 October 1947, letter from Stencek to D. J. Bruinsma, now of the International Court of Justice, regarding the removal of Lars Jorstad's furniture from The Hague, R5291 17/42922/2989.
32 The French Foreign Ministry did not grant their approval to start making arrangements until mid-September: LNA, 15 September 1947, letter from French Foreign Ministry to Stencek, R5502 18B/40793/40793.
33 The vases were valued, for the purposes of insurance, at 25,000 Swiss francs, increasing costs: LNA, 29 September 1947, letter from Stencek to Mademoiselle Arthurion, R5502 18B/40793/40793. The air traffic delays meant the vases were eventually transported by land over a weekend, leading to an increase in the original invoice, for a total of 21,000 French francs – the equivalent of 2,377 Swiss francs (exchange rate of 1 Swiss franc = 9.76 French francs, as used by Véron, Grauer & Cie, the Geneva removals firm). See LNA, 13 October 1947, letter from J. Véron, Grauer & Cie to Mademoiselle Arthurion, R5502 18/40793/40793.
34 LNA, 2 October 1947, letter from Stencek to Lester, R5813 50/44139/43262.
35 LNA, 23 October 1947, letter from Stencek to Lester, R5813 50/44139/43262.
36 Stencek provided a full explanation of the situation in a letter transferring the debt to the Pensions Administrative Council: LNA, 9 October 1947, letter from Stencek to the president of the Staff Pensions Administrative Council at the ILO, R5353 17/44138/44138.
37 There are several examples of the League paying sums to the UN in September and October, including 1,725 Swiss francs for the period of July and August: LNA, 2 September 1947, letter from 'The Treasury' to Lloyds & National Provincial Foreign Bank Ltd, R5299 17/3934/3933.2; and a further 232 Swiss francs for the costs accrued in September for postage of items to the Board of Liquidation: LNA, 2 October 1947, letter from Stencek to H.W. Salisbury, Finance Officer of the United Nations European Office, R5299 17/3934/3933.
38 LNA, 4 September 1947, letter from H. Gallois, Assistant special du Directeur général at the ILO, to Stencek, confirming receipt of the 31,024.70 Swiss francs, R5385 18A/44108/3471. Meanwhile the Library Building Fund was transferred to Arthur Breycha-Vauthier in his position as the chief of the Library of the United Nations European Office which he noted, in his official acknowledgement of the 1,924.15 Swiss francs transfer, would be especially used in the 'preparation and printing of a pamphlet explaining the various exhibits' [of the Historical Collection]: LNA, 2 October 1947, letter from Breycha-Vauthier to Stencek, R5265 16/33082/33080.
39 Percy Watterson, still guarding the League's remaining financial assets in the United States, confirmed the outstanding Rockefeller Grant balance – of

$5,184.77 – was transferred to the UN account at the Chemical Bank and Trust Corporation in New York: LNA, 8 October 1947, letter from Watterson to Pelt, C1741.

40 The full breakdown of the League's assets – both fixed and liquid – and how they were distributed to members and the UN organizations was published in a communique in early September. The liquid assets amounted to 15,238,794.32 Swiss francs: LNA, 9 September 1947, communique distributed to members of the League titled 'Distribution of League Assets' C.6.M.6.1947, S923.

41 LNA, 25 October 1947, League of Nations, Supplementary Accounts for the Winding-Up Period after the Close of the League Accounts on 31 July 1947. C.7.M.7.1947, R5353 17/44134/44093.

42 The letters to the Geneva Telephone Service, the Geneva Postal Service, the Geneva Telegraphy Service, and the Geneva Customs Service, were all – bar the recipients' names – identical: LNA, 17 October 1947, letter from Stencek to Fritz Jöhr, Directeur des téléphones, R5813 50/44139/43262; LNA, 17 October 1947, letter from Stencek to Edouard Sägesser, Directeur des postes, R5813 50/44139/43262; LNA, 17 October 1947, letter from Stencek to Hermann Gimmi, Chef du télégraphe, R5813 50/44139/43262; LNA, 17 October 1947, letter from Stencek to Adolphe Zoller, Directeur des douanes, R5813 50/44139/43262.

43 LNA, 17 October 1947, letter from Stencek to Louis Casaï, R5813 50/44139/43262; LNA, 21 October 1947, letter from Casaï to Stencek, R5813 50/44139/43262; LNA, 21 October 1947, Stencek to Gallois, R5813 50/44139/43262.

44 For example, see LNA, 16 October 1947, letter from Stencek to Secrétan, R5813 50/44139/43262; LNA, 15 October 1947, letter from Stencek to Lachavanne, Directeur-conservateur du Registre foncier, R5813 50/44139/43262.

45 The supplementary accounts for the winding-up period following 31 July, sent to members at the end of October, noted: 'there remained outstanding on the date of the Board's dissolution on July 31st, 1947, a few matters of secondary importance, for the settlement of which a small staff was retained': LNA, 25 October 1947, League of Nations, Supplementary Accounts for the Winding-up Period after the Close of the League Accounts on 31 July 1947, C.7.M.7.1947, R5353 17/44134/44093.

46 Stencek noted in a letter to Brunskog that he would be absent on leave between 1 and 12 October, but this holiday never materialized: LNA, 24 September 1947, letter from Stencek to Brunskog, R5265 16/33082/33080.

47 LNA, 29 September 1947, Stencek to Lester, R5353 17/44093/44093; LNA, 2 October 1947, Stencek to Lester R5813 50/44139/43262.

48 Stencek also described Lester as someone 'to whom I could turn in all my troubles for advice and help, being sure that these will be readily and most generously extended to me'. Lester's Diary, 24 October 1947, letter from Stencek to Lester.

49 Ranshofen-Wertheimer, Egon F., *The International Secretariat: A Great Experiment in International Administration* (Washington, DC: Carnegie Endowment for International Peace, 1945), 242.
50 LNA, 23 October 1947, letter from Stencek to Lester, R5813 50/44139/43262.
51 LNA, 12 November 1947, letter from Stencek to Watterson, R3748 3A/41136/705.
52 The full name on the account was confirmed in a letter from the Princeton Bank and Trust Company: LNA, 28 October 1947, letter from Lilian V. S. Stout, assistant treasurer, to Watterson, C1784-4. In addition, it is not clear why Watterson – living in Washington, DC – decided to use the Princeton Bank and Trust Company for this last League account. He noted, in a letter to the bank in early October 1947, that he had previously been a personal banking customer of theirs – presumably when based in Princeton between 1940 and 1946, but why he chose to open an account with them again in 1947 is unclear: LNA, 7 October 1947, letter from Watterson to Princeton Bank and Trust Company, C1784-4.
53 See Chapter 4 for more on the San Yo-Sha debt, and in addition: LNA, 29 September 1947, letter from Ragnar Nurkse to Watterson, asking the latter to forward on fifteen diagram drawings for the French publication of 'Inflation Volume' being issued from Geneva, C1784-4; LNA, 25 November 1947, letter from Aldo Caselli, Comptroller at Haverford College, to Watterson, querying whether the display material for the tapestries might also be recalled to Geneva, C1784-4; LNA, 15 January 1948, letter from David L. Bazelon, assistant attorney general and director of the Office of Alien Property, to Watterson, regarding the San Yo-Sha publications debt, C1784-4.
54 See both: LNA, [unknown date], letter from Office of Commissioner of Internal Revenue, US Treasury Department, to Renborg, C1784-4; LNA, 14 October 1947, letter from Watterson to Renborg, C1784-4.
55 LNA, 12 September 1947, cable from Ranshofen-Wertheimer to J. G. Schumacher confirming Rosenborg's return to New York, C1741; LNA, 29 September 1947, letter from Rosenborg to Owen, C1741.
56 LNA, 29 September 1947, memo from Ranshofen-Wertheimer to Rosenborg confirming that Watterson has been instructed to transfer the money to the UN, C1741; LNA, 24 September 1947, letter from Norvell B. Samuels to Rosenborg, C1741.
57 LNA, [unknown date], invoice from Princeton University Press for publication and distribution of *Europe's Population in the Interwar Years*, C1741; LNA, 1 October 1947, letter from Rosenborg to Samuels expressing concern over invoice total, C1741.
58 Samuels explained that had the Princeton University Press accounted for its usual profit on the publication, the bill 'should have been in the neighbourhood of $12,000': LNA, 21 October 1947, letter from Samuels to Rosenborg, C1741.

59 LNA, 11 December 1947, letter from Samuels to Rosenborg, C1741; LNA, 19 December 1947, letter from Rosenborg to F. P. E. Green of the UN Economic Affairs Department, C1741.
60 The agreement signed by former officials stated:

> In consideration of the matters above set forth I hereby confirm the understanding and agreements therein states and hereby agree, on behalf of myself, my heirs, executors, personal representatives, administrators or assigns, to conform thereto and to perform and make, execute and deliver the acts, assignments, agreements and payments therein set forth, in the contingencies and according to the conditions therein provided, as and when called upon by the Trustee and Liquidating Agent or substitute or successor Trustee or Liquidating Agent.

LNA, 26 August 1947, letter from Watterson to Loveday, C1784-4.
61 LNA, 10 September 1947, letter from Stencek to Watterson sending instructions on next steps, C1784-4 3A/41136/705.
62 Giraud wrote: 'The claim, to my mind, has no legal ground and the suit will be lost.' LNA, 22 October 1946, memo from Giraud to Lester, S567.
63 LNA, 9 October 1947, The tax court ruling: 9 T. C. No. 87, The Tax Court of the United States, John Henry Chapman v Commissioner of Internal Revenue, Docket number 10121, promulgated 9 October 1947, C1784-4.
64 LNA, 22 October 1947, unsigned letter from Edwards & Smith to John Henry Chapman confirming the outcome of the lawsuit, R3748 3A/41136/705; LNA, [unknown date], sample letter sent from Watterson to former League officials based in the United States during the Second World War, R3748 3A/41136/705.
65 LNA, 3 November 1947, letter from Watterson to Stencek, R3748 3A/41136/705.
66 LNA, 25 October 1947, letter from Edwards & Smith to Watterson, C1784-4.
67 See both: LNA, 4 November 1947, letter from Watterson to Edwards & Smith, C1784-4; LNA, 18 November 1947, letter from Watterson to Edwards & Smith, C1784-4.
68 LNA, 12 November 1947, letter from Stencek to Watterson, R3748 3A/41136/705.
69 Watterson explained to Stencek that preparing copies of the Court Judgement for members 'will take some little time': LNA, 25 November 1947, letter from Watterson to Stencek, R3748 3A/41136/705.
70 LNA, 31 January 1948, letter from Watterson to thirty-six member states and nine Board of Liquidation Members, C1784-4.
71 LNA, 12 April 1947, League of Nations: Board of Liquidation, Provisional Minutes of Twentieth Meeting B.L./P.V.20, S569.
72 LNA, 26 August 1947, list of US-based League officials, prepared by Watterson, affected by the income tax lawsuit and the consequent fallout, R3748 3A/41136/705.

73 LNA, 26 January 1948, letter from Watterson to Stencek outlining the 'grave problem', R3748 3A/41136/705.
74 Upon Watterson's request for assistance, Seymour Jacklin suggested that the UN could reimburse these officials as the new organization had received 'the balance of the funds from the League'. This was not true – as later confirmed in a letter from Stencek – League members had received the balance of funds from the League as UN credits, but the UN itself did not have any former liquid assets with which to refund officials. See: LNA, 26 January 1948, letter from Watterson to Stencek, R3748 3A/41136/705; LNA, 4 February 1948, letter from Stencek to Watterson in which the former explains Jacklin's error, R3748 3A/41136/705.
75 LNA, 4 February 1948, letter from Stencek to Lester, R3748 3A/41136/705.
76 LNA, 8 April 1948, letter from Hambro to Watterson, C1784-4.
77 LNA, 4 February 1948, letter from Stencek to Lester, R3748 3A/41136/705.
78 One such example is Stencek's letter to Watterson dated 4 February 1948: LNA, 4 February 1948, letter from Stencek to Watterson, C1784-4.
79 LNA, 4 February 1948, letter from Stencek to Lester, R3748 3A/41136/705.
80 See both: LNA, 20 February 1948, letter from Chapman to Watterson, C1784-4; LNA, 24 February 1948, letter from John F. Dailey Jr, of Edwards & Smith, to Watterson, C1784-4.
81 Watterson first raised the question with Lilian Stout at the Princeton Bank and Trust in late February, and the matter was only confirmed as settled in April: LNA, 28 February 1948, letter from Watterson to Lilian Stout, C1784-4; LNA, 13 April 1948, letter from Watterson to Dailey Jr., C1784-4.
82 LNA, 13 April 1948, letter from Watterson to Stout, C1784-4.
83 Samuels wrote in his reminder, dated 10 February, that 'We think we have been extremely patient as regards payment of this bill but we feel that the United Nations is imposing on us.' LNA, 10 February 1948, letter from Samuels to Rosenborg, C1741.
84 The first reminder can be found at: LNA, 25 March 1948, invoice for $1 from Columbia University Press to 'League of Nations, Princeton, New Jersey', C1784-4. The second, somewhat passive-aggressive reminder – 'We know you will realize how each outstanding account handicaps us and why we ask that you send us your check promptly' – was sent several weeks later: LNA, 16 April 1948, letter from Mrs L. E. Scanlan, Assistant Treasurer, to League of Nations, Princeton, C1784-4.
85 LNA, 28 April 1948, letter from Rosenborg to Watterson, C1784-4.
86 Watterson suggested to Scanlan that, as the League's accounts were well and truly closed, she refer the matter to Charles Proffitt, the Press's director, and consider writing off the $1 bill: LNA, 3 May 1948, letter from Watterson to Scanlan, C1784-4.
87 Driscoll's original letter stated: 'I hardly know how to approach the matter without asking for your help. With apologies for troubling you again.' LNA, 6 February

1948, letter from A. M. Driscoll to Peter Welps, R5291 17/42922/2989. Jenny's response meanwhile was dismissive, mistakenly assuming Driscoll was asking for her removals compensation – which she was not – and instructed her to 'address your request direct to Mr. Bruinsma', something Driscoll had already been trying for over six months. LNA, 11 February 1948, letter from Jenny to Driscoll, R5291 17/42922/2989.

88 LNA, 22 September 1949, letter from R. Adams, chief accountant UNESCO, to 'The Secretary, Board of Liquidation, League of Nations, Geneva', R5816.4 50/44117/43844.

89 LNA, 4 October 1949, letter from J. R. Conway, UN Finance Officer, to Adams, R5816.4 50/44117/43844.

90 Taken from the UN Library at Geneva list of goals, under the section heading 'Preserving the Institutional Memory of UN Geneva', United Nations Office Geneva Archives webpage: https://www.ungeneva.org/en/knowledge/archives (retrieved 15 March 2021).

91 Auberer, Benjamin, 'Digesting the League of Nations: Planning the International Secretariat of the Future, 1941–1944', in *New Global Studies* (2016), 1–13; Royal Institute of International Affairs, *The International Secretariat of the Future: Lessons from Experience by a Group of Former Officials of the League of Nations* (London: Royal Institute of International Affairs, 1944); J. V. Wilson, 'Problems of an International Secretariat', *International Affairs* 20, no. 4 (October 1944), 542–54.

92 Carnegie Endowment for International Peace, *Proceedings of the Exploratory Conference on the Experience of the League of Nations Secretariat, Held in New York City on August 30, 1942, under the Auspices of the Carnegie Endowment for International Peace* (Washington, DC: Carnegie Endowment for International Peace, 1942); Carnegie Endowment for International Peace, *Proceedings of the Conference on Experience in International Administration, Held in Washington on January 30, 1943, under the Auspices of the Carnegie Endowment for International Peace* (Washington, DC: Carnegie Endowment for International Peace, 1943).

93 Finch quoted from Winston Churchill's speech to the UK House of Commons on 27 February 1945, in his preface to Egon Ranshofen-Wertheimer's review of the League Secretariat: Ranshofen-Wertheimer, *The International Secretariat*, vii.

94 Ibid., xiii, viii. There were nine other works, alongside Ranshofen-Wertheimer's, published by the Carnegie Endowment under this banner: Butler, Nicholas Murray, *The International Law of the Future: Postulates, Principles, Proposals* (Washington, DC: Carnegie Endowment for International Peace, 1944); Manley O. Hudson, *International Tribunals: Past and Future* (Washington, DC: Carnegie Endowment for International Peace, 1944); Vladimir D. Pastuhov, *A Guide to the Practice of International Conferences* (Washington, DC: Carnegie Endowment for International Peace, 1945); P. de Azcárate, *League of Nations and National Minorities: An*

Experiment (Washington, DC: Carnegie Endowment for International Peace, 1945); Hill, Martin, *The Economic and Financial Organization of the League of Nations: A Survey of Twenty-five Years' Experience* (Washington, DC: Carnegie Endowment for International Peace, 1946); Bertil A. Renborg, *International Drug Control: A Study of International Administration by and through the League of Nations* (Washington, DC: Carnegie Endowment for International Peace, 1947). Martin Hill, *Immunities and Privileges of International Officials: The Experience of the League of Nations* (Washington, DC: Carnegie Endowment for International Peace, 1947); H. Duncan Hall, *Mandates, Dependencies and Trusteeship* (Washington, DC: Carnegie Endowment for International Peace, 1948); Jacob Viner, *The Customs Union Issue* (Washington, DC: Carnegie Endowment for International Peace, 1950).

95 LNA, 25 March 1946, memo by Ranshofen-Wertheimer titled Employment of Nationals of Non-Member States with the Secretariat, S568; LNA, 29 April 1946, report by Ranshofen-Wertheimer titled Transfer of Functions: Notes on some Problems Raised by the Continuation of certain League Activities, S568.

96 Trygve Lie, thanking Lester for releasing Lukac from his League contract, wrote: 'he will be most valuable to the United Nations': LNA, 9 April 1946, letter from Lie to Lester thanking the latter for releasing Lukac from his position, S568. Hill meanwhile, described by Lester as an 'exceptional' case, was released immediately following the twenty-first Assembly, again at the request of Lie: LNA, 17 June 1946, letter from Lester to Stencek, S568.

97 LNA, 17 June 1946, letter from Lester to Pelt, S922.

98 Lester wanted to hang onto Giraud for longer – he wrote to Pelt in early November 1946 describing him as 'my last Legal Adviser' – but agreed to release him before the end of that year. LNA, 6 November 1946, letter from Lester to Pelt, S567. Meanwhile Erim was offered a role in October 1946 but having asked Lester to intervene in order to secure a higher salary, he did not depart until the spring of 1947. He wrote to the secretary general: 'that as a result I may be enabled to put my capacities and experience at the disposal of the United Nations for work which I have very much at heart'. LNA, 11 October 1946, letter from Erim to Lester, S567.

99 LNA, 17 July 1946, letter from G.A. Johnston at the ILO, to Lester, S568.

100 In a letter to Phelan, Lester referred to Jenny as 'really indispensable'. LNA, 29 October 1946, letter from Lester to Phelan, S567.

101 *The Washington Post*, 18 February 1979, [unknown author], 'Ansgar Rosenborg, Was UN Official' (retrieved online 10 March 2021: https://www.washingtonpost.com/archive/local/1979/02/18/ansgar-rosenborg-was-un-official/b2b58e13-1a1a-44b4-9113-43d639580a1f/).

102 United Nations World Health Organization Interim Commission, *Official Records of the World Health Organization No. 4: Minutes of the Second Session of the Interim*

Commission, Held in Geneva from 4 to 13 November 1946 (Geneva: United Nations, 1947), 39, 74–5.

103 The details of Siegel's positions at the WHO are taken from his 1982 interview: World Health Organization Archives Unit, 15 November 1982, Transcript of oral interview with Professor Milton P. Siegel, moderated by Gino Levy, Chief of News Media Relations at the WHO, and with the participation of Mr Norman Howard-Jones, 3: https://www.who.int/archives/fonds_collections/special/milton_siegel_tapes.pdf (retrieved 21 February 2021).

104 Ibid., 10, 26.

105 Ibid.

106 Information regarding Stencek's numerous positions and the dates of his employment was provided by the WHO Archives Service, 21 November 2019.

107 Lester's Diary, 22 May 1946, letter from Lester to James Tyrrell, Lester's brother-in-law. In addition, in a report to Eamon de Valera, dated 11 June 1947, Lester closed his letter with the statement 'I have never been ambitious, I sought none of these positions.' Lester's Diary, 11 June 1947, Lester to Eamon de Valera, Minister of External Affairs, Dublin.

108 The letter from J. T. Walshe, of the Irish Department of Foreign Affairs, offering these postings to Lester has been lost from his files. In a handwritten entry in Lester's Diaries, his daughter, Ann Gorski, wrote: 'I have mislaid this letter in which SL was offered posts in either New York, Brussels, Stockholm, or Pretoria. And SL had noted in the margin that he was not interested in any of these offers. As I remember this.' Lester's Diary, 4 April 2005, handwritten note by A. Gorski.

109 Lester's Diary, 9 July 1947, personal memo by Lester.

110 See: Lester's Diary, 8 June 1948, letter from Lie to Lester; Lester's Diary, 9 June 1948, telegram from Lester to Lie.

111 Gram-Skjoldager, Ikonomou, and Kahlert (eds), *Organizing the 20th-Century World*; Reinalda, *International Secretariats: Two Centuries of International Civil Servants and Secretariats* (London: Bloomsbury, 2020).

112 For more on Weber's definition and praise for bureaucratic administrations see: Max Weber, *Economy and Society: A New Translation*. Edited and translated by Keith Tribe (London: Harvard University Press, 2019), 347–54.

Conclusions

1 League of Nations Archives, 4 August 1945, proposed timetable of UN/League of Nations meetings and negotiations 1945–6, S565.

2 LNA, 21 February 1946, letter from Lester to Hambro, S565.

3   LNA, 6 April 1946, letter from Lester to Jacklin querying some wording in the latest British draft of the Dissolution Resolution, S565.
4   LNA, 12 February 1946, letter from Lester to Hugh McKinnon-Wood, S565.
5   League of Nations, *Official Journal Special Supplement No. 194: Records of the Twentieth (Conclusion) and Twenty-First Ordinary Sessions of the Assembly* (Geneva: League of Nations, 1946), 281.
6   For examples, see: LNA, 20 May 1947, letter from Hambro to Lester congratulating the latter on the birth of his grandson, S567; Lester's Diary, 24 October 1947, letter from Stencek to Lester; LNA, 13 June 1947, letter from Lester to the director general of UNESCO regarding job opportunities for League Secretariat officials, S942.
7   'There has scarcely been one good days [*sic*] weather for weeks here and all Switzerland seems to be more or less under floods.' LNA, 6 September 1946, letter from Lester to Hambro, S567.
8   LNA, 11 September 1946, letter from Lester to Moderow thanking the latter for his 'excellent collaboration' in the transfer work, R5813 50/43874/43262. UNOG Archives, 28 January 1947, letter from Lester to Moderow commiserating over their shared lack of information from UN headquarters relating to outstanding transfer questions, G.I. 4/4 (26).
9   For examples, see: LNA, 13 June 1947, letter from Lester to Phelan, S916; LNA, 13 June 1947, letter from Lester to the Executive Secretary of the Preparatory Commission for the Refugee Organisation, S927; LNA, 13 June 1947, letter from Lester to Moderow, S927; LNA, 13 June 1947, letter from Lester to Lie, S927.
10 In a private journal entry dated 2 August 1940, recalling a conversation with Adolfo Costa du Rels about his taking up the post of secretary general, Lester wrote: 'I explained my personal views, pointing out that the job was not an enviable one … I said I would think it over and I had never yet refused moral responsibilities ….' Lester's Diary, 2 August 1940, personal diary entry.
11 In a report to Eamon de Valera, dated 11 June 1947, Lester closed his letter with the statement 'I have never been ambitious, I sought none of these positions'. Lester's Diary, 11 June 1947, Lester to de Valera, Minister of External Affairs, Dublin.
12 Stencek's personal details come from his personnel file: LNA, [no date and unknown author], Stencek's Carrière au Secrétariat held by the personnel office, S887.
13 In a letter to Stencek in June 1947, Watterson said, 'I have felt that I owed it to the League and the Board of Liquidation to satisfactorily wind up matters as a fitting termination to the many years of service I enjoyed with the Organization.' LNA, 4 June 1947, letter from Watterson to Stencek, C1784-4.
14 Information kindly provided by Harris's family suggests she may have worked for the International Red Cross in Geneva following her League departure, but this thus far remains unconfirmed.

15 The League was often referred to as 'a great experiment' during this period. Just two examples are in the title of Ranshofen-Wertheimer's review of the Secretariat: Egon F. Ranshofen-Wertheimer, *The International Secretariat: A Great Experiment in International Administration* (Washington, DC: Carnegie Endowment for International Peace, 1945); and in a letter from Arthur Sweetser to Frank Aydelotte – head of the Princeton Institute for Advanced Studies – where the former describes Frank Walters' history of the League as a vivid account of 'the first great experiment': White and Levy Archives, 15 November 1948, letter from Sweetser to Frank Aydelotte, Director's Office: General Files: Box 39: League of Nations Invitation to the Economics Group, 70159 Princeton I.A.S. files.
16 World Health Organization Archives Unit, 15 November 1982, Transcript of oral interview with Professor Milton P. Siegel, moderated by Gino Levy, Chief of News Media Relations at the WHO, and with the participation of Mr Norman Howard-Jones, 26: https://www.who.int/archives/fonds_collections/special/milton_siegel_tapes.pdf (retrieved 21 February 2021).
17 LNA, 14 February 1947, Board of Liquidation: Provisional Minutes of Sixteenth Meeting (Private), B.L./P.V.16, S569; LNA, 15 April 1947, Board of Liquidation document, prepared by Verchère de Reffye, titled Rapport sur la liquidation de l'office international Nansen, B.L.124, S569.
18 Bob Reinalda, *Routledge History of International Organizations: From 1815 to the Present Day* (Abingdon: Routledge, 2009), 756–8; Susan Strange, 'Why Do International Organizations Never Die?' in Bob Reinalda and Bertjan Verbeek (eds), *Autonomous Policy Making by International Organizations* (London: Routledge, 1998), 213–20.
19 Lester's Diary, 5 August 1947, letter from Sweetser to Lester.

Bibliography

Archives

Carnegie Endowment for International Peace New York and Washington Offices Records 1910–1954, Columbia University Libraries, New York (CEIP)
League of Nations Archives, Geneva (LNA)
League of Nations Photograph Collection
League of Nations Secretariat, 1919–1946
Seán Lester's Diary, Geneva
Shelby White and Leon Levy Archives Center, Princeton
The National Archives, Kew (TNA)
United Nations Archives Geneva, Geneva (UNOG)
United Nations Archives, New York (UNA)
World Health Organization Archives Unit, Geneva

Press

Belfast Telegraph
Manchester Guardian
New York Times
Times of London
Tribune de Genève
Washington Post

Published primary and secondary sources

Alcock, A., *History of the International Labour Organisation*. London: Palgrave Macmillan, 1971.

Amrith, Sunil S., 'Internationalising Health in the Twentieth Century', in Glenda Sluga and Patricia Clavin (eds), *Internationalisms: A Twentieth-Century History*. Cambridge: Cambridge University Press, 2017, 245–64.

Amrith, Sunil S., and Glenda Sluga, 'New Histories of the United Nations', *Journal of World History* 19, no. 3 (2008): 251–74.

Archer, Clive, *International Organizations*, Third Edition. Abingdon: Routledge, 2001.

Ariffin, Yohan, Jean-Marc Coicaud and Vesselin Popovski (eds), *Emotions in International Politics: Beyond Mainstream International Relations*. New York: Cambridge University Press, 2016.

Armstrong, David, Lorna Lloyd and John Redmond, *From Versailles to Maastricht: International Organisation in the Twentieth Century*, Second Edition. Basingstoke: Macmillan, 1996.

Armstrong, David, Lorna Lloyd and John Redmond, *International Organisation in World Politics*, Third Edition. Basingstoke: Macmillan, 2004.

Auberer, Benjamin, 'Digesting the League of Nations: Planning the International Secretariat of the Future, 1941–1944', *New Global Studies* 10, no. 3 (2016): 393–426.

Barcroft, Stephen, 'The International Civil Servant: The League of Nations Career of Sean Lester, 1929–1947'. Unpublished doctoral thesis, Trinity College Dublin, 1973.

Barros, James, *Betrayal from Within: Joseph Avenol, Secretary-General of the League of Nations, 1933–1940*. New Haven, CT: Yale University Press, 1969.

Bendiner, Elmer, *A Time for Angels: The Tragicomic History of the League of Nations*. New York: Book World Promotions, 1975.

Bennett, LeRoy, and James Oliver, *International Organizations: Principles and Issues*. Upper Saddle River: Prentice Hall, 2002.

Betts, Paul, 'Humanity's New Heritage: UNESCO and the Rewriting of World History', *Past & Present* 228, no. 1 (2015): 249–85.

Biltoft, Carolyn N., 'Decoding the Balance Sheet: Gifts, Goodwill, and the Liquidation of the League of Nations', *Capitalism: A Journal of History and Economics* 1, no. 2 (2020): 379–404.

Biltoft, Carolyn N., *A Violent Peace: Media, Truth, and Power at the League of Nations*. Chicago: University of Chicago Press, 2021.

Boje, David, 'Globalization Antenarratives', in Albert J. Mills, Jean C. Helms Mills, Carolyn Forshaw and John Bratton (eds), *Organizational Behaviour in a Global Context*. Peterborough: Broadview Press, 2007, 505–50.

Borowy, Iris, *Coming to Terms with World Health: The League of Nations Health Organisation 1921–1946*. Frankfurt: Peter Lang, 2009.

Brydan, David, and Jessica Reinisch (eds), *Internationalists in European History: Rethinking the Twentieth Century*. London: Bloomsbury, 2021.

Butler, Nicholas Murray, *The International Law of the Future: Postulates, Principles, Proposals*. Washington, DC: Carnegie Endowment for International Peace, 1944.

Caine, Barbara, *Biography and History*. Basingstoke: Palgrave Macmillan, 2010.

Campbell, Thomas, and George Herring, *The Diaries of Edward Stettinius Jr., 1943–46*. New York: Littlehampton, 1974.

Carnegie Endowment for International Peace, *Proceedings of the Exploratory Conference on the Experience of the League of Nations Secretariat, Held in New York City on August 30, 1942, under the Auspices of the Carnegie Endowment for International Peace*. Washington: Carnegie Endowment for International Peace, 1942.

Carnegie Endowment for International Peace, *Proceedings of the Conference on Experience in International Administration, Held in Washington on January 30, 1943, under the Auspices of the Carnegie Endowment for International Peace*. Washington, DC: Carnegie Endowment for International Peace, 1943.

Carr, E. H., *The Twenty Years' Crisis 1919–1939: An Introduction to the Study of International Relations*. London: Palgrave Macmillan, 2016.

Cecil, Robert, *A Great Experiment: An Autobiography*. London: Jonathan Cape, 1941.

Clark, Christopher, *Time and Power: Visions of History in German Politics, from the Thirty Years' War to the Third Reich*. Princeton: Princeton University Press, 2019.

Claude, Inis L. Jr., *National Minorities: An International Problem*. Cambridge: Harvard University Press, 1955.

Claude, Inis L. Jr., *Power and International Relations*. New York: Random House, 1962.

Claude, Inis L. Jr., *Swords into Plowshares: The Problems and Progress of International Organizations*, Fourth Edition. New York: McGraw-Hill, 1984.

Clavin, Patricia, 'Europe and the League of Nations', in Robert Gerwarth (ed.), *Twisted Paths: Europe 1914–1945*. Oxford: Oxford University Press, 2007, 325–54.

Clavin, Patricia, 'Introduction: Conceptualising Internationalism Between the World Wars', in Daniel Laqua (ed.), *Internationalism Reconfigured: Transnational Ideas and Movements Between the World Wars*. London: Bloomsbury, 2011, 1–14.

Clavin, Patricia, *Securing the World Economy: The Reinvention of the League of Nations, 1920–1946*. Oxford: Oxford University Press, 2013.

Clavin, Patricia, and Jens-Wilhelm Wessel, 'Transnationalism and the League of Nations: Understanding the Work of Its Economic and Financial Organisation', *Contemporary European History* 14, no. 4 (2005): 465–92.

Coicaud, Jean-Marc, and Veijo Heiskanen (eds), *The Legitimacy of International Organizations*. Tokyo: United Nations University Press, 2001.

Cox, Robert W., and Harold K. Jacobson (eds), *The Anatomy of Influence: Decision-making in International Organization*. New Haven, CT: Yale University Press, 1973.

Craig, Gordon A., 'Diplomats and Diplomacy during the Second World War', in Gordon A. Craig and Francis L. Loewenheim (eds), *The Diplomats, 1939–1979*. Princeton: Princeton University Press, 1994, 11–37.

Craig, Gordon A., and Francis L. Loewenheim, 'Introduction', in Gordon A. Craig and Francis L. Loewenheim (eds), *The Diplomats, 1939–1979*. Princeton: Princeton University Press, 1994, 3–8.

Dale, H. E., *The Personnel and Problems of the Higher Civil Service*. London: Oxford University Press, 1945.

de Azcárate, P., *League of Nations and National Minorities: An Experiment*. Washington, DC: Carnegie Endowment for International Peace, 1945.

Dijkstra, Hylke, and Maria J. Debre, 'The Death of Major International Organizations: When Institutional Stickiness Is Not Enough', *Global Studies Quarterly* 2 (2022): 1–13.

Divine, Robert A., *Second Chance: The Triumph of Internationalism in America during World War II*. New York: Atheneum, 1967.

Dubin, Martin D., 'Transgovernmental Processes in the League of Nations', *International Organization* 37, no. 3 (1982): 469–93.

Dubin, Martin D., 'Towards the Bruce Report: The Economic and Social Programs of the League of Nations in the Avenol era', in United Nations Library (ed.), *The League of Nations in retrospect: Proceedings of the Symposium. Organized by the United Nations Library and the Graduate Institute of International Studies, Geneva, 6–9 November 1980*. Berlin: de Gruyter, 1983.

Dunbabin, J. P., 'The League of Nations' Place in the International System', *History* 78, no. 254 (October, 1993): 421–42.

Duncan Hall, H., *Mandates, Dependencies and Trusteeship*. Washington, DC: Carnegie Endowment for International Peace, 1948.

Dykmann, Klaas, 'How International was the League of Nations Secretariat', *International History Review* 37, no. 4 (2015): 721–44.

Edwards, Emma Mary, *The Wartime Experience of the League of Nations, 1939–1947*. Unpublished doctoral thesis, University of Ireland Maynooth, 2013.

Eichelberger, Clark, *Organizing for Peace: A Personal History of the Founding of the United Nations*. London: Harper and Row, 1977.

Eilstrup-Sangiovanni, Mette, 'Death of International Organizations. The Organizational Ecology of Intergovernmental Organizations, 1815–2015', *Review of International Organizations* 15 (2020): 339–70.

Eilstrup-Sangiovanni, Mette, 'What Kills International Organisations? When and Why International Organisations Terminate', *European Journal of International Relations* 27, no. 1 (2021): 281–310.

Endres, Anthony M., and Grant A. Fleming, *International Organizations and the Analysis of Economic Policy, 1919–1950*. Cambridge: Cambridge University Press, 2002.

Fleming, Robin, 'Writing Biography at the Edge of History', *American Historical Review* 114, no. 3 (2009): 606–14.

Fosdick, Raymond, *Chronicle of a Generation: An Autobiography*. New York: Harper & Bros, 1958.

Fosdick, Raymond, *Letters on the League of Nations*. Princeton: Princeton University Press, 1966.

Fosdick, Raymond, *The League and the United Nations after Fifty Years: The Six Secretaries-General*. Newtown: Raymond B. Fosdick, 1972.

Fosse, Marit, and John Fox, *Sean Lester: The Guardian of a Small Flickering Light*. Lanham: Hamilton Books, 2016.

Fried, John H. E., 'Relations between the UN and the ILO', *American Political Science Review* 41, no. 5 (1947): 963-77.

Gageby, Douglas, *The Last Secretary-General: Sean Lester and the League of Nations*. Dublin: Townhouse, 1999.

Geyer, Martin, and Johannes Paulmann (eds), *The Mechanics of Internationalism: Culture, Society and Politics from the 1840s to The First World War*. Oxford: Oxford University Press, 2001.

Ghebali, Victor-Yves, 'La transition de la Société des Nations à l'Organisation des Nations Unies', in United Nations Library (ed.), *The League of Nations in retrospect: Proceedings of the Symposium. Organized by the United Nations Library and the Graduate Institute of International Studies, Geneva, 6-9 November 1980*. Berlin: de Gruyter, 1983.

Ghebali, Victor-Yves, *Organisation Internationale et Guerre Mondiale. Le Cas de la Société des Nations et de l'Organisation Internationale du Travail Pendant la Second Guerre Mondiale*. Édité par Robert Kolb. Bruxelles: Bruylant, 2013.

Gladwyn, Lord, *The Memoirs of Lord Gladwyn*. London: Weidenfeld and Nichols, 1972.

Goodrich, L., 'From League of Nations to United Nations', *International Organization* 1, no. 1 (1947): 3-17.

Gram-Skjoldager, Karen, ' "A Great Experiment": Professional Self-Perceptions and Working Conditions in the Secretariat', in Haakon A. Ikonomou and Karen Gram-Skjoldager (eds), *The League of Nations: Perspectives from the Present*. Aarhus: Aarhus University Press, 2019.

Gram-Skjoldager, Karen, and Haakon A. Ikonomou, 'Making Sense of the League of Nations Secretariat – Historiographical and Conceptual Reflections on Early International Public Administration', *European History Quarterly* 49, no. 3 (2019): 420-44.

Gram-Skjoldager, Karen, and Torsten Kahlert, 'The Men Behind the Man: Canvassing the Directorship of the League of Nations Secretariat', in Haakon A. Ikonomou and Karen Gram-Skjoldager (eds), *The League of Nations: Perspectives from the Present*. Aarhus: Aarhus University Press, 2019, 19-29.

Gram-Skjoldager, Karen, Haakon A. Ikonomou and Torsten Kahlert, 'Introduction', in Karen Gram-Skjoldager, Haakon A. Ikonomou and Torsten Kahlert (eds), *Organizing the 20th-Century World: International Organizations and the Emergence of International Public Administration, 1920-1960s*. London: Bloomsbury, 2020, 1-12.

Greenwood, Royston, and C. R. (Bob) Hinings, 'Radical Organizational Change', in Stewart R. Clegg, Cynthia Hardy, Thomas B. Lawrence and Walter R. Nord (eds), *The Sage Handbook of Organization Studies*, Second Edition. London: Sage, 2006, 814-42.

Grigorescu, A., 'Mapping the UN-League of Nations Analogy: Are There Still Lessons to Be Learned from the League?', *Global Governance* 11 (2005): 25-42.

Groom, A. J. R., and Paul Taylor (eds), *Frameworks for International Cooperation*. London: Pinter, 1990.

Habermann-Box, Sigrun, 'From the League of Nations to the United Nations: The Continuing Preservation and Development of the Geneva Archives', in Madeleine Herren (ed.), *Networking the International System: Global Histories of International Organizations*. Heidelberg: Springer, 2014, 15–30.

Hambro, C. J., *How to Win the Peace*. London: Hodder & Stoughton, 1943.

Henig, Ruth, *The League of Nations*. London: Haus, 2010.

Herren, Madeleine, 'Governmental Internationalism and the Beginning of a New World Order in the Late Nineteenth Century', in Martin Geyer and Johannes Paulmann (eds), *The Mechanics of Internationalism: Culture, Society and Politics from the 1840s to The First World War*. Oxford: Oxford University Press, 2001, 121–44.

Hilderbrand, Robert C., *Dumbarton Oaks: The Origins of the United Nations and the Search for Post-war Security*. Chapel Hill: University of North Carolina Press, 1990.

Hill, M., *The Economic and Financial Organisation of the League of Nations: A Survey of Twenty-Five Years' Experience*. Washington, DC: Carnegie Endowment for International Peace, 1946.

Hill, Martin, *Immunities and Privileges of International Officials: The Experience of the League of Nations*. Washington, DC: Carnegie Endowment for International Peace, 1947.

Hinsley, F. H., *Power and the Pursuit of Peace: Theory and Practice in the History of Relations between States*. Cambridge: Cambridge University Press, 1963.

Hobsbawm, Eric, *The Age of Extremes: The Short Twentieth Century, 1914–1991*. London: Abacus, 1994.

Holsti, Kalevi, 'Change in International Politics: The View from High Altitude', *International Studies Review* 20, no. 2 (2018): 186–94.

Hopkins, Keith, 'What Is Social History?', *History Today* 35, no. 3 (1985): 38–9.

Housden, Martyn, *The League of Nations and the Organisation of Peace*. Harlow: Longman, 2012.

Hudson, Manley O., *International Tribunals: Past and Future*. Washington, DC: Carnegie Endowment for International Peace, 1944.

Hughes, E. J., 'Winston Churchill and the Formation of the United Nations Organization', *Journal of Contemporary History* 9, no. 4 (1974): 177–94.

Hugill, Peter J., *World Trade Since 1431: Geography, Technology, and Capitalism*. Baltimore: Johns Hopkins University Press, 1995.

Ikonomou, Haakon A., and Karen Gram-Skjoldager, 'Introduction: The League of Nations – Perspectives from the Present', in Haakon A. Ikonomou and Karen Gram-Skjoldager (eds), *The League of Nations: Perspectives from the Present*. Aarhus: Aarhus University Press, 2019.

International Labour Organization (ed.), *Edward Phelan and the ILO: The Life and Views of an International Social Actor*. Geneva: International Labour Organization, 2009.

International Labour Organization, *Minutes of the 102nd Session of the Governing Body, Geneva. 13 June-10 July 1947*. Geneva: International Labour Organization, 1947.
Iriye, Akira, *Cultural Internationalism and World Order*. Baltimore: Johns Hopkins University Press, 1997.
Iriye, Akira, *Global Community: The Role of International Organizations in the Making of the Modern World*. Berkeley: University of California Press, 2004.
Jackson, Simon, and Alanna O'Malley (eds), *The Institution of International Order: From the League of Nations to the United Nations*. Abingdon: Routledge, 2018.
Jordanova, Ludmilla, *History in Practice*. London: Arnold, 2000.
Kahlert, Torsten, '"The League Is Dead, Long Live the United Nations": The Liquidation of the League and the Transfer of Assets to the UN', in Haakon A. Ikonomou and Karen Gram-Skjoldager (eds), *The League of Nations: Perspectives from the Present*. Aarhus: Aarhus University Press, 2019, 256-66.
Kahlert, Torsten, 'Prosopography: Unlocking the Social World of International Organizations', in Karen Gram-Skjoldager, Haakon A. Ikonomou, and Torsten Kahlert (eds), *Organizing the 20th-Century World: International Organizations and the Emergence of International Public Administration, 1920-1960s*. London: Bloomsbury, 2020, 49-69.
Karns, Margaret P., Karen A. Mingst, and Kendall W. Stiles, *International Organizations: The Politics and Processes of Global Governance*, Third Edition. Boulder: Lynne Rienner, 2015.
Kennedy, Paul, *The Parliament of Man: The Past, Present, and Future of the United Nations*. New York: Random House, 2006.
Keohane, Robert O., *International Institutions and State Power*. Boulder: Westview Press, 1989.
Kessler-Harris, Alice, 'Why Biography?', *The American Historical Review* 114, no. 3 (2009): 625-30.
Kosseleck, Reinhart, *Futures Past: On the Semantics of Historical Time*. English translation by Keith Tribe. New York: Columbia University Press, 2004.
Kott, Sandrine, 'Fighting the War or Preparing for Peace. The ILO during the Second World War', *Journal of Modern European History* 12, no. 3, International Organisations during the Second World War (2014): 359-76.
Langrod, Georges, *The International Civil Service: Its Origins, its Nature, its Evolution*. Leyden: Oceana Publications, 1963.
Laqua, Daniel (ed.), *Internationalism Reconfigured: Transnational Ideas and Movements between the World Wars*. London: Bloomsbury, 2011.
Laqua, Daniel, 'Student activists and international cooperation in a changing world, 1919-60', in David Brydan and Jessica Reinisch (eds), *Internationalists in European History: Rethinking the Twentieth Century*. London: Bloomsbury, 2021.
Laqua, Daniel, 'Transnational Intellectual Cooperation, the League of Nations, and the Problem of Order', *Journal of Global History* 6 (2011): 223-47.

Laqua, Daniel, Wouter Van Acker and Christophe Verbruggen (eds), *International Organizations and Global Civil Society: Histories of the Union of International Associations*. London: Bloomsbury, 2019.

Lauren, Paul Gordon, 'The Diplomats and Diplomacy of the United Nations', in Gordon A. Craig and Francis L. Loewenheim (eds), *The Diplomats, 1939–1979*. Princeton: Princeton University Press, 1994.

Lavelle, Kathryn, 'Exit, Voice, and Loyalty in International Organizations: U.S. Involvement in the League of Nations', *Review of International Organizations* 2 (2007): 371–93.

League of Nations, *Board of Liquidation Final Report, Presented to States Members of the League of Nations in accordance with the Requirement of the Final Article of the Resolution for the Dissolution of the League of Nations adopted by the Assembly on April 18th, 1946, at its Twenty-first Ordinary Session*. Geneva: League of Nations, 1947.

League of Nations, *Official Journal Special Supplement No. 194: Records of the Twentieth (Conclusion) and Twenty-First Ordinary Sessions of the Assembly*. Geneva: League of Nations, 1946.

League of Nations, *Official Journal Special Supplement: Records of the First Session of the Assembly*. Geneva: League of Nations, 1920.

League of Nations, *Official Journal Special Supplement: Records of the Tenth Session of the Assembly*. Geneva: League of Nations, 1929.

League of Nations, *Report on the Work of the League 1941–1942, Submitted by the Acting Secretary-General*. Geneva: League of Nations, 1942.

League of Nations, *Report on The Work of the League 1942–1943, Submitted by the Acting Secretary-General*. Geneva: League of Nations, 1943.

League of Nations, *Report on the Work of The League 1943–1944, Submitted by the Acting Secretary-General*. Geneva: League of Nations, 1945.

League of Nations, *Report on the Work of the League during the War: Submitted to the Assembly by the Acting Secretary-General*. Geneva: League of Nations, 1945.

Long, David, and Brian Schmidt (eds), *Imperialism and Internationalism in the Discipline of International Relations*. Albany: State University of New York Press, 2005.

Loveday, Alexander, *Reflections on International Administration*. Oxford: Clarendon Press, 1956.

Luard, Evan, 'The Process of Change in International Organizations', in Evan Luard (ed.), *The Evolution of International Organizations*. London: Thames & Hudson, 1966, 9–24.

Luard, Evan, *A History of the United Nations: The Years of Western Domination, 1945–55 Vol. 1*. London, Macmillan, 1982.

Luard, Evan, *The United Nations: How It Works*, Second Edition. Basingstoke: Macmillan, 1994.

Lyons, F. S. L., *Internationalism in Europe, 1815–1914*. Leyden: A. W. Sythoff, 1963.

Martin, Lisa, and Beth Simmons (eds), *International Institutions: An International Organization Reader*. Cambridge: MIT Press, 2001.

Macfadyen, David, Michael D. V. Davies, Marilyn Norah Carr and John Burley, *Eric Drummond and His Legacies: The League of Nations and the Beginnings of Global Governance*. London: Palgrave, 2019.

Matt, Susan J., and Peter N. Stearns (eds), *Doing Emotions History*. Urbana: University of Illinois Press, 2014.

Maul, Daniel, *The International Labour Organization: 100 Years of Global Social Policy*. Berlin: De Gruyter Oldenbourg, 2019.

Mazower, Mark, 'An International Civilization? Empire, Internationalism and the Crisis of the Mid-Twentieth Century', *International Affairs* 82, no. 3 (2006): 553–66.

Mazower, Mark, *Governing the World: The History of an Idea*. London: Penguin, 2012.

Mazower, Mark, *No Enchanted Palace: The End of Empire and the Ideological Origins of the United Nations*. Princeton: Princeton University Press, 2009.

McAllister, William B., *Drug Diplomacy in the Twentieth Century*. London: Routledge, 2000.

Meisler, Stanley, *The United Nations: The First Fifty Years*. New York: Atlantic Monthly Press, 1995.

Menzies, A. A., 'Technical Assistance and the League of Nations', in United Nations Library (ed.), *The League of Nations in Retrospect: Proceedings of the Symposium. Organized by the United Nations Library and the Graduate Institute of International Studies, Geneva, 6–9 November 1980*. Berlin: de Gruyter, 1983.

Meron, Theodor, *The United Nations Secretariat*. Lexington: D.C. Heath, 1977.

Mills, Albert J., 'Introducing Organizational Behaviour', in Albert J. Mills, Jean C. Helms Mills, Carolyn Forshaw and John Bratton (eds), *Organizational Behaviour in a Global Context*. Peterborough: Broadview Press, 2007.

Moraes, Marco, *Internationalism as Organizational Practice. The League of Nations Secretary-General, 1918–1946*. Unpublished doctoral thesis, University of Oxford, 2020.

Morse, David A., *The Origin and Evolution of the I.L.O. and Its Role in the World Community*. Ithaca: W. F. Humphrey Press, 1969.

Murray, Gilbert, *From the League of Nations to the U.N.* London: Oxford University Press, 1948.

Myers, Denys P., 'Liquidation of League of Nations Functions', *The American Journal of International Law* 42, no. 2 (1948): 320–54.

Nasaw, David, 'Introduction', *American Historical Review* 114, no. 3 (2009): 573–8.

Noel-Baker, Philip, *The League of Nations at Work*. London: Nisbet, 1926.

Nord, Walter R., Thomas B. Lawrence, Cynthia Hardy and Stewart R. Clegg, 'Introduction', in Stewart R. Clegg, Cynthia Hardy, Thomas B. Lawrence and Walter R. Nord (eds), *The Sage Handbook of Organization Studies*, Second Edition. London: Sage, 2006, 1–16.

Northedge, F. S., and M. D. Donelan, *International Disputes: The Political Aspects*. London: The David Davies Memorial Institute of International Studies, 1971.

Northedge, F. S., and M. J. Grieve, *A Hundred Years of International Relations*. London: Duckworth, 1971.

Northedge, F. S., *The League of Nations: Its Life and Times 1920–1946*. Leicester: Holmes & Meier, 1986.

O'Connor, Emmet, 'Edward Phelan: A Biographical Essay', in International Labour Organization (ed.), *Edward Phelan and the I.L.O.: The Life and Views of an International Social Actor*. Geneva: International Labour Organization, 2009.

Parker, Barbara, and Stewart Clegg, 'Globalization', in Stewart R. Clegg, Cynthia Hardy, Thomas B. Lawrence and Walter R. Nord (eds), *The Sage Handbook of Organization Studies*, Second Edition. London: Sage, 2006.

Parry, Ken W., and Alan Bryman, 'Leadership in Organizations', in Stewart R. Clegg, Cynthia Hardy, Thomas B. Lawrence and Walter R. Nord (eds), *The Sage Handbook of Organization Studies*, Second Edition. London: Sage, 2006.

Pastuhov, Vladimir D., *A Guide to the Practice of International Conferences*. Washington, DC: Carnegie Endowment for International Peace, 1945.

Paul, T. V., 'Assessing Change in World Politics', *International Studies Review* 20, no. 2 (2018): 177–85.

Pedersen, Susan, 'Back to the League of Nations', *American Historical Review* 112, no. 4 (2007): 1091–117.

Pedersen, Susan, *The Guardians: The League of Nations and the Crisis of Empire*. Oxford: Oxford University Press, 2015.

Piguet, Myriam, 'Gender Distribution in the League of Nations: The Start of a Revolution?' in Haakon A. Ikonomou and Karen Gram-Skjoldager (eds), *The League of Nations: Perspectives from the Present*. Aarhus: Aarhus University Press, 2019.

Plesch, Dan, *America, Hitler, and the UN: How the Allies Won World War II and Forged a Peace*. London: I. B. Tauris, 2011.

Porter, Louis H., *Cold War Internationalisms: The USSR in UNESCO, 1945–1967*. Unpublished doctoral thesis, University of North Carolina at Chapel Hill, 2018.

Purves, Chester, *International Establishments: Some notes on the Experience of the Internal Administration of the League of Nations Secretariat*. London: Royal Institute of International Affairs, 1945.

Ranshofen-Wertheimer, Egon F., 'International Administration: Lessons from the Experience of the League of Nations', *American Political Science Review* 37, no. 5 (1943): 872–87.

Ranshofen-Wertheimer, Egon F., *The International Secretariat: A Great Experiment in International Administration*. Washington, DC: Carnegie Endowment for International Peace, 1945.

Ranshofen-Wertheimer, Egon F., *Victory is Not Enough: The Strategy for a Lasting Peace*. New York: W. W. Norton, 1942.

Ravndal, Ellen J., *In the Beginning: Secretary-General Trygve Lie and the Establishment of the United Nations*. Bristol: Bristol University Press, 2023.

Reinalda, Bob, *International Secretariats: Two Centuries of International Civil Servants and Secretariats*. Abingdon: Routledge, 2020.

Reinalda, Bob (ed.), *Routledge Handbook of International Organization*. Abingdon: Routledge, 2013.

Reinalda, Bob, *Routledge History of International Organizations: From 1815 to the Present Day*. Abingdon: Routledge, 2009.

Reinalda, Bob, and Kent J. Kille, 'The Evolvement of "International Secretariats, Executive Heads and Leadership in Inter-Organizational Relations"', in Rafael Biermann and Joachim A. Koops (eds), *Palgrave Handbook of Inter-Organizational Relations in World Politics*. London: Palgrave Macmillan, 2017.

Reinisch, Jessica, 'Internationalism in Relief: The Birth (and Death) of UNRRA', *Past & Present* 210, Issue Supplement 6 (2011): 258–289.

Reinisch, Jessica, 'Introduction: Relief in the Aftermath of War', *Journal of Contemporary History* 43, no. 3 (2008): 371–404.

Renborg, Bertil A., *International Drug Control: A Study of International Administration by and through the League of Nations*. Washington, DC: Carnegie Endowment for International Peace, 1947.

Reynolds, P. A., and E. J. Hughes, *The Historian as Diplomat: Charles Kingsley Webster and the United Nations, 1939–1946*. London: Martin Robertson, 1976.

Rochester, Martin J., 'The Rise and Fall of International Organization as a Field of Study', *International Organization* 40, no. 4 (1986): 777–813.

Rovine, Arthur, *The first fifty years: The Secretary-General in World Politics 1920–1970*. Leyden: A. W. Sijthoff, 1970.

Royal Institute of International Affairs, *The International Secretariat of the Future: Lessons from Experience by a Group of Former Officials of the League of Nations*. London: Royal Institute of International Affairs, 1944.

Salter, Arthur, *Memoirs of a Public Servant*. London: Faber & Faber, 1961.

Samuel, Raphael, 'What Is Social History?', *History Today* 35, no. 3 (1985): 34–8.

Scaglia, Ilaria, *The Emotions of Internationalism: Feeling International Cooperation in the Alps in the Interwar Period*. Oxford: Oxford University Press, 2020.

Schlesinger, Stephen C., *Act of Creation: The Founding of the United Nations. A Story of Superpowers, Secret Agents, Wartime Allies and Enemies and Their Quest for a Peaceful World*. Boulder, CO: Westview, 2003.

Scott, George, *The Rise and Fall of the League of Nations*. London: Hutchinson, 1973.

Seidenfaden, Emil Eiby, 'From the Gallery to the Floor: The League of Nations and the Combating of "False Information"', in Haakon A. Ikonomou and Karen Gram-Skjoldager (eds), *The League of Nations – Perspectives from the Present*. Aarhus: Aarhus University Press, 2019, 188–200.

Seidenfaden, Emil Eiby, 'Legitimizing International Bureaucracy: Press and Information Work from the League of Nations to the UN', in Karen Gram-Skjoldager, Haakon A. Ikonomou and Torsten Kahlert (eds), *Organizing the 20th-Century World: International Organizations and the Emergence of International Public Administration, 1920–1960s*. London: Bloomsbury, 2020, 129–43.

Seidenfaden, Emil Eiby, *Message from Geneva: The Public Legitimization Strategies of the League of Nations and their Legacy, 1919–1946*. Unpublished doctoral thesis, University of Aarhus, 2019.

Seidenfaden, Emil Eiby, 'The League of Nations' Collaboration with an 'International Public', 1919–1939', *Contemporary European History* 31, no. 3 (2022): 368–80.

Sinding, Knud, and Christian Waldstrom, *Organisational Behaviour*, Fifth Edition. Maidenhead: McGraw-Hill Education, 2014.

Sinha, Aseema, 'Building a Theory of Change in International Relations: Pathways of Disruptive and Incremental Change in World Politics', *International Studies Review* 20, no. 2 (2018): 195–203.

Sluga, Glenda, 'Women, Feminisms and Twentieth-Century Internationalisms', in Glenda Sluga and Patricia Clavin (eds), *Internationalisms: A Twentieth-Century History*. Cambridge: Cambridge University Press, 2017, 61–84.

Sluga, Glenda, and Patricia Clavin, 'Rethinking the History of Internationalism', in Glenda Sluga and Patricia Clavin (eds), *Internationalisms: A Twentieth-Century History*. Cambridge: Cambridge University Press, 2017, 3–14.

Stearns, Peter N., 'Emotion and Change: When History Comes In', in Yohan Ariffin, Jean-Marc Coicaud and Vesselin Popovski (eds), *Emotions in International Politics: Beyond Mainstream International Relations*. New York: Cambridge University Press, 2016, 48–64.

Steiner, Zara S., *The Lights That Failed: European International History, 1919–1933*. Oxford: Oxford University Press, 2005.

Stöckmann, Jan, *The Formation of International Relations: Ideas, Practices, Institutions, 1914–1940*. Unpublished doctoral thesis, University of Oxford, 2017.

Stone, Lawrence, 'Prosopography', *Daedalus* 100, no. 1, Historical Studies Today (1971): 46–79.

Stopford, Martin, *Maritime Economics*, Third Edition. London: Routledge, 2008.

Strange, Susan, 'Why Do International Organizations Never Die?', in Bob Reinalda and Bertjan Verbeek (eds), *Autonomous Policy Making by International Organizations*. London: Routledge, 1998, 213–20.

Sweetser, Arthur, 'From the League to the United Nations', *Annals of the American Academy of Political and Social Science* 246 (1946): 1–8.

Sweetser, Arthur, *The League of Nations at Work*. New York: Macmillan, 1920.

Tollardo, Elisabetta, *Fascist Italy and the League of Nations, 1922–1935*. London: Palgrave Macmillan, 2016.

Tournes, Ludovic, 'The Rockefeller Foundation and the Transition from the League of Nations to the UN (1939-1946)', *Journal of Modern European* History 12, no. 3 (2014): 323-41.

United Nations World Health Organization Interim Commission, *Official Records of the World Health Organization No. 4: Minutes of the Second Session of the Interim Commission, Held in Geneva from 4 to 13 November 1946*. Geneva: United Nations, 1947.

United Nations, *Report of the Preparatory Commission of the United Nations*. London: United Nations, 1946.

Viner, Jacob, *The Customs Union Issue*. Washington, DC: Carnegie Endowment for International Peace, 1950.

Walters, F. P., 'The League of Nations', in Evan Luard (ed.), *The Evolution of International Organizations*. London: Thames & Hudson, 1966, 25-41.

Walters, F. P., *A History of the League of Nations*. Oxford: Oxford University Press, 1952.

Walters, F. P., *Administrative Problems of International Organization*. Oxford: Oxford University Press, 1941.

Weber, Max, *Economy and Society, A New Translation*. Edited and translated by Keith Tribe. London: Harvard University Press, 2019.

Wegener, Jens, *Creating and 'International Mind'? The Carnegie Endowment for International Peace in Europe, 1911-1940*. Unpublished doctoral thesis, European University Institute, 2015.

Weiss, Thomas G., 'The United Nations: Before, During and After 1945', *International Affairs* 91, no. 6 (2015): 1221-35.

Wilkinson, Paul, *International Relations: A Very Short Introduction*. Oxford: Oxford University Press, 2007.

Williams, Andrew J., Amelia Hadfield and J. Simon Rofe, *International History and International Relations*. Abingdon: Routledge, 2012.

Wilson, J. V., 'Problems of an International Secretariat', *International Affairs* 20, no. 4 (1944): 542-54.

Winchmore, Charles, 'The Secretariat: Retrospect and Prospect', *International Organization* 19, no. 3, The United Nations: Accomplishments and Prospects (1965): 622-39.

Online sources

British Pathé, 'Last Meeting of the League of Nations 1946'. https://www.britishpathe.com/video/VLVA72PEE0JN6QAYCJBACTUKP2CKG-NO-INFORMATION/query/%22league+of+nations%22

Laqua, Daniel, 'Internationalism', *European History Online (EGO)*, published 4 May 2021, 1–28. http://ieg-ego.eu/en/threads/transnational-movements-and-organisations/internationalism/daniel-laqua-internationalism (retrieved 10 November 2021).

United Nations Dag Hammarskjöld Library, 'How many people work for the United Nations Secretariat?'. http://ask.un.org/faq/14626 (retrieved 17 January 2023).

United Nations Geneva Archives, 'Preserving the Institutional Memory of UN Geneva'. https://www.ungeneva.org/en/knowledge/archives (retrieved 4 December 2021).

Index

assets
    distribution of liquid 34, 143, 173–4
    transfer of fixed 33–5, 50–3, 69–70, 77
    value of 53, 79–80, 87–8, 137
Avenol, Joseph 5, 25–6, 42, 66

Babington, Cecily 92–3, 120, 124
Biraud, Yves 54, 61, 125
Board of Liquidation 9, 46–50
    dissolution of 131, 133, 135, 140, 160
    financial concerns of 63, 98, 116–18, 129
    fortnightly progress reports 48, 87
    Interim Reports to members 84, 89, 100
    limitations of 48–50, 86–7
    meetings 48, 80, 82–3, 97, 115–16, 123
    membership of 47, 62
    negotiations with ILO 88, 98, 101, 112–18
    and procedure 117–19, 123, 125–6, 128
    relationship to the League of Nations 49, 124–5
    relationship with Secretariat 48–9, 98–9, 108, 119, 124–8, 131
    and reputation concerns 84, 98–109, 112–13, 117–18, 129–30, 174–5
    roles and responsibilities 48–9, 76, 81–4, 86–9, 165
Board of Liquidation Documents 49, 87
Boiteux, Marie 128, 140, 145
Breycha-Vauthier, Arthur 105, 106–8
Bruce Report 5, 35
Brunskog, Uno 139, 143

Carnegie Endowment for International Peace 6, 155
Chapman, John Henry 88, 122, 148
Charvériat, Émile 47, 135
Common Plan for the Transfer of League of Nations Assets 34–5, 50, 87–8

communications
    problems 58–9
    with League members, *see* League of Nations Membership
Communications and Transit Section 54, 57
Costa du Rels, Adolfo 25, 47, 82–3, 86
Curry, Evelyn 91–2, 128, 138–9

Distribution Service 55–6, 79
Drug Control Service 27, 29, 54, 58, 78–9
Drug Supervisory Body 25, 54, 78
Drummond, Eric 4, 25, 155
Dumbarton Oaks Conference 30, 35, 110

Economic and Financial Organization 24, 27, 54, 57, 65–70
ECOSOC, *see* United Nations Economic and Social Council
Edwards & Smith 122, 148–9
Elkin, Alexander 61, 63, 80
emotions in decision-making 11–12, 97–8, 109, 115–6, 117–19, 130–1
Erim, Tevfik 105, 156
Europe's Population in the Interwar Years 121, 143, 147–8

failure 6–8, 13
FAO, *see* Food and Agriculture Organization
Final Report to Members 9, 128–9
    completion of 100–1, 133, 135
    delays 135–6
    obfuscation of events 100–1, 118, 136
Food and Agriculture Organization 81, 121, 157
French Government 4, 141

Giraud, Émile 52, 88, 93, 122, 156

Hambro, Carl 37–8, 47, 81–3, 86, 122–3, 151

Harris, Constance 25, 28, 119, 128, 138, 171–2
Hill, Martin 6, 13, 61, 67, 156
Hudson, Manley O. 6, 85–6

ILO, *see* International Labour Organization
Information Section 99, 108
Institutional memory 134, 154–9, 161
International civil service 4, 12, 17, 119, 159
International Labour Organization 10, 27, 34, 109–19, 127
  and Pensions Funds 88, 112–16
  relationship with UN 100–12
International Labour Organization Governing Body 113–14, 115–16, 118
International organizations 6, 8, 11, 134, 175
internationalism 3, 6

Jacklin, Seymour 27, 32, 48, 62, 86
Jenny, Otto 138, 153, 157

Kisch, Cecil 47, 86, 104, 108, 118
Kopecky, Jaromír 25, 48, 83, 135

League of Nations
  bank accounts 121–2, 139, 143, 147, 152
  central services 55–6, 79
  functions 35, 54
  increasing irrelevance 29, 110
  and the International Labour Organization 109–19
  leadership of 17, 76, 80–9, 98–9, 145, 151, 165
  legacy 98, 99–109, 124–5, 129, 174–5
  Library 55, 63, 105–6, 108
  New Delhi Office 91, 139
  publications 28, 69–70, 79–80
  public relations 99–102
  time of death 133–5, 159–62
  and women 105, 107, 120
League of Nations Administrative Tribunal 63–4
League of Nations Archives 55–6, 102, 104, 108, 154–5
  transfer of 102–4
League of Nations Assembly 5, 24, 165–6
  21st Assembly 1–2, 9, 39–43, 60
  delegated authority 26, 47, 89, 97–8
League of Nations Health Organization 54, 58, 78–9
League of Nations Historical Collection, *see* League of Nations Museum
League of Nations membership 1, 41, 137
  communications with 101–2, 146, 149
  financial contributions 115–16
League of Nations Museum 76, 105–9, 129, 139
League of Nations Permanent Exhibit, *see* League of Nations Museum
League of Nations Secretariat
  budget 4–5, 90
  camaraderie 18, 27, 92, 168
  commitment of officials 18, 60, 92, 119–21, 154, 160–1, 168–72
  concerns of officials 61, 64–5, 67–9, 92–3
  contracts 37–8, 57, 60–1, 64, 66–9
  departure of officials 60–5, 68–9, 93–4, 138–9, 156–7
  dissolution of 140–5, 160–1
  exclusion from legacy 108, 124–5, 131
  experience of dissolution 9, 16, 46, 61, 74, 90–4, 98–9, 119, 128, 130–1, 138–9
  income tax 76, 88
  indemnity payments 64, 66
  knowledge transfer 55, 155–8, 172–3
  removal of furniture 64, 86–7, 90–1, 111, 139–41, 143
  repatriation of officials 66–8, 76
  requests for financial compensation 125–7
  salaries 92–3, 127
  size 5, 24–5, 27, 36–7, 41, 60, 65, 119
  Staff Committee 64, 125
  Staff Pensions Fund 76, 88, 101, 112–16, 126
  transfer of officials to the United Nations and agencies 37, 57–65, 67–9, 156–7
  wartime voluntary contributions 125
Lester, Seán 3, 13, 17, 25, 31, 111, 136, 168–9
  experience of liquidation 56–65, 71–5, 78, 84–5, 138, 145, 169–70

experience of Second World War 26–9, 63, 85
relationship with Board of Liquidation 71–2
relationship with Secretariat 27–8, 37–8, 63–5, 67–8, 106, 127–8, 131
relationship with Seymour Jacklin 38, 62, 86
relationship with Trygve Lie 77–8, 81, 85, 137–8
relationship with Valentin Stencek 82, 127–8, 142, 144–5, 151–2
relationship with Włodzimierz Moderow 51–2, 72–3, 78, 103, 168
retirement 138, 158–9
in the United States in 1946 81–7
Lie, Trygve 51, 67
liquidation
delays to 114, 117–18, 129–30, 140, 161
misunderstanding of process 59, 76, 87, 167
planning for 36, 42, 73, 89–96, 164–8
Loveday, Alexander 24–5, 27, 66, 86–7, 155
Lukac, Branko 57, 61, 156

Moderow, Włodzimierz 33, 51–3, 103
relationship with the League of Nations 51, 108–9
Myrddin-Evans, Guildhaume 113–18

Nansen Office for Refugees 104
News media, *see* press
Non-political activities, *see* Technical activities
Nonin, Cosette 81, 127

Owen, David 32, 36, 57, 68–9

Palais des Nations 1, 41, 50, 59–60, 80, 93, 102
PCIJ, *see* Permanent Court of International Justice
Pelt, Adriaan 58, 103, 155
Permanent Central Opium Board 25, 54, 78–9
Permanent Court of International Justice 42, 86, 153
Judges' Pension Fund 101, 114–15, 142

Phelan, Edward 109–11
post-war planning 28, 29–39, 110
precedence 46, 94–6, 164–8
presentism 46, 59, 89–90, 94–5, 118, 164–8
press 43, 108–9, 136–7
Princeton University 27, 65–70, 79
Printing and Publications Department 55–6, 63, 79–80
Purves, Chester 48, 81–2, 89–90, 103, 120, 135–6, 157–8

Ranshofen-Wertheimer, Egon 5, 6, 12, 24, 28, 55, 85, 155
registry 55–6, 79, 102
Renborg, Bertil 6, 29, 92, 103, 147
Resolution for the Dissolution of the League of Nations 40, 42, 47, 84, 112, 166
Rockefeller Foundation 7, 66, 143
Rosenborg, Ansgar 66–9, 121–2, 147–8, 152–3, 157

San Francisco Conference 30, 110
Second World War 10, 23–9, 66
Secrétan, Daniel 48, 105–6, 135
Social Questions Section 24, 28, 54, 58, 78–9
Steinig, Léon 25, 61, 91, 127
Stencek, Valentin 13, 17, 37, 67, 105
experience of dissolution 90–2, 140–5, 170
post-Secretariat 146, 149, 150–2, 157–8
relationship with Secretariat 91–3, 120, 131
Supervisory Commission 24, 26, 33, 47, 63, 115
Sweetser, Arthur 106, 137, 155
relationship with Seán Lester 85, 137–8
support for the League of Nations 39–41, 66, 99–100
Swiss Government 35, 52–3, 143–4

technical activities 5, 8, 24
continuation of 42–3, 55
transfer to the UN 35–6, 53–9, 69–70
treasury 27, 66
Trustee and Liquidating Agent, *see* Percy Watterson

UK Government 4, 40
UNESCO, *see* United Nations Educational, Scientific and Cultural Organization
United Nations
  distancing from the League of Nations 29, 31, 35, 54, 164
  impact on liquidation of League of Nations 38–9, 56–9, 73, 84–9
  internal communications 59, 73, 83
  links to League of Nations 3, 10, 14, 30, 45, 173–4
  recruitment of League officials 60–5, 66–9, 156–8
  transfer from the League to 45, 51–65, 77–80, 108–9
United Nations Committee on League of Nations Assets 33, 51
United Nations Economic and Social Council 32, 35–6, 54, 56
United Nations Educational, Scientific and Cultural Organization 127, 153–4
United Nations General Assembly 32, 39, 42, 73, 80–6, 89–90
United Nations Negotiating Committee 51–2
United Nations Preparatory Commission 32, 35–6, 54
United Nations Relief and Rehabilitation Administration 29, 54, 93

United Nations Secretariat
  establishment 57–65, 77–80, 165
  relationship with the League 32
United Nations Secretary-General, *see* Trygve Lie
United States Government 4, 5, 28–9, 31, 35, 42
  Inland Revenue Service lawsuit 88, 101, 122–4, 147–51
  unreliable narrator 101–2, 129–30, 146
USSR Government 24, 31, 35, 42, 53–4

van Asch van Wijck, Willem 105–6, 138–9
Vilatte, Henri 63, 92–3

Walters, F. P. 7, 104, 155
Watterson, Percy 17, 66, 69–70, 79, 93, 125–6, 152, 157
  commitment to the League 120–4, 171
  as North American liaison for the League of Nations 81, 107, 116–17, 121–4
  as Trustee and Liquidating Agent 124, 146–9, 150–1
Welps, Peter 140, 145, 153
WHO, *see* World Health Organization
Working Capital Fund 111–12, 114–15
World Health Organization 157–8

www.ingramcontent.com/pod-product-compliance
Lightning Source LLC
Chambersburg PA
CBHW071819300426
44116CB00009B/1374